The Conflict That Was A War

IN VIETNAM AND AT HOME

★

Nineteen Vietnam Veterans open their locked inner selves
to tell what they experienced

FOREWORD

The journeys these combat veterans describe in The Conflict That Was a War are a tribute to all Vietnam veterans who served their country when asked. The experiences of these men highlight resolve, courage, and sacrifice that I, as an Iraq War veteran, admire. The service members in today's conflicts are better cared for, appreciated, and understood because of the Vietnam veterans who have gone before us. We all will remain grateful for your service and sacrifices.

Every veteran copes with and finds answers to the combat experience in his unique way. The men whose stories fill this book took up a mission. They sought to express their experiences both to find answers for themselves and to share that experience with others. If you are reading this to find answers for your combat experience, these Vietnam veterans want you to know you are not alone. Please embrace their experiences and learn from them. Develop an understanding of your own traumatic experiences and have the courage to seek support. As combat veterans of the United States Armed Forces, you have earned a better quality of life and it is honorable to seek services to embrace it.

I am honored to be in the presence of these veterans, and I wish to thank the authors for writing their journeys. Your wisdom, insight, and experiences are valued. The combat veteran is a servant, and by writing this book you continue your service by helping your fellow combat veterans in their journey home. These written words transcend our lives. They will outlast us and help service members and veterans of future conflicts to heal and find understanding. This document reminds my generation of combat veterans of the importance of supporting the next generation of our nation's warriors. I thank all of you for writing these powerful experiences.

Derek McGinnis
Readjustment Counselor
Modesto Vet Center

TABLE OF CONTENTS

DEDICATION

We would like to dedicate this book to the more than fifty-eight thousand fellow comrades who paid the ultimate price of war and to the families of these soldiers who never got to see their loved ones walk back through the door. This dedication is also to the more than 153,000 veterans who were wounded in action and still live with the scars of battle. Not to be forgotten are all the veterans who served on the battlefields of Vietnam and did return—but returned to a life that was never the same as before their tour of duty. Finally, this dedication is also to the spouses and family members who stuck by their loved ones when they returned, battered, from the war.

Wednesday Morning PTSD Group
Veterans Center
Modesto, California

PREFACE

Many books have been written and movies have been made that depict what authors and moviemakers believe went on in Vietnam during the war. Some have come close to capturing that experience, but none has fully grasped what it was like to spend a year or more of your life surviving the heat, rain, rice paddies, and an elusive enemy in a foreign country.

The Vietnam War was a highly debated conflict that left a lasting memory in the minds of a generation of Americans. However, to the men and women who served in the armed forces, it wasn't just a memory but a nightmare—and in more ways than one. First, unlike many wars, especially the two large world wars that preceded it, in Vietnam no battle lines separated the opposing forces. The enemy lived behind the closed doors of houses in the villages and cities. They owned or worked in the businesses of the community. They worked in the rice paddies and fields. They dug tunnels and lived below ground. The enemy could pop up from anywhere, at any time, and they could end your life. No matter where we were, they had us surrounded. We learned to live with our heads on a swivel, to fight a war against an enemy who could disappear back into the thick jungle just as quickly as they emerged from it, leaving behind deadly mines and booby traps in the underbrush. This was guerrilla warfare, a new and deadly kind of fighting that many of us knew nothing about. It was a type of warfare that we learned on the job—a reliable, but dangerous, way to learn to stay alive.

The other fact that distinguished the combat experience of Vietnam is that, unlike veterans of earlier wars, returning military personnel were spit on, called warmongers and child killers, and harassed by their own countrymen, their fellow Americans. It was bad enough that theses brave and courageous men and women had to leave some friends behind, pack up their own scars, and try to recoup their lives. Worse was that they had to do it alone. Their countrymen, people who called themselves loving, Bible-reading, caring, and responsible individuals, turned their collective back on returning Vietnam veterans. They said, "Look at what you did, shame on you!" From the West Coast to the East Coast and from the Gulf of Mexico to the Canadian border, veterans were told, Fend for yourself. Don't look to us for help. If this sounds harsh, it is. Veterans didn't take lightly to being chastised for serving in the armed forces of our country, and many still feel bitterly toward those who treated them like criminals. Memories, both of combat and of returning home, have made life hell for many, many veterans.

We hope that reading these stories from a group of veterans will show the country what it was like to be a veteran and a survivor of combat. We hope it will show what it means for returning military personnel to be treated like the heroes they are. And finally we hope our stories will help assure that military men and women returning from the Middle East are not treated as criminals but welcomed with a big Thank you for your service!

WE HAVE BEEN ASKED; WHY DID WE GO?

Some were drafted into military service for their country. Some volunteered. No matter how they found themselves in the armed forces of the United States, almost every single soldier who served in the Republic of Vietnam was ordered to the war zone. And every one of us raised our right hand and took the following oath:

OATH OF ENLISTMENT

I (STATE YOUR NAME), DO SOLEMNLY SWEAR THAT
I WILL SUPPORT AND DEFEND THE CONSTITUTION
OF THE UNITED STATES AGAINST ALL ENEMIES,
FOREIGN AND DOMESTIC; THAT I WILL BEAR TRUE
FAITH AND ALLEGIANCE TO THE SAME; AND THAT
I WILL OBEY THE ORDERS OF THE PRESIDENT OF
THE UNITED STATES AND THE ORDERS OF THE
OFFICERS APPOINTED OVER ME, ACCORDING TO
REGULATIONS AND THE UNIFORM CODE OF
MILITARY JUSTICE. SO HELP ME GOD.

Whether out of patriotism or commitment, every one of us took the Oath of Enlistment, and we are extremely proud to have followed this oath to the letter. We live in the greatest country in the world, a country that deserves to have citizens willing to sacrifice in order to assure the pursuit of freedom and happiness remains available to all within its borders.

CHAPTER ONE

WAR, WHAT IS IT GOOD FOR? ABSOLUTELY NOTHING!

William Bruno
Spec. 4
US Army
Eleventh Armored Calvary Regiment
July 1968–July 1969

In 1967, I joined the army after unsuccessfully trying to join the national guard, navy, air force, and so on. A friend of mine, who worked for the Selective Service, warned me that my name was coming up to be drafted. During this time, the draft was on and the army was taking anyone that they could get, including dropouts, prisoners, and physically unfit people. I had to make some decisions and quick. However, my choices were few. I could fail to report and face a $10,000 fine along with ten years in prison. I could retreat to Canada and dishonor my family. Or I could join the army, volunteer for an extra year, and receive some free schooling. I chose the third option and signed up for avionics school.

I completed my basic training at Fort Lewis, Washington. I must confess at this time that the military life was not at all what I expected. As the days went on, I found that I hated every second of it. There is something about not having control of your own life. It seemed like every second, we were being yelled at or told how "fucked-up" we were. I didn't like the idea of being punished for things that other people did. If a person could not do push-ups or run fast enough, the whole group, platoon, company would be punished. The poor guy that caused the punishment would also be punished by the rest of the group that night.

I went on to Fort Gordon, Georgia, for schooling. Things did not seem to get much better. At school, the instructors kept threatening that anyone who flunked out would be sent to the infantry, a place that I didn't want to go. Toward the end the school, they picked the top ten students to attend a top-secret school at Fort Dix, New Jersey, which required a secret clearance. They told us that they would be contacting our parents, schools that we attended, and friends back home. I never did hear of anyone being contacted. There at Fort Dix, in a classroom built inside a big mesh cage of copper wire with loud music playing outside and armed guards, we were instructed in the intricacies of a special new radio. There were few of these radios in Vietnam, but in case we ran into one, we needed to know what to do. We were also taught how to enter the secret communications codes that changed at least once a day. We were warned that should we ever be captured by the enemy we must never divulge this information. Just knowing it put a bounty on our heads. When our training finished at Fort Dix, we went back to Georgia to finish up and graduate. I would later learn that the subject matter I'd been taught was nothing I really wanted to know. But it was already too late to do anything about that.

One weekend we were restricted to the base with no passes to leave. One of our platoon leaders snuck off base and returned with some booze and a few local girls. The platoon leaders had a separate room at the end of the barracks, and they decided to have a party. They came through the barracks and picked a few people they could trust to join them. Not knowing what was going on (only that I had been invited to join them) I walked into the room and was handed a drink. I didn't even get the drink to my lips before the door burst open and the CO (company commander) came in with his assistant and yelled, "You're all busted!" The CO was a second lieutenant (the lowest grade of a military officer) right out of OCS (officer candidate school) and trying to make a name for himself. He threatened that we would all be court-martialed. It was later decided, by a person higher than he, that we all would be given regimental article fifteens. This meant, among other things, that we were all busted in rank to private E-1, the lowest rank there is. When giving me my punishment, the officers tried to make a deal with me. They said that if I told them the name of the soldier who'd left base that night, I would be punished less severely than the others. My response to this, as cordial and respectful as I could muster, was "Fuck you, sir."

After basic training and my schooling, I was sent home for a two-week leave. I got married to a girl that I had gone with for about four years. Everyone told me that I was making a big mistake. I wish I had listened to them. In being married, I had to sign an allotment that would automatically send half of my salary home to my wife. I had no control over this and could not alter this until I reached the rank of E-5 (pay grade), which I never did.

I arrived in Vietnam as a private E-1, and the first letter that I received was from my new mother-in-law, informing me that my new wife was going out on me. I had to carry this knowledge with me because there was nothing else that I could do. It seemed like a lot of guys were getting Dear John letters, but most of them were not married.

We landed at Long Bien Airbase, near Bien Hoa. Immediately I understood that Vietnam was nothing like I had been told or was prepared for. When the door was opened on the TWA 707 plane, we stepped from the seventy-degree air-conditioned cabin into 110-degree heat with 95 percent humidity. The stench was unbelievable. The buses that met us at Long Bien Airport had heavy mesh screen over the windows. My first thought was that even the bases weren't safe. It was a short trip to the Bien Hoa processing center where hundreds of "new guys" were sitting under the biggest tents that I had ever seen. Names were being called out, and I was instructed to sit and wait until my name was called. Finally, after about four hours, my named was called.

I was told that there was a big board, up front, where I could locate the appropriate shoulder patch. Mine would be for the Eleventh Armored Calvary Regiment. Once I found my patch, I was to proceed down a dusty road to a tent (hootch) with the same patch and make arrangements to get to the regiment's base. I had never heard of this unit. On my way to the hootch I saw soldiers with the Eleventh Cavalry patch on their upper arm. Bear in mind that I was still in my stateside fatigues, shiny boots and all. These guys were loaded with weapons, belts of ammo, and covered in probably twenty pounds of red dirt.

I made the mistake of asking what it was like in the Cav. They asked me where my weapons were and what I was trained to do (my MOS). I said I was trained to work on aircraft. They told me the Eleventh Cav had no aircraft, only armored vehicles, and that I was screwed. They also told me to get a weapon because the Eleventh Cav's base (Xuan Loc) had no runway. Instead I would be dropped off in the jungle close to the base, which meant I would need at least a rifle and knife, as some guy named "Charlie" would be trying to kill me.

The whole time I was in-country, I never felt more frightened than I did then. After I got over my thoughts of going AWOL and stealing orders off a guy going back to the states, I found the Cav tent and was told that a plane would be coming for me within an hour.

While I waited I got a drink of water from a big canvas bag with faucets at the bottom. The chlorine was so strong I felt like I had just drunk out of a swimming pool. I got violently ill.

The plane was a C-123 Caribou, and we flew about an hour to our destination. I kept my eyes glued to the window, too scared to ask anybody anything. We arrived at a base that from the air looked like San Francisco Airport, with runways, towers, and aircraft all over the place. I guess the Cav guys I met earlier had a good laugh over feeding me that story about getting dropped in the jungle. But it wasn't all a joke; upon exiting the aircraft, the pilot showed me several new bullet holes from our flight.

The Eleventh Cav's home base was called Xuan Loc. I was assigned a bunk in a hootch where about twenty infantry troops lived. They told me there was some kind of arrangement with the local "Charlie" that we would not attack them and visa versa. They said that the base hadn't sustained a rocket attack in over a year. Yeah, right! We were hit with rockets pretty good that night.

Back in the world, we had been instructed about what to do in the event of a rocket attack. We were to get below the level of the sandbags that surrounded our hootch, then dress, grab our weapon, and proceed to the nearest bunker. I followed those instructions and noticed that all of a sudden, I was the only one still in the hootch. I ran outside, not even knowing what a bunker looked like, and spotted a big pile of sandbags with an entryway and smoke coming out. Upon investigation, I found all of my roommates naked, playing cards, and smoking. All I could hear over the laughter was, "Here is the FNG" (fucking new guy).

I learned that the base was hit at least once a week. I also learned that I could not believe anything that anyone told me. When they told me to stay dressed because we would get hit again. I thought, Yeah, sure, and got undressed and went back to bed. Two hours later, when we got hit again, I was the naked one in the bunker, and everyone else was dressed. I knew what they were thinking: "Here comes the new guy again!" Seeing everyone dressed, I noticed that some of the infantry troops wore strings from their belts hung with what appeared to be dried apricots. I later found out they were ears, taken from dead (I hope) Viet Cong. To this day, I have trouble shopping the dried fruit section of my grocery store.

The next day I reported to a Major Cunningham. He told me that the army could not send a private E-1 to a combat zone. I was hoping that they were going to send me home. Fat chance! They promoted me to private E-2 on the spot (big deal).

My first task was to figure out why radio range between camp and the aircraft was no better than twenty miles. I noticed that the various antennae were mounted on top of a one-story operations shack. I had also noticed, when first flying in on the Caribou, an old metal tower lying on its side about a mile from the base. I suggested that they sling-load the tower to the base, lay it on its side so I could mount the antennas and coaxial cable, and then sling it vertical again. When this was completed, the range of the radio communication more than doubled, and I was promoted private E-3 (private first class—PFC) (big deal). I never did understand why the avionics people couldn't figure this out, because it must have been a problem for some time. I also received the Army Commendation Medal at this time (big deal).

Everything seemed bigger in this strange land including the mosquitos. Before Vietnam, I had never had to sleep under a mosquito net. There must be a trick to keeping them from getting under the net, but I hadn't learned it. Inevitably, at least one and sometimes a squadron would dive bomb a sleeper under the cover of darkness. I swear that one night I saw red-bodied mosquitos with yellow stars painted on their fuselages and rifle barrels sticking out of their noses.

The bees were a bigger problem because I was allergic to their sting. One day, we were to move the Avionic Unit closer to the flight line. Everything was mounted on deuce and half trucks with the avionic shops looking like huge camper shells on their backs. The move would have been easy except that we had to drive through a small grove of trees. Lucky me, I drove the truck with the whip antennas sticking up about thirty feet. The canvas roof was down and I had the windshield folded down. As I drove beneath the trees, one of the antennas mounted on the front bumper severed a beehive. We were only traveling about five miles per hour, which was slow enough for the hive to crash onto the hood and break into many pieces. Those bees were pissed. They were also big, probably three times larger than any I had ever seen. The bees swarmed and stung me. The truck was still rolling when I jumped from it and ran to the aid station. They kept me there for a while to see if I would have a reaction, but I didn't. The doctor surmised that I probably got such a large dose, that in the future I would be immune (I was not).

Spiders were pretty hefty too. One type of spider was about an inch around, not counting its legs. It looked like a crab, and if you put two of them together they would fight to the death. We built a coliseum for them out of Plexiglas, painted dots on their backs tell them apart, and wagered on them. It was kind of like a sixteen-legged cockfight. I had a winner (called Orange Dot) for quite a while, until it lost a few legs and I released it for compassionate reasons.

Rhinoceros beetles were pretty cool. They could grow eight inches long and had large horns on their heads. One guy had glued string to one and wanted me to take moving pictures of him flying it around like a model airplane. He said nobody back home would believe it. With their large wings, it almost sounded like they had a small motor.

I can't forget about those fucking lizards. It is the strangest thing. When you are all alone and you think you hear someone say fuck you. You look around and see nobody. I began to wonder about myself but I later found out that this small lizard was the culprit. It made a sound like it was talking. I felt better.

After about a month, I was sent to our forward position at Bien Hoa. I met the Avionics guy that I was replacing. He was a small man nicknamed Indian. He looked exactly like the proverbial cigar store wooden Indian. He gave me the twenty-five-cent tour, showed me where the tools were, and could not leave fast enough to go back to Xuan Loc. I soon found out that there was only one Avionics person in the forward position, while there were about ten sitting on their asses back at base camp. It was like being on a twenty-four-hour no-sleep shift.

One day, I was working on a helicopter, my upper body stuck in an access hatch in the tail boom, standing in a puddle of water. They always told us in avionics school to remove our dog tags while working on electronic systems. Remember, I am the guy that wasn't going to believe anybody. As I was working on the unit, my tags slipped out of my shirt and fell inside the transponder that I was working on. At about the same time, the transponder keyed (activated). The jolt threw me ten feet. My dog tags were virtually welded together. Then and there I decided that I didn't want to do avionics anymore.

But what I liked about avionics was the flying. Quite often, problems would arise with the communications systems due to the vibration from the helicopter. I would have to go up with a pilot and try to figure out what was wrong. Quite often, I would lie about having a problem just to be able to take a short flight. I can honestly say it was like going on a ride at Disneyland with no lines or tickets. Those flights were the one thing that I enjoyed in the military.

One time, Major Cunningham took me up in his OH-6 Loach. He told me that every time he fired the mini-gun that his FM radio would go out. Sitting on the left hand side of the aircraft, two feet away from a firing weapon is an experience not to be forgotten. On the way back to the base, I looked over to see the pilot slumped over like he had been shot. I seized the controls. I had always watched how pilots controlled the aircraft. I could control it, but I know I wouldn't be able to land. I glanced quickly at the pilot, and he was laughing hysterically, tears running down his cheeks. He liked to play that game on captive audiences.

I liked flying so much, I figured I would volunteer to be a door gunner on a Huey—the job was in high demand. For my first flight out as a door gunner, I had lied and said that I was familiar with the M60 machine gun. In reality, I had never even seen one before. I figured I could look around the transmission housing and copy what the crew chief on the opposite side was doing. When I looked around, I saw that the crew chief had the feed tray open and was putting the belt of ammunition in the weapon. I looked at my weapon and tried to figure out how to open the feed tray. I finally figured that one of the levers might do it, but when I pushed a lever, the brass bag (a canvas bag attached to the weapon to collect spent shell casings), flew off. I tried to grab the bag, but didn't realize that I had forgotten to strap myself in the seat, and almost fell out of the aircraft. After losing the brass bag, I figured out how to get the feed tray open and load the ammo. After getting the belt in and closing the tray, I sat back to enjoy the ride, proudly thinking that I had figured everything out. We were the last ship in the formation so no one could see how inept I really was. Our mission was to pick up some ARPs (aero rifle platoon). These were soldiers that had been dropped off a couple of days earlier. After some daydreaming during the flight, I could here a metallic clanging noise. Unbeknownst to me, I had not put the belt into the machine gun far enough and was losing all of my ammunition, which was flying out the door. The long string of belted shells was flopping in the wind beside the aircraft. If the wind carried it under the aircraft it would fly into the tail rotor. I had to free the belt. I knew that if I pulled a shell out, I could break the belt and let it go free. I did it and was left with only five bullets.

When we took our turn to go into the landing zone to pick up the last of the ARPs, the pilot told us over the intercom to pepper the area. I had no idea what that meant. All I knew was that the crew chief was firing like crazy out his side of the aircraft as we were lifting off. I assumed that we were being attacked on his side of the aircraft, so I grabbed a small rifle (an M1 with the stock cut off) that we each had in case of an emergency, and tried to wade through the guys sitting on the floor in an attempt to reach the crew chief's side. I had my flight helmet on and couldn't hear what anyone was saying, but they were all pointing back to my side of the aircraft. Oh shit, I thought, we're getting hit on both sides. Then I realized that there was nobody out there, and that I had made a real fool of myself (now I knew what "pepper the area" meant). I fired off my five rounds, and we headed back to

Bien Hoa. I hoped that we would just keep flying so that I wouldn't have to face anyone.

But the crew decided that if I was stupid enough to volunteer to do this, it was worth the time to train me, which they did. I always felt bad that I had put those brave souls at risk and that I had lost 595 out of six hundred shells, which probably were used to kill some of my fellow, brave Americans. Even though we laughed about it, it really was not a laughing matter. After that, I was used as a fill-in door gunner. This meant that I would fly as a replacement when someone was sick, or on rest-and-relaxation leave. This meant that I would fly a lot on different types of missions with different crews and different aircraft.

One of our pilots liked to fly at treetop level along the many canals. Being strapped into the seat on the side of the helicopter was the weirdest sensation. As the aircraft banked around the curve of the canal, you would instantly see trees, then water, then sky, then water, then trees. This pilot believed flying fast made us a more difficult target to hit. I thought that he was right so I always wanted to fly with him. Plus it was a lot of fun.

Someone told me that the Viet Cong had been told that our tanks were made out of heavy cardboard. I didn't believe this until we flew convoy cover. Being an armored unit, we would have a convoy perhaps a quarter of a mile long rumbling down the road. We would fly the length of the convoy, over and over, looking for possible problems. Once in a while Charlie would come running out of the elephant grass with a machete and try to stab one of our track vehicles. Unfortunately for Charlie, this act made for good target practice.

One time we were flying over a rice paddy, and I noticed a guy walking around with what appeared to be a pole on his shoulder. We were up about three thousand feet and I couldn't make out what it was. In order to fire our weapons, we would have to let the pilot know first. I called to the pilot over the intercom, "Hey, look down at four o'clock" (the approximate location for this guy). The pilot looked through his binoculars and started laughing. He asked the crew if we wanted to see a magic trick. Before waiting for an answer, the pilot dropped in altitude and began to hover at five hundred feet directly over the guy. I leaned out and could see the guy, but I still couldn't make out what he had on his shoulder. The pilot knew the guy had some sort of a rocket launcher. However, he was holding it upside down. He fired, and after the smoke cleared from where he had been standing, there was no sign of him. Unfortunately for him, the rocket had detonated at his feet. It was a pretty good trick.

We also flew medevac missions and carried a supply of medical equipment and morphine syringes to administer for pain. I don't know which I hate more, giving or getting shots. We were to give patients one per hour, but usually they were at an aid station or field hospital before I had to stick them again.

Until they found a replacement for me, I still had my avionics duties to fulfill. This worked out well for the military because when downed aircraft were found they could use me to retrieve the avionics gear and keep it out of the hands of the enemy. They always sent someone with me to watch my back, but retrieving equipment was a scary proposition. If the aircraft had been down for very long, it would be occupied by rats, snakes, or spiders—all of which I was more afraid of than I was of Charlie.

One of those infamous secret radios was in our commanding officer's helicopter with whom I flew with a few times. His name was Colonel Patton and yes, he was the son of General Patton of World War II fame.

Along the way I met a fellow soldier and quickly discovered that we had a lot in common. His name was Bob Mingle and he, like me, had volunteered to become a door gunner. We started competing for flight hours so that we could get an air medal. He had arrived in country shortly after I had, and we planned to get together at some point after we rotated back to the world. At this time, I was assigned to a new forward position called Quan Loi, up by the Cambodian border. It was nicknamed Rocket City because we sustained at least one rocket attack each day, sometimes more. Through a third party, Bob and I were still able to keep track of each other's flight hours.

While at Quan Loi, I had a crazy idea. In town I had seen a couple of vases I liked made from spent artillery shells. The civilian selling them wanted $100 each. We were paid with MPC (military payment certificates—play money), which would change every so often to help curb the black market. No one ever knew what the new money was going to look like, but I had a feeling that a change might be coming. I wrote to my folks and asked them to send me a Monopoly game because it was very popular in Vietnam. The timing could not have been more perfect, and I purchased those vases, as well as a couple of other items, and gave the man a $100 tip, all in Monopoly money. I expected to hear bullets flying over our heads as we left town, but we didn't. I never did go back to town for fear of being shot when the store owner found out.

While stationed at the Eleventh Armored Cav's forward base at Quan Loi, I acquired a pet monkey from another soldier who had completed his tour of duty and was about to rotate home. At this time there was only one airline that would handle wild animals, and it was very expensive. The animal also would have to be placed in quarantine for six months, and I was also told that after all of that, the monkey would probably not survive anyway. The noise, stress, and temperature difference would probably be too much. The monkey was named Garfunkel and became quite an interesting pet. He was curious about everything. I usually kept him on a leash to keep him out of trouble. At night he was a real terror. He would get into a pack of gum, toss the gum, and eat the foil. He would eat the nose rests off my flight glasses (which were hard to acquire). And if he was upset, he would poop in his hand and throw it at you. Finally I had to keep him in my metal wall locker at night. During the day he accompanied me on my daily duties—including flying in the helicopter, as I was still a door gunner and avionics tech.

One night, while stationed at Quan Loi, I heard a metallic tapping that sounded like it was coming from directly below our hootch. A rumor had been circulating that the enemy was digging tunnels under our base. A fellow soldier was awake, and we stood in the dark, trying to figure out what the noise was and where it was coming from. All of a sudden, the other soldier let out a laugh and said, "Get your flashlight." He opened the wall locker really fast and I shined the light inside. Lo and behold we caught the monkey masturbating—his elbow was hitting the side of the metal locker. Garfunkel sure looked guilty, but we had a good laugh. Monkeys are famous for mimicking people, and I was teased a lot by everyone asking me how the monkey learned to do that.

One day we were assigned to drop our ARPs into one of the Michelin Rubber Plantations. The Viet Cong had stationed snipers in the trees and they were firing at anything that came along, including aircraft. Our aircraft and three others dropped off enough ARPs so that there was a platoon for each row of trees. They were to walk every row in the plantation and find the snipers in the trees. While the other helicopters went back to base, ours landed in a clearing and stayed in case there were any casualties. After about an hour, I guess one of the troopers was bored and not paying attention, he walked into a giant spider web. Huntsman spiders are known to grow to twelve inches in size. Like me, with great fear of spiders, the soldier drew his .45 caliber pistol and shot it. Everyone panicked and started firing everything from M60 machine guns to M79 grenade launchers. In the confusion, we could not reach anyone on the radio, but it sure looked like the Fourth of July. Fortunately no one was injured, and no other spiders were found that day.

During the month of May, 1969, we were hit with a great rocket attack. This was followed by an even greater ground attack. The first sergeant came into our hootch looking for volunteers to help guard the perimeter of our base. We told him, "No way, we're ED" (exempt from duty) meaning we were on a flight crew and didn't have to perform these duties. The first sergeant explained that some NVA (North Vietnamese soldiers) had already been found on the base, and that a couple of our troops have had their throats slashed while they were sleeping. One NVA had been captured and during interrogation revealed the plans of the ground attack. As we were getting our gear and loading our magazines, the siren went off and red flares filled the sky. We took our positions for the impending onslaught. It was pretty crazy. It was like killing a swarm of ants with a toothpick. The NVA soldiers would run to the barbed wire and dive on top of it to allow the soldiers following, a way to cross over the wire. It seemed like there was no end to their numbers because we fought all night. They had run large animals into the berm (protected area around the base) in order to destroy our booby traps and land mines.

The next day, the attack was over, and we did a body count. Most of the hundreds of dead enemy were kids, perhaps teens, dressed in their under shorts, and some without weapons. Among the dead bodies we spotted our barbers as well as other Vietnamese civilians that were cleared to work on our base. I always wondered what they were thinking while they were shaving us with those sharp straight razors and doing the chop, chop thing on our backs and cracking our necks. To this day I cannot go to a male barber.

During my last week in Vietnam I was sent back to base camp (Xuan Loc). I guess the unit figured that I was too short (time wise) to be flying anymore. I was assigned CQ duty. This was a job answering the phones at night and running troops to the clinic who had contracted the clap or any other STD. I was required to witness the gruesome procedures used to treat these poor souls. I then went back and told everyone, "It's not worth it, stay away from the girls."

I ran into my friend, Bob Mingle, and tried to convince him not to fly anymore because he did not have that much time left do in country either. One night, I got the call that the helicopter that he was on had gone down, and there were no survivors. I later found out that Major Cunningham (the major that feigned injury while we were flying) was also killed when his helicopter was shot down. Later, in 2011, I found and made etchings of their names from the Vietnam Veterans Memorial (the Wall) in Washington DC.

I did leave Vietnam as an E-4 and with a Good Conduct Medal (big deal). Later I was sent to Georgia and on to Germany before being honorably discharged at Fort Dix, New Jersey. I never did turn in my many flight hours as a door gunner or report a small wound sustained while flying in to perform a medevac in a hot LZ called Holiday Inn. I just wanted to go home and return to the life I had known. But I found that life as I had known it didn't exist any more.

Upon coming home I wore my uniform with pride. We didn't hear very much about the demonstrations while in the Nam. The first civilian I encountered at the Oakland Bus Depot spit on me with no explanation. Our war was not called a war. It was identified as a "conflict" or a "police action." It was directed by a bunch of clowns in the big top (Washington, DC), who in most cases had never been in a combat situation. The news media didn't help much either. They painted us as a bunch of doped-up baby killers. Vietnam was the first conflict televised to American viewers, and the media depicted soldiers in a very negative way. We didn't get to enjoy the tickertape parades of World War II or the hero status given to Korean War veterans. We couldn't enjoy the simple fact that we made it through, or that we'd helped protect the "American way of life." More than fifty-eight thousand brave young Americans made the ultimate sacrifice, and I felt that it was all for nothing. Nobody cared! I never did meet a person, while in country, that wanted to be in the conflict. I call it a war and I defy anyone who claims it was not.

One final aspect of the war that needs to be mentioned is something that wasn't known about by all those who served in Vietnam. It wasn't until long after US forces officially left Vietnam that veterans began to comprehend one of the war's hidden dangers. This was the danger of repeated exposure to concentrated chemical herbicides and pesticides. Operation Ranch Hand was conducted from 1962 through 1971, and it remains a controversial subject to this day. The operation consisted of the spraying of herbicides over large portions of Vietnam (see enclosed map). It was designed to kill all plant life, which would deny the enemy food and the jungle canopy in which to hide. Unfortunately it also killed people and is still killing people today. Herbicides were sprayed on roads, canals, and food-production areas, as well as around the perimeters of our bases. A total of nineteen million gallons of herbicide were sprayed, eleven million of which was a chemical called Agent Orange. There were also fifteen different mixtures of dioxins and arsenic, which accounted for Agents White, Blue, Purple, and so on. The potency of Agent Orange used in Vietnam was thirteen times higher than the legal USDA limits. Spraying was primarily conducted by US aircraft, boats, and backpack sprayers. The heaviest spraying occurred from 1967 through 1969, and the areas most heavily contaminated with dioxins were the sites of US bases. Bien Hoa, where I was stationed in 1968 and 1969, recorded the largest leak (7,500 gallons) of toxins from underground storage tanks. Three other leaks were also recorded at Bien Hoa.

During Operation Flyswatter, another chemical Malathion was sprayed on military bases and local cities every nine days to eliminate mosquitoes. Over the course of 1,300 missions, 1.7 million liters of Malathion concentrate were sprayed. Various maladies that have surfaced in US veterans and Vietnamese citizens, including diabetes, various forms of cancer, skin problems, birth defects, and breathing problems are all considered by the Veterans Administration to be connected to spraying operations in Vietnam.

I can still remember Papa San with that backpack sprayer, spraying around our hootches. And I remember a time when the crew chief and I loaded two leaking fifty-five-gallon drums onto a pallet to be sling-loaded under a helicopter and dropped into the jungle. We had that shit all over us, and we didn't have a clue how dangerous it was. No one told us about the dangers of these chemicals. We only learned many years later, when we began to develop symptoms. Those symptoms came in two forms—physical and emotional. The question in my mind is, If the opportunity arises to do this again, should it be done? Unequivocally no!

Bill Bruno with his pet monkey

Bill Bruno in the door gunner seat on his chopper

Herbicide Spray Map

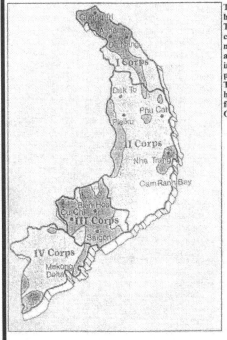

This map is a representation of herbicide spray missions in Vietnam. The dark areas represent concentrated spraying areas. This map only represents fixed-wing aricraft spraying, and does not include helicopter spraying of perimeters, or other spray methods. The III Corps area received the heaviest concentations of spraying, followed by I Corps, II Corps and IV Corps.

CHAPTER TWO

THE WAR
PEOPLE LOVE TO FORGET

Chet Brassart
Sergeant
US Army
First Infantry Division, Dog Handler
1969-1970

The breezes were hot at Fort Benning, Georgia, where I was awaiting my orders for Vietnam. I thought I was in hell. Later I would long for that Georgia weather. An NCO (noncommissioned officer) called out asking anyone within earshot, "Anybody here with experience around dogs?" I broke the cardinal sin of the army: I raised my hand indicating that I had some experience with dogs. This cardinal sin was called *volunteering*, and it put me on my way to dog-training school.

At the school, different types of dogs and handlers received different types of training. Army dog types included scouts, trackers, and sentries, with land mine and booby trap detection thrown in for good measure. I was assigned a scout dog. A scout dog was used as the point for an infantry unit. We received training in early alert of ambush, along with booby trap and land mine location—a wonderful job that included a tight asshole thrown in at no extra charge. Upon completion of the training, I headed home for a short leave. My parents were so excited to have me back they took a three-week vacation without me. My vacation consisted of drinking, girls, and headaches—none in the amounts I'd hoped for.

I was scheduled to report to Oakland Army Base in California for shipment to Vietnam. My parents refused to go with me. My dad said nothing to me, and my mom wouldn't even look at me. So a neighbor took me. This wasn't the kind of send off I had envisioned. I spent over a week in Oakland waiting for the shipment orders to come and listening to all the old guys trying to scare the hell out of all of us FNGs (fucking new guys). I boarded a bus in Oakland for the trip to Travis Air Base with visions of a commercial flight to Vietnam. However, upon arrival at Travis we boarded a Flying Tiger Freight Plane, which turned out to be a converted cargo plane with seats bolted into it. I only remember one stewardess, but I am sure there were others. My memory fails me here.

The flight was routed by way of Alaska, which was fun if you liked five-degree weather while wearing jungle fatigues. I was soon to realize how much I would miss the five-degree weather. I played cards and dined on a sandwich that tasted left over from the Korean War. After another brief stop in Japan, we ran into a large storm that stayed with us all the way to Tan Son Nhut Air Base in Vietnam. The storm was so bad I was sure I'd never reach Vietnam and die a shark-bait hero instead.

Arriving in Vietnam was no different from any other trip you can take in the army. I truly believe that all military transport planes arrive at their destination at the required time of 12:00 midnight to 2:00 a.m. The temperature in the plane was very comfortable. However, at 0100 hours (1:00 a.m.) when the doors of the plane opened my, face began to feel like it was melting in an oven. And it smelled like all the shit in the world had been dumped in Vietnam. Why I had the idea that Vietnam could not be hotter than Georgia, I don't know, but I sure learned fast.

I boarded what appeared to be an old prison bus. The process at Tan Son Nhut would take three days and the impression was that they had nothing for us to do. With an Infantry MOS (military occupational specialty), I was selected for guard duty. Wow, I though, my first day in country, and I was to guard the Doughnut Dolly Compound (headquarters of Red Cross volunteers who visited units with coffee and doughnuts, delivered Red Cross packages and emergency messages from home). They gave me one magazine for my M16 and told me to call before I shot anyone. But with no radio and no other instructions, I was glad I didn't meet some poor son of a bitch because I would have shot him and worried about it later.

We received our unit assignments, but we wouldn't be going to our units until we got our dog and received some training with the animal. This would let the dog get used to his handler as well as showing us (the handler) what the dog was capable of. My dog's name was Smokey but he was known as 5A8A, as all dogs were required to have dog tags just like the soldier. The dog was army property, but he was another soldier to me and later my friend. The team (the dog and I) was assigned to the First Infantry Division at Lai Khe. We rode to the location of the camp in a two-and-a-half-ton truck, commonly known as a duce and a half. After arriving in Lai Khe, which was an old French rubber plantation, I was wondering if this country's temperature was always set on London broil. They assigned me to the Forty-First Infantry Scout Dog Platoon, which was on call to all infantry units in the division.

The first thing I learned was, *if you're going to be an infantryman, be a Big Red One infantryman.* The Big Red One was formed on May 24, 1917. It is the oldest infantry division in the army and is highly decorated. The division's motto is *no sacrifice to great, no mission to difficult, duty first.* It was special to be assigned to the division. The second thing I learned was some of the local slang. This slang consisted mainly of *boom boom,* which meant sex; *didi mau*, which indicated you had better get the fuck out of there; and *dinky dau*, which meant you were crazy. The others have slipped my mind. I realized later that we all were dinky dau to a degree. But that craziness really kept us sane (combat vets know what I mean).

My first experience in the field was alongside an experienced handler whose main job was to cover me and show me the real mission of a dog handler. This experienced guy, a large redheaded man who was short (meaning he had little time left in country), wasn't exactly excited about being in combat with a FNG. However, he did help with many ideas and ways to stay alive, which Smokey and I greatly appreciated. When we (Smokey and I) began accompanying the infantry units without the short timer, we found it a lonely experience. Infantry units were together long enough for members to bond and gain trust. But Smokey and I moved from unit to unit. We were outsiders, but they treated us with respect and were generally kind. I always had the utmost respect for all infantry units as there was very little time for the bullshit that went on at some base camps. The dogs were a recent addition to these units, and most members didn't even know dogs were being used in Vietnam. How the dogs were used in combat was a learning experience for most people.

Vietnam was divided into different areas of operation for various combat units. Our unit operated in what was called III Corps. This area extended from Central Vietnam to the Delta in the south. III Corps included an area called the Iron Triangle located between the Thi-Tinh and Saigon Rivers, next to the Cu Chi District. At times we would work near or with unit such as the Eleventh Armored Cavalry, Twenty-Fifth Infantry Division.

A lot of my tour of duty—sorry, that sounds like a view from a cruise ship with a buffet, lets say *my time in country*—was with the First Infantry, but later the First Infantry was rotated back to the United States. Then I served with the Forty-Ninth Infantry Scout Dog Platoon of the 199th Light Infantry Brigade. The jobs were the same and constantly meeting and working with new people was tough. Some of our First Infantry Platoons went to the 101st Division, while others were scattered throughout Vietnam.

Ecologically, there were many different areas of Vietnam ranging from farms and rice paddies to double canopy jungle. When an infantry squad was setting out, a call would be made to our platoon leader, and Smokey and I would be assigned to a squad. This would make for an interesting trip. First, we would hitch a ride to a firebase camp, hook up with a unit, and then proceed out to the field. The exact amount of time we would spend out in the jungle depended on the type of mission. We would board Hueys (helicopters) that landed in a dirt area at the firebase and travel to an LZ (landing zone).

I disliked flying tremendously, but when it came to helicopters that fear disappeared. Helicopters provided a one of a kind rush. The side doors were removed, and the wind against my face was a feeling I grew to love. Smokey with his head in the wind and his legs over the edge was a site I would never forget. The Huey was four or five feet off the ground at the LZ when we would hear the word *out*. I pushed Smokey and jumped onto what I hoped was grass or soft ground. This wasn't always the case. Sometimes it was soft, and sometimes it was hard. We would hit the ground, run to the edge of the LZ, and start the "hump" through the jungle. This was OK unless the LZ was hot (hot meaning it was receiving enemy fire). If the LZ was hot, it was a whole different—and pretty dangerous—situation.

I grew up watching movies about World War II and had a young person's fantasy of what the jungle would be like. However, reality set in fast. The heat of the jungle beneath the double canopy (one layer of jungle grown over another) was almost unbearable. We were always working in darkness, whether it was nine in the morning or four o'clock in the afternoon. Only the occasional small patch of light ever broke through the mass of growth. The jungle meant living with bugs, snakes, and plant life I had seen only in National Geographic or on TV. There were mosquitoes with their own area code and bugs bigger than most animals at home. There were snakes that could kill you and others that could eat you. Green vipers and cobras made my hatred of snakes grow more intense. And I can't forget the wonderful elephant grass that caused the cuts and infections while also being a pain in the ass. Or the ants that crawled down your neck, the scorpions that crept into your boots, and wasps that buzzed in your face. I hope I didn't leave anyone out because I want to give full credit to all that made life pleasant.

On one night mission, it was late in the evening and everyone was on edge because we had found a basecamp that the NVA (North Vietnamese Army) had left just before our arrival. When we made camp that night, guard duty was assigned and everyone took their turn watching for the enemy. When it was my turn for guard duty, I left Smokey on my poncho liner (the plastic sheet we slept on) and proceeded to a position near a trailhead. It was almost pitch black when in the moonlight I saw the outline of a cobra's head, just in front of me. I reached for my weapon, but when I looked back he was gone. I still remember the image of that deadly snake—as much I remember as any image of the war.

The jungle had its own soundtrack, and it changed with the hours of the day. But the AK-47, the preferred weapon of the NVA and VC, had a sound of its own, one that penetrated the thick air and cut through the other noises around you. It is amazing how much energy you feel at the sound of rounds fired from a weapon.

The jungle is absolutely beautiful as long as you can view it from afar. From afar you never smell the jungle's stench of rot, as if there is death and beauty, all in the same place. The smells are sharpened by the heat and the wet. During my time in country, I was beginning to tolerate the heat when the rainy season broke. It was hot and wet, which was good with a woman but not in the jungle. I will credit that line to *Good Morning, Vietnam* so you won't sue me. Oh, to hell with it. All someone can sue me for is dysentery, malaria, Parkinson's, and a healthy distrust of 99.9 percent of the human race. I need to focus here because war is not fun. But when you are a little dinky dau, certain things become more tolerable. I do have a respect for all who served in Vietnam, and a hatred for the "fuck job" we received for doing our job.

I am rambling on. It was the best of times, and it was the worst of times. Where am I going with this? Now I'm stealing from old novels. It was the rainy season, and God poured buckets of water on all of Vietnam. The biggest problem was sleeping in the jungle with rivers running around your poncho liner. At times many things were bad all at once: the weather, the war, the heat, and all those people you would never know again. It gave me a much larger appreciation for my dog and the loyal way he performed his duty. He was a friend who never complained, and I have never met a better soldier.

In the field, the basic necessities of life were all you cared about. The meal of C-rations heated with C-4, your friendly explosive heat source, with a low flame and a nice smokeless burn, was what you had to eat. I shared my C-rations with Smokey, even though I had dog food for him, too. At times the dog food was better than the C-rations, especially when the dog food was made into nice patties and cooked over the C-4 flame.

I worked with all types of infantry units including an Armored Unit of the Eleventh Cavalry. I discovered these soldiers were "boo coo dinky dau." I learned never take a ride with them. They drove through jungle, woods, and dirt roads with a rush hour LA mindset. I discovered religion that day. I thought my time had finally come, and asked for help from whoever would give it. The Buddha didn't even help.

I was around fewer Vietnamese than other soldiers because the dog was trained to "alert" on them and became very aggressive around them. One night on patrol after an arc light raid by B-52s, we captured two gooks with Ho Chi Minh sandals and paperwork that we knew was phony. Locals were to stay out of the areas known as free fire zones, where anyone seen could be considered the enemy. The lieutenant was the only one who believed those assholes, and he let them go. Sure enough we got hit that night. That was one of the problems of "friend by day and enemy by night." This game of cat and mouse went on throughout my time in Vietnam.

Lieutenants could be very good at times, and at other times they could be horrible. The time of Smokey's revenge was one of those hit and miss times. I had hooked up with a squad, and we were to leave the next morning. The lieutenant was fascinated with Smokey. I told him "a pet he was not" and was best left alone, but the lieutenant thought he knew better and went behind the hootch to pet Smokey. It was glorious! The next sound I heard was screaming and yelling. I slowly walked to the other side of the hootch to rescue the lieutenant. The incident got us an extra day in camp, and it got the lieutenant a set of marks he can treasure forever. It will be the gift that keeps on giving.

It wasn't until later in life that I discovered what was called Agent Orange. This herbicide is the gift that will keep on giving death to my brothers. I always wondered why the firebases had nice dirt landing areas and there was no vegetation around the hootches. The answer was that Agent Orange was used to destroy anything that grew and this included humans. The effects of being in an area sprayed with this chemical will keep affecting veterans until their lives finally end. It is strange that life gives you things you can't describe or you never dreamed of. Many would say the circumstances of their lives are not what they wanted. However, be it bad, good, or horrible, it is who we are today. Nothing can or will explain that reality.

The time had come to head home, and I was in a very strange position. I wanted to go, but I could remember times of being left alone and not fucked with, which made being there somewhat bearable. I felt a dark attraction to stay and not face home.

Home later became a hell all its own. I missed the snakes, spiders, ants, and elephant grass in a strange way that nobody could understand. At home I met my wife and started my family, and they were my ticket to staying alive. However, the guilt I feel for those brothers who never got the chance I did never goes away.

I could not continue without mentioning the family aspect of my homecoming. My dad fought the battle of Los Angeles during WWII. He spent 1941–1945 in California. To this day it is a mystery how he accomplished this. When he passed away, he was thought of as a WWII veteran. I will give him credit for his service, but he was not a veteran of the war. When I first came home my dad told me he was glad I didn't fight in a real war, and he was happy I had an easy job in the army. Then he asked me how long it would be before I got a job. This was on my first day home. I found a job I hated and moved out almost immediately. His family treated me like I had a contagious disease and moved to the other side of the room when I visited them.

These experiences helped contribute to my view of hating most of the human race. I have had people tell me that Vietnam vets are whiners who need to just suck it up and forget the past. The people who say this never heard a shot fired in anger. The American public hated us, ignored us, wanted us to just disappear. So we went silent and buried our feelings. Now that we are dying at a rate higher than any other veteran group, and will vanish into the vacuum of history, we will have our say. The world can go fuck itself. All that we wanted was to be welcomed home as your father, son, sister, brother, friend, and to be left to lead our lives as a part of this country. Instead we were marked as crazy, dangerous, uneducated, and outside the mainstream of society. We were called baby killers and dope fiends. When we dared to speak up for ourselves, people called us whiners or complainers, and acted like we didn't have a right to speak of our experiences. I say that when people share a personal part of their lives, you can ignore it, or listen. But I will never again accept the disrespect. I will not tolerate this ever happening to any other generation.

We all wish for better things, but sometimes I think of bad times as good, and I know that the world will continue to move on with or without us, so just remember, *and Fuck it. It doesn't mean a thing!*

Chet Brassart along with his dog Smokey

Chet Brassart holding the assigned name and number of his dog

WHY I HATE YOU

By a soldier

Chet Brassart
Sergeant
US Army
First Infantry Division
1969-1970

I remember you as the one who had to be right. The appearance of the high moral ground was your fortress. The facts of right and wrong were always gray. The tradition of yesterday was to be laughed at, and the moral structure of my life was a myth. I wanted to learn, you wanted to tear down; I wanted to discuss, you wanted to initiate; I believed that there was evil in the world, and you saw only evil in the very country I loved and would give my life to preserve. Did you have the right to believe these things? Yes, but that right doesn't extend to the destruction of the freedom that others have fought and died for and also the extension of freedom throughout the world.

I hate you for cheering when the ROTC building burnt down at Cal. I hated it when you carried a Viet Cong flag. When you chanted, Ho, Ho, Ho Chi Min, the NLF is going to win. The protests were large when I went to Vietnam and were large when I returned. I hated you for the medals you threw over the fence at the White House, and the fifty-eight thousand brothers you dishonored by joining the chorus of hate that infested your movement. I was not the uneducated, I was not the poor, and I was not the colonial power arm for empire. I was the America you hated; The America of my ancestors; The America of hard work; The America of freedom, and not one of the unwashed mass you claimed to lead. I hate your elitist, righteous view you that only you carry the torch of moral superiority, and that only you can decide the path of my country, and my life.

I am told that you can like the person, but hate what they believe. I say you are what you believe. Can one change? Yes! I do believe that change can happen in a person, but that will never change what was done: I may forgive, but I will never forget. You were the neighbor I knew who was kind and soft spoken, who may have seemed a little odd, but likeable. In the coming years you were the one who called a family and told them you were glad that their son had died in Vietnam. You were the one who said that we were baby killers, haters, not to be honored but to be separated from the rest of the Good People who had the courage to oppose the war.

Did I like war? No! Did I feel that we fought a war that was constantly interfered with by politicians whose actions were guided by thoughts of re-election, right or wrong? Yes! This does not excuse you, or make you right. You have the right to believe, but not to use me as a whipping boy for your elitist views. Never again will I let this happen to any soldier. I will always hate you for your relative morals. Where were you with the massive protests when Pol Pot murdered two million people in the name of agrarian communism? Where were you when hundreds of thousands died in re-education camps in Vietnam? Where was the outrage? I spoke and was told it was my fault because we were there. You were the guilt-free moralist sitting in an ivory tower of self-righteousness.

I hate you because in many ways you have forced me into a life of isolation. I came back to an America that wanted no part of my kind. It was not an issue of *we will forget you*, but an issue of putting me in a box and locking it for all times. Not one of us wanted to be held on a pedestal or set aside as someone different from you. We had a brotherhood, and all we asked was to be your son, father, hard worker, lover, countryman, and to experience life in the country we loved. You wouldn't allow this, and that is why I hate you.

CHAPTER THREE

VIETNAM MENACE: BOOBY TRAPS, LAND MINES, AND TUNNELS

Jim Money
Sergeant
US Army
Company B
Sixty-fifth Engineer Battalion
Twenty-fifth Infantry Division
January 1967–January 1968

I wanted to talk about what I went through in Vietnam but from a different perspective, from a perspective of one soldier who put his life on hold for our country and world freedom. I wanted to give you an idea of what it was like to be an ordinary young man who was born in the early forties, grew up in the fifties, and found who he was during the sixties. What made him voluntarily enter the military service? What he went through. What he went through upon return to the United States.

It is really hard to believe that I am alive and able to compile this accounting of Vietnam. Many of the soldiers who returned home from their tour in the Republic of Vietnam left friends over there who didn't make it home. I had friends who never made it home. There were many times when I thought my own time had come, but I made it. It has been over forty years, and my mind has blocked out some of what happened to me while in Vietnam. I am going to do my best to put things in the correct timeline, but I can't promise anything. What I do remember is that I spent the majority of my time out in the jungles. As you will see, any time infantry (foot soldiers) or armored cavalry (mechanized infantry) went out in armored personnel carriers in search of the Viet Cong, I was with them. There were several of these types of fighting units at the base camp where I was sent, which kept us pretty busy. It seemed that as soon as we returned to base camp another unit was heading out, and looking for demolition help.

I should have known what kind of year it would be when everything started happening before I even set foot in Vietnam. We had been sitting on the chartered jet liner for what seemed years when a quick glance at the watch on my wrist showed it had only been a few hours. The flight from Oakland, California, to South Vietnam was scheduled to take fifteen hours. I told myself this was going to be a long day.

We made a couple of stops on the way to refuel. I must have dozed off because something jarred me awake, and I found myself struggling to decode the odd noise entering my ears. Instead of the drone of the jet engines from the airplane, a different sound was attempting to get through to the brain. Suddenly I realized it was an actual voice attempting to get inside my head. It took a minute for my mind to realize that it was the captain speaking to us, but before I could translate what he was saying the plane took a sudden nose dive towards the ground, and just when I thought that the ground was going to come up and slam into the plane, we leveled out and touched down on the airport runway. Suddenly I realized that we were in Vietnam. The soldier next to me said, "Wasn't that something. I mean the way we had to land." Gasping for a breath, I nodded my agreement. He added, "This is my second trip over here. They have to land that way because the planes are shot at if they came down gradually like a regular plane." This should have told me something.

I survived the landing and the sudden influx of heat that entered through the door in the plane. The next couple of days were spent getting an orientation to Vietnam. Finally, we were loaded on a truck and convoyed to a place called Cu Chi, escorted by two MP gun jeeps.

The Cu Chi base camp was fairly large, and just outside the perimeter was the city of Cu Chi, which was northwest of Saigon. In order to be able to use soldiers for what they are trained to do, the camp used local villagers to do some of the work on the base. Viet Cong mortar crews knew exactly where they wanted the rounds to land because the inside of the camp was precisely mapped out for them by the people working on the base. We found out, too late, that they had dug tunnels under the camp. We found out, the hard way, that nobody could be trusted.

My first look at what combat was all about and the art of staying alive began just days after landing in Vietnam and being assigned to the Sixty-fifth Engineer Battalion, Twenty-fifth Infantry Division. Upon arrival at the unit, I was asked if I would like to become a demolition specialist (someone who blew things up). I had no idea how to use explosives. My only experience as a combat engineer was bridge building, which I learned while assigned to an engineer battalion in West Germany. The unit told me that as a demo specialist, I would be teamed up with a partner, and then we would accompany infantry units on search and destroy missions. Our particular duty on these missions would be to destroy any booby traps, mines, and tunnels that were found with an explosive called C-4. It sounded interesting so I accepted the offer.

I was introduced to my platoon sergeant, Sergeant Hensley, who took me to my hootch and introduced me to my partner (who also was fairly new). Hensley explained to me that one of the squad's missions was to sweep one of the roads leading into the base camp on a daily basis.

However, since I was going to be a demolition specialist, I wouldn't have to worry about the mine sweeping because I wouldn't be around much.

He wasn't kidding. The next day, my partner and I were assigned to a company from one of the armored cavalry units who were going out on a search and destroy mission. We gathered our equipment, which included a .45 caliber pistol, M16 rifle, and an M79 grenade launcher. We also picked up some C-4 plastic explosive, fuse, and detonating caps, which would be used to destroy any mines, booby traps, and tunnels we came upon.

We left the area of our unit and walked to where we were to meet the unit we were going out with. This was our first assignment, and we were unsure of what to expect. We arrived a little apprehensive but ready and were told to find a track (APC-armored personnel carrier) to ride on. Not knowing any better and not being advised by anyone, we hopped on the second vehicle in the convoy which had a 105 recoilless weapon mounted on it. We had no idea what type of weapon this was. Normally, the vehicle had a hatch on top which opened exposing the interior. There also was a ramp which opened the rear of the vehicle allowing soldiers or supplies to be loaded into it. Because of the weapon mounted on top we had to sit on top of the closed hatch. Besides having to get used to sitting on top of a large running piece of metal and bouncing with every ditch or hole the monster ran into, we had to dodge low hanging branches from trees and jungle growth that came at us as we made our way forward. Besides hiding the Viet Cong, these branches held other surprises for us. Very large, nasty, and hungry red ants fell on everyone riding in or on the vehicle, along with the occasional snake. These snakes could sometimes be lethal. Most of us would have rather faced the Viet Cong in a fight than run into an agitated poisonous snake.

For the first few hours everything seemed to be going fine (at least we hadn't been shot at yet). The convoy busted out of the jungle into a small clearing. Our track vehicle had reached the center of the clearing when the convoy took fire. One of the vehicle's crewmembers yelled at us to jump off the track. We hesitated a second, thinking in our heads that this guy must be crazy. Then he yelled, "This is a 106 recoilless and you can't be on the vehicle when it's fired." Needless to say we jumped off the vehicle as it made its way towards the source of the enemy fire. Then it dawned on us that here we were out in the middle of this clearing, with nowhere to hide and bullets flying through the air. We both looked at each other, and then we tried to bury ourselves in the six-inch-high grass.

The air was ringing with gunfire and loud explosions. The track we'd just jumped off of charged the wall of jungle in front of it. Just as it seemed to reach the edge of the jungle the track lurched to a sudden stop. Amazed, we watched one of the crewmen jump from the vehicle, run around to the front, and toss something into the jungle. It turned out to be a hand grenade. A loud bang and a cloud of dust showed where the grenade had landed, exposing a small hole. After the explosion all the rifle fire stopped, and a few minutes later we were called forward to rejoin our vehicle.

When we reached the spot where the vehicle had stopped, we could see two mangled bodies, which we found out were Viet Cong (VC), lying in front of a small hole from which they had been dragged. We were amazed that only two enemy soldiers had opened fire on a convoy of armored track vehicles carrying a company of infantrymen.

That was my first encounter with war and with the enemy I would come to know. The company commander called for a lunch break and we pulled out our C-rations, sat down and ate, all the while staring at the dead bodies. I then experienced a second lesson of war: Don't let blood and broken bodies stop you from eating your lunch at the normal time. Strangely it didn't seem to bother any of us.

After we finished lunch the company commander told us to load up, and we were back in the jungle. The rest of the mission went off without a major hitch. We all returned to base camp smiling and in one piece.

I must have had a sign on me that said Leave Me because something similar happened on another mission. My partner and I joined a company of infantry nicknamed the Wolfhounds. We were airlifted to a clearing about thirty minutes flying time from base camp. We knew something big was up because of the amount of explosives they wanted. Thank heavens for helicopters.

It seemed that a patrol had located an enemy underground base camp. The unit we were with was ordered to reinforce the patrol, and we were brought along to destroy the tunnels. As soon as we jumped off the choppers, the company surrounded the tunnel complex and dispatched a couple of patrols to make sure we weren't surprised while my partner and I were in the process of destroying the complex. It was getting close to the end of the day when we finished. Just as we finished blowing up the last tunnel, the helicopters were returning to pick everyone up for the trip back to base camp. Before we knew it, the choppers were on the ground and people began loading in them. My partner and I reached the line of choppers only to find there was no more room on them. Someone yelled from the last bird, "Someone will be right back to get you."

"Well, this is great!" I said to no one in particular. Here we were, the two of us in the middle of a clearing again, only this time alone. And somewhere out in the jungle was a very upset group of Viet Cong, mad as hell at the soldiers who had just blown up their homes. Needless to say we were a little nervous. We decided to sit down with our backs together, which gave us the best area of vision, and we watched for any movement. It seemed like hours passed before we could hear the rotor noise of a returning helicopter. We found out later that one of the other helicopters radioed back to base that we were still in the mission area and needed a ride. The ride home actually arrived about forty-five minutes after the company had left the area. After we were back in our hootch, it dawned on us that it really wouldn't have done us any good sitting back to back out in the middle of this field because the VC could have shot us before we would have seen movement. We felt a little dumb, but it had made us feel better while we were out there. We were getting a little tired of ending up in the middle of clearings with no cover.

Another mission called on us to join a leg unit on a search-and-destroy trek through the jungle. We spent several days trying to locate the elusive gook (another name for a VC) without success. However, we did find the mines and booby traps they left for us on the trail. Some of them were found by unlucky soldiers who had to take a ride back to the base hospital. Enough were found by watchful eyes to keep the demo team busy destroying the traps without destroying anybody else. Booby traps were especially hard because, a lot of times, the trap was a hand grenade resting precariously on a thin branch of a bush. A wire stretched across the trail. If a soldier tripped the wire, the grenade would explode. When we found this type of trap, I would have to set a piece of C-4 explosive with a blasting cap next to the grenade, without shaking the grenade from the branch, then light the fuse and get out of range before the explosion. What made this more difficult was that we had to run for cover back the way we had come. We couldn't run further up the trail because we might step on a land mine or another hidden booby trap. However, running back the way we had come usually meant hurdling the trip wire that was strung across the trail.

Another mission found us walking down a trail when we came to a fifteen-foot-thick hedgerow that was as long as the eye could see. The infantry company commander didn't want to attempt to go around the hedgerow because he couldn't see the end of it, and we would waste too much time. Our orders were to locate and destroy any booby traps so the unit could get through. The area was about thirty feet in length. Even with a couple of the infantrymen helping us search, it took four hours to get through the hedgerow. We destroyed ten booby traps and uncovered two tilt-rod land mines. I was shaking so much by the time the last booby trap was erased that it was hard to walk. My partner drank a whole canteen of water.

We all moved through the hedgerow and had been walking about an hour when we came to a small stream. The soldier in front of me was going down the bank to the streambed when he stepped on a land mine sending a hot piece of shrapnel into the can of blasting caps that was in the side pocket of my fatigues. When I took it out of my pocket, the can was bent completely in half. How the heat and the collision hadn't set off the blasting caps, I didn't know at the time, but later I thought that God must have been watching. I was sure thankful for Him watching over me.

Later that day we came upon an artillery shell that was standing upright. A dud shell that doesn't explode usually lands pointed toward its target. The shell raised our suspicions because it was sitting, pointed straight up, like someone had put it there, which meant it was probably booby-trapped. The company commander told us to get rid of it. We couldn't see any booby traps around the shell, but we didn't want to pick it up. Not wanting to cause it to explode while the infantrymen were walking by, we gathered some rope from the unit and put a noose over the round. We waited until the whole unit has passed our location. After assuring the unit's last soldier had reached a safe distance, we pulled the rope and knocked the shell over. To our surprise and happiness, nothing happened. We checked the fallen shell and found no booby traps. We set a small charge and blew it apart in order to ensure the Viet Cong could not use it.

Upon return to base camp at Cu Chi, we were getting some needed rest and cleaning our equipment when word came from the orderly room (company headquarters) that Sgt. Hensley had just been killed on the morning minesweeping mission. The sweepers had missed a landmine, and he had found it. It was a complete shock to us, and the platoon took it pretty hard. He was a good man and a fine soldier. A couple of days later, as we were getting his belongings ready to be shipped back to his family, word came from his wife that we should keep the radio and television for the platoon. I never knew what they had on TV because I never watched it. My squad leader became the platoon sergeant and I took over the squad. However, the new position didn't relieve me of my demolition duties. I still had to blow things up, and things went on as usual.

Another search-and-destroy mission was with the Eleventh Armored Cavalry Unit during Operation Junction City. The date was April 27, 1967, a day that is embedded in my mind forever. This was the day I received my first and thankfully, my only, Purple Heart. I do feel somewhat responsible because my partner and I pulled the biggest no-no anyone could pull. I believe we were told to meet the armored cavalry unit at the back gate of the base, which was called Ann Margaret. Upon arrival at the unit's location, we were told the usual: Find a ride. We walked the line of armored personnel carriers and found that no room was available on any vehicle except the lead track. Riding on the lead track was the big no-no. This was because the lead vehicle was the first over the road, or the first into the jungle. The other vehicles following the lead one are taught to stay in his tracks on the ground. The lead track would be the one to find any trouble, whether it was buried in the ground or coming from the side. My partner and I reluctantly climbed aboard and were seated atop an open hatch that folded over the area where the troops rode.

The convoy left base-camp, and we proceeded out into what was called the Iron Triangle. The Iron Triangle was a 120 square mile area twenty-five miles north of Saigon. The triangle was formed by three provinces. It was a VC stronghold and a main infiltration route for the enemy. The mission was uneventful for the first couple of hours. We began to think the danger of riding in the lead vehicle was just a myth. We crossed a fairly large clearing and entered the jungle. The lead APC led the convoy along a path past a mound of earth. This mound was little higher than the top of the APC. We had traveled approximately a quarter of a mile when there was a loud boom and I was lifted into the air. That was the last thing I remember until I woke up inside the APC with the hatch closed above me. When I came to my senses, the inside of the vehicle was a mess and full of dust. My partner and I were on our backs on top of a bunch of gear that had been tossed around.

We didn't know how long we had been out, but we knew we had to get out of there. I quickly pushed the hatch open. We grabbed our rifles and looked out the hole toward voices coming from the top of the mound of dirt. A group had gathered, and they were hollering, "Get out! Get out! They said we should jump across the open space between the APC and the mound so as not to step on the path in case there were other mines. Lacking the strength we needed, we made the jump and landed about three fourths of the way to the top. The soldiers immediately grabbed us and pulled us up over the top. Someone said that the vehicle had hit a land mine and that the driver was dead. They thought that we were also dead because we weren't answering their screams. The lieutenant, who was riding on the track behind us, told us that when the mine was hit, the hatch had come up and hit us, knocking us inside. We were told to walk to the end of the convoy to get on a medevac chopper for transport back to the base hospital. I remember all of the men of the unit giving us the thumbs up as we walked pass. Later, back at the hospital, we found out that one of the sergeants, who had given us the thumbs up, stepped on another mine just in front of his APC and was killed. I was checked out by the medical staff, bandaged from head to foot, and sent back to my unit. I felt like a walking bandage factory. But I was still alive!

After being release from the hospital, I reported back to my unit to find that they had been sent out on a mission. The sergeant who was in charge of the small attachment left behind was thrilled to see me and my partner. We soon found out that he was happy only because he had two more people to pull guard duty at night. That night, bandages and all, I was in the bunker pulling my shift on guard duty. No rest for the weary. However, it was a break from walking through the jungles, and I wasn't complaining.

There was another mission that stands out in my mind. My partner and I had joined the Wolfhounds on a search and destroy mission. We had humped through the jungle all day and had nothing but the heat to talk about. It was getting late in the afternoon, and the unit was looking for a place to set up camp for the night. We were walking through an open area that was surrounded by jungle. The area was in the shape of an L and when we reached the lower end of the long part of the L, we made a left turn into the smaller part of the L, and the commanding officer chose to set up at the far end of the short leg of the L. There was jungle on three sides of us and the unit was deployed into the jungle to set up defensive positions. We soon discovered that there were tunnel entrances/exits all through the jungle where the unit was setting up their perimeter. Some of the entrances/exits were located inside the perimeter, which proved fatal later that evening. The command post was in the open clearing where the commanding officer and the first sergeant were located along with the radio operator and the medics.

As soon as darkness engulfed the area, the Viet Cong hit us with mortars, and then they began coming up inside the perimeter. There were always two men to a position and the word was passed to stay in your position and shoot anything that moves. The fight lasted until daylight the next morning. We were told that the unit had lost over half of its strength, largely due to the fact that no medevacs could get in to evacuate the more seriously wounded or bring help in. It seemed that the helicopters had to fly down the length of the short leg of the L to get in to us because the command post was located close to the jungle for safe landing. Furthermore, they were pummeled with enemy fire when they tried to enter our location.

There were many more missions, but my memory has faded somewhat. However, there is one last trip I would like to mention. This account will give you another look at what happened to us over there. The unit had received a call from an infantry unit that had come across an underground location that went down six stories into the ground. Our platoon was sent out to assist, and when we arrived at the scene the infantry commander said they had spent hours trying to talk several VC out of the underground hideout. It seemed that the underground building was a hospital and that there were wounded soldiers who didn't want to come out and surrender. The commander decided that enough time had been wasted and told us to flood the underground hospital with the VC still down in it. Several tanker trucks of water soon arrived plus we had water from a small river flowing nearby. We pumped as much water as the place would hold. In fact, the water was coming out of the ground at the entrance. I didn't have much time to reflect on what had just happened because the platoon leader called me over to his location and said that he and I were going out to recon a possible bridge site.

I grabbed a radio, and we jumped into a jeep and left the location escorted by two MP gun jeeps. The trip out was uneventful, but on the way back to camp we were ambushed just outside of a small village. We jumped from the jeep into a ditch on the side of the road and returned fire out into a field where the rounds were coming from. One of the gun jeeps called for help, and reinforcements arrived to get us out of the scrape. After returning to camp we noticed a small group of women at the front gate. They were animated and screaming something to guards. We were told that the women had just complained that we had killed their relative who had been in the field farming.

Finally I was able to sit down and go back over the events of the day. The fact that I had a hand in killing wounded and unarmed VC who wouldn't come out of the underground hospital really didn't sit well with me. It bothered me until recently, when I was reminded about the fact that if they hadn't been killed, they probably would have killed some American soldiers later. I guess that is war. At least that is what I am now telling myself.

I can remember another occasion we were out with a leg unit. We had been pushing our way through jungle and rice paddies when we came across a small village. We noticed some villagers watching us cross a rice paddy and climb a small hill to reach the village. We secured the village and the infantry soldiers made a hootch-to-hootch search. A few booby traps were found, and we took care of them. One search team returned to the area where my partner and I were located along with the company commander, first sergeant, and radio operator. They had two local, male villagers with them. They were interrogated, using an RVN Scout, but no information was forthcoming. The company commander put a request in for a helicopter gun ship to be flown to our location. When the chopper arrived, a platoon sergeant and the interrogator escorted the two gooks to the chopper, and they all got on. Soon the chopper was up in the air and after a short time it returned with only the platoon sergeant and the interrogator on board. I asked one of the soldiers, whom I had come to know, what happened to the two male gooks. He informed me that normally, when two go up in a chopper, one usually returns. This is because if they refuse to give the interrogator the information he is looking for, one is pushed out and before the scream can no longer be heard, the other one is talking his head off. He said that this time, neither one must have talked so they both went out the door. Before my time was up in Vietnam, this happened a few other times. I guess it was another fact of life in war.

There were many, many more days and operations out in the jungle blowing things up and getting shot at, but my memory has faded mainly because it has been suppressed for over forty years. No one wanted to know what that year was like, in fact, we were told not to speak of it because it was a war the country wanted to forget.

There was one lighter moment that happened sometime during the middle of my tour of duty. I was told that it was time for me to take an R&R and get away from things. I decided to go to Hawaii. It sounded like a good place. While on the plane to Hawaii, I became acquainted with another soldier on his way to Hawaii. I don't remember how or why but we talked about home and how nice it would be to see everyone. I mentioned that I had a son born in March, which was during my third month in Vietnam. I hadn't seen him yet. Before we landed the subject of leaving Hawaii and going home came up and it sure sounded good. We quickly decided to attempt to buy tickets after we landed and continue to go home. He was going to the State of Washington and I was going on to Boston. We landed, and to our dismay there were Military Police all over the place.

After discussing the situation, we decided to try anyway, reasoning that if we were caught, what would they do, send us to Vietnam? We slipped into the restroom and changed our clothes and proceeded to the ticket counter. To our amazement and relief nobody questioned us, and after making plans to meet up upon our return, we proceeded to our respective gates.

Naturally, everyone was surprised to see me, and it was great to see my son. My parents were a little upset but didn't let on. To my surprise a minister from a church showed up at the house to talk to me. My parents thought I was going AWOL. After I finally assured them that I had all intentions of returning, they relaxed and we had a good reunion. I returned to Hawaii with about fifteen hours to spend in Hawaii before my plane left for Vietnam. I met my newfound friend at the airport, and we spent the last few hours sitting on the beach.

I spent my last month and a half in country with my squad, pulling a minesweeping operation on a road leading into a forward artillery base camp located northwest of Tay Ninh, close to the Cambodian border. Every morning the squad would sweep the road leading into the basecamp for mines.

They did an excellent job but had a lapse on one morning. The minesweeping detail missed a mine on Christmas day of December 1967, and an escort vehicle hit it. Thankfully, no one was injured. Later that day the near miss was all but forgotten when the daily resupply run arrived with a surprise gift for the squad from the company commander. It was a case of champagne! It was a pleasant surprise that the company commander would think of us. We didn't usually have diversions like that. Normally, the days were long and quiet with the only excitement coming just after dark. Every day about one hour after darkness, everybody would assemble at positions on the perimeter and participate in what was called a "mad minute." At a given signal, every weapon in camp would fire for a solid minute into the surrounding jungle. I know we made a lot of noise and killed a lot of water buffalo. It was the most excitement I saw during the last month of my tour of duty.

I was convoyed from Tay Ninh to Cu Chi on about the January 20, 1968, but before leaving the camp I was told to turn in my weapons and ammunition to the company's headquarters. The ride to Cu Chi was uneventful, and I reported to the company's rear detachment. Not having a weapon was a little worrisome, and it proved to be down right crazy. I had just lain down for the night when mortar rounds began pounding the base. The Orderly Room sent a runner to wake us up and at the same time he was telling us to get to the supply room and obtain some type of weapon. The VC had breached the perimeter on the other side of the base, and we were to get to our perimeter bunker in case they tried to come through our area. I was able to get a hold of a .45 caliber pistol but realized it would do me little good if they came through the barbed wire because of the distance from the bunker. They would have to get a lot closer for me to be effective. To my relief, after about two hours the attack was over with no attempt by the VC to come through our sector. Several enemy soldiers that had reached the airfield were either captured or killed.

There was one last experience to go through before getting on the plane, and at the time we didn't know anything about it. Two trucks were used to transport everyone who was going home from Cu Chi to Saigon. We would be escorted by two gun jeeps. Because we had all turned in our weapons as ordered, the machine guns on the jeeps would be the only weapons in the convoy. The icing on the cake was finding out later that there had been a 99.9 percent chance that the NVA and VC were already in place for the Tet Offensive and could have wiped us out. I remember joking with the other men on the truck about riding through Vietnam without any weapons. I felt naked during that ride and, after finding out about Tet, really lucky that Charlie had decided not to expose himself early by attacking a basically unarmed convoy.

I boarded my plane home on January 25, 1968. The Tet Offensive began a few days later. I was told, after getting to my next duty station, that during the Tet Offensive the artillery camp where I had left my squad had been overrun and my entire squad was killed. Some days it is hard to get past that memory. I feel bad that I can't remember all their names. I was proud to have served with them, and I pray for them every day.

However, the war didn't stop there. Another war was waiting for me in the United States. I had a thirty-day leave, to pick up my family, before traveling for another tour of duty in West Germany. I feel lucky to have only spent thirty days at home. I soon found out that it was unwise to wear my uniform in public. I was on a subway train headed to downtown Boston when I was accosted by several young men. They were calling me baby killer and warmonger and were waiting for me to reply. Suddenly, three very husky men wearing hardhats stepped between them and myself and told them that they would have to go through them to get to me. I thank God for these men because I was ready to take the group on and probably would have been severely injured. This was one of a few incidents that I had experienced, and I thank God there were some who didn't despise me and the uniform.

I was a lucky one because I didn't have to put up with that stuff for long, at least not as long as some of my fellow soldiers. I went to West Germany for three years and when I returned, I went directly to Fort Leonard Wood in Missouri. I spent just shy of fifteen years in the army, and my duty stations provided some insulation from a lot of the bad feelings directed towards soldiers who were returning from Vietnam, but not all of it. I saw some of the demonstrations and heard the insults directed to those in uniform. I was upset then, and I am still angry towards those who berated and scolded those of us who served our country. All of the angry words may not have been directed toward me, in person, but I felt all the nasty rhetoric that was directed toward my brothers. I join them in telling you how disappointed and angry we were at the way we were treated by our own countrymen.

However, the war was not confined to the jungles of Vietnam or the streets of America. I, as well as most war veterans, fought another war against a hidden disease upon our return to regular living. It is called PTSD (post-traumatic stress disorder). The daily grind of fighting off sudden spurts of anger brought on by the most minimal stressor, the nightly dreams and nightmares of being shot at or seeing others wounded, maimed, or killed. PTSD made me go through life without friends, jumping from job to job, always giving 110 percent, but never realizing that something was wrong with me. One job was right up my alley. It was long-haul truck driving. I was alone, with my truck, driving five hundred miles a day and answering only to a delivery date. I drank heavily (not while on the road), which messes up your mind, and causes a person to do things he or she wouldn't normally do. My current wife—my third—has often wondered why I never had any male friends. I know now that I didn't want to become close to anyone for fear they would die or suddenly be out of my life (this included being close to family). A PTSD sufferer is always looking over his or her shoulder, always expecting someone to sneak up on him or her. They jump (some will actually dive to the ground) when a loud noise surprises him or her. They also will try to drink the local bar and liquor store dry.

Another souvenir veterans brought home from Vietnam was Agent Orange. This was an herbicide the government sprayed to destroy the jungle in order to minimize the areas where the VC could hide. The government is still finding health issues caused by contact with the stuff, but one major result is a disease called ischemic heart disease. I should have known something was wrong when I had to have a couple of balloons put in my arteries when I was about forty-eight years old, and then suffered a heart attack at fifty-eight years old that required a five-artery bypass.

We live the Vietnam War every day of our lives and quite frankly would like to be left alone. Being alone is our comfort zone and we will share our comfort zone with our fellow soldiers, but no one else. The war and what we saw, along with the name-calling from the citizens of this great country, put my brothers and me on the road of loneliness. Thanks!

That is war from one set of eyes. Learn from it. Soldiers suffer greatly from combat. Some effects can be seen, but others are hidden. Don't let the soldiers returning from Iraq and Afghanistan suffer any more than they already are. Welcome them home!

Jim Money outside his barrack in the Cu Chi base camp

Jim Money relaxing next to the wall of sandbags protecting his hootch in Cu Chi

CHAPTER FOUR

SO THAT OTHERS MAY LIVE

James Carlo Calibro
Spec. 4
US Army
First Calvary Division
Medevac
June 1967–June 1968

I was born and raised in Woodland, California. At that time Woodland was a small farming community with tomatoes and sugar beets as its main crops. I grew up on cowboy and WW II war movies, and these guys were my heroes. I graduated from Woodland High School in June 1966, and I was ready to travel to places I had never been and see things I had only dreamed of. The week I graduated I went to the recruiting office located in the old downtown post office with every intention of enlisting in the USMC (United States Marine Corps). The recruiters were all out to lunch (can you imagine that?), so I went to the draft board in the basement of the building volunteered for the draft and entered the army. My dad couldn't believe that I would do anything so foolish. After all, I was only eighteen years old. My basic training was at Fort Lewis, Washington, followed by AIT (advanced individual training) at Fort Eustis and Fort Story, Virginia. I was training to be a stevedore which was a person trained to unload vessels in port. We were training for duty in Vietnam and were going to ship over as a unit until the 409th Transportation Company disbanded. I received separate orders, from the rest of the unit, and was destined for Vietnam. After a thirty-day leave I departed for the experience of a lifetime.

Everyone has a story about their time in Vietnam. Their story may be humorous or it may be sad, but here is my story as I recall it.

I arrived in Vietnam in June of 1967. Our plane landed at Bien Hoa, where we were processed into country and received our assignments. I felt that I had stepped into an oven when we left the air-conditioned plane and the heat slapped us in the face. I will never forget the smell; it was a stench full of heat, dirt and rotten air. It was totally unexpected. The soil was red dirt, dry and dusty. They herded us into a bus with metal screens covering the windows and drove us through town en route to the processing center. I couldn't believe people could live like this, much less survive. Their hootches were put together with scrap lumber and whatever else they could find. People were getting water out of a community well. They milled about in traditional clothing and squatted in doorways.

We arrived at our location and had lunch in a mess area. I about threw up when I took a drink of the warm milk on our dinner table. I found out it was powdered milk because fresh milk was unavailable. They had a water tank with wheels on it referred to as a "water buffalo." I tried to drink the water, and it was green and tasted like chlorine.

I was assigned to my unit and transported to An Khe . I was put on detail to "burn shit," as they put it, which meant I had to clean out the shit houses. The army had taken a fifty-gallon drum, cut it in half and then slid through a door at the bottom of the outhouses to catch human waste. The only way to dispose of the waste was to burn it. In order to burn it, we used a formula of about three parts JP4 (helicopter fuel), one part diesel, and a dab of gasoline. I put on gloves and got a long pole to stir the shit. Then I would stand back, start the fire, and start stirring the mess. I made every attempt to avoid the black smoke and stink, and keep from getting it on my clothes. Afterward I had to shower. That was a shitty job!

An Khe

I was assigned to the Fifteenth Medical Battalion, First Calvary Division, located in An Khe. I questioned why I was assigned to a medical unit since I didn't have a medical background. When I reported in, the first sergeant explained to me that they had a shortage of door gunners for their medevac choppers. He asked me if I could handle the job. He then explained to me that the door gunner I was to replace had been killed the previous day. He was shot by a sniper. The aircraft commander also took a round to his right shoulder and was medevaced out. That afternoon I attended a small service for the door gunner.

The medevac unit was unique, as it was the only unit of its kind in the history of the US Army. This unit was ordered to Vietnam in the fall of 1965 by President Lyndon Johnson. Its insignia, a yellow patch with a black stripe and a horse's head, was considered to be feared by the Viet Cong and the North Vietnamese Army because the unit arrived during the Vietnamese Year of the Horse on the lunar calendar.

The medevac platoon consisted of twelve UH-1H air ambulance helicopters. The aircraft were marked with a red cross and a white background. General John J. Tolson said he was tired of his medevac's being shot up and ordered the white background removed and the aircraft armed with two M60 machine guns—7.62 mm—one on each side of the aircraft. We were a crew of five consisting of an aircraft commander, pilot, crew chief, medic, and door gunner. Two aircraft were assigned to Headquarters Company, which was in base camp. Two aircraft were assigned to each of three combat brigades in the field of operations. The other four were usually in for scheduled maintenance or repair from enemy fire or being held in reserve. We carried up to four litter patients and three "walking wounded." We rescued not only First

Cav troopers but also other Americans in various units as well as ARVNs and POWs. This was extremely dangerous duty as the enemy had put a twenty-five-thousand-dollar bounty on any air ambulance shot down. In my twelve months, my aircraft was shot up numerous times; we made one hard landing due to enemy fire, and were shot down near Khe Sanh on April 4, 1968.

My first crew chief was a short timer they called Barney, he didn't relish the idea of going to the field with a FNG. He came into the hootch I was assigned to and asked for Calibro. I said, that's me, what's up? He responded, Get your things together we're going to LZ Uplift, which meant nothing to me on my first day in the unit. I asked him how long we would be gone, and he responded, who knows maybe a month or more. I thought he was joking and didn't realize that he was serious. Another FNG commented that I had better listen to him and pack up to go, which I did.

Barney and I walked to the armory where I was issued a rifle and two brand new M60 machine guns, I was told that I was responsible for them until I either went home or got killed—what a thrilling thought that was. When I told him I had never flown in a helicopter or fired a machine gun, Barney got upset and started talking to himself. "Why me? I'm too short for this shit," he kept saying. He gave me a crash course on the 60s and my duties, and he soon discovered that I was a quick learner and a natural for the job. We flew out at dusk headed for LZ Uplift. I was taught to wear my chest plate, a two- or three-inch plate of armor for protection, referred to as "chicken plates." There was also a chicken plate for your back. However, due to the weight, we chose to sit on it, rather than wear it, in case any rounds came up from under the aircraft.

Most crewmembers were issued a sidearm, usually an S&W .38, which we used to place between our legs while holstered to protect the family jewels. My first helicopter ride as a door gunner was on the right side of the aircraft, with open doors. I took to it like a duck to water. The wind blowing in your face, people looking like ants on the ground. Most of all I liked the fresh air up there.

LZ Uplift

It was dark when we arrived at LZ Uplift. We headed for the aid station, which was a large tent with wood pallets for floors and numerous patients waiting to be evacuated to a larger hospital at a secure location. We weren't there long when we got our first mission. There had been a firefight somewhere west of our location. That was all I knew. I was scared shitless. However, I showed no fear around all the seasoned vets. It didn't help a lot when my crew chief told me that the "gooks" had green tracer rounds and we had orange: "So, if you see green tracers shoot at them, but keep in mind they also have red and orange tracers, like us." My biggest fear was I didn't want to get confused and shoot our own troops.

We flew two missions that night. The first one we were told to wait because they were receiving enemy fire. I'm not ashamed to say I was scared as we circled and waited, after all this was my first mission. When they said it was clear, the fear went away and I did my job. We made it in without any problems, never had to fire a shot. As we landed with the walking wounded at LZ Uplift, we received another radio call to return. We picked up a "Cho Hoy." It was the first time I actually saw the enemy. He didn't look so big and bad, but I knew not to misjudge them. They had been fighting their war for years and were deadly. We returned to Uplift and managed to grab a few hours of sleep before our next mission.

The next morning, my second day on the job, we got a hoist mission right out of the barn. The wounded trooper was located on the side of a mountain with tall trees. Hoist missions are the most dangerous as you have to hover in the air above the trees on the side of a mountain and lower a jungle penetrator below the treetops. Usually all communication is by radio because you can't see what is below you. We brought up two people. The first was a wounded GI. The second was a female VC in black pajamas. She had shot the GI, and another GI returned fire and wounded her. She was a mean one. When the medic got her in, he had to fight her. Her hands and feet were tied but she was a kicker. I thought it would be easier to throw her out, but we didn't do those things. As the pilot was getting ready to pull pitch a sniper fired a round that hit me in the left knee and ricocheted off, striking the medic in the forehead. I was not injured but the medic was treated at the base hospital and received the Purple Heart.

After almost a month in the field at LZ Uplift, we returned to base camp for scheduled maintenance on our helicopter. I was under the impression that we would be able to relax with nothing to do for a few days. Boy, I was wrong! The medic and I were reassigned to another aircraft. I met my new crew chief and liked him really well. He was killed in action along with four other crewmembers on September 9, 1967. They were flying into LZ Uplift with a load of wounded soldiers when their medevac exploded, no survivors. I met my friend's sister in 2009 at a Vietnam reunion for our unit in Myrtle Beach, South Carolina. She told me that the family was notified of his death by a telegram delivered by taxi.

After LZ Uplift I soon found out that I would see things in one year that most people wouldn't see in a lifetime. Our job was to go into an LZ no matter the situation. Many times we received heavy enemy gunfire, and we witnessed a lot of hostilities. That was the nature of our mission. We weren't a heartless bunch of guys with no feelings. However, we had a job to do, and that was to get the wounded out of combat and to an aid station so the medical personal could make every attempt possible to save their lives. Many times while en route to the aid station, you had men grabbing your arm, pant leg, shirt, and crying out, don't let me die! Some cried for their family members, usually their mother, some called out for either their wife or girlfriend. It wasn't unusual for a door gunner to hold his M60 with one hand and with his other hand hold an IV bottle or apply direct pressure on a wound.

As a door gunner I was responsible for both M60 machine guns on the medevac. If the gun jammed it was useless so I cleaned and maintained my guns on a daily basis. To better maintain them, I practiced breaking them down and putting them back together blindfolded. It wasn't unusual to go into a hot LZ and fire two or three hundred rounds—not once but on several occasions over the course of a day. We were on call 24/7 with little time to eat, sleep, or relax. Many a time cooks brought sandwiches out to us to eat while flying.

Another responsibility I had was to check the right side of the engine deck every time we started up the helicopter. We were checking for fuel leaks and fires. The whine of the turbines was loud—ear shattering. To this day I still have ringing in my ears, commonly known by its official name, tinnitus.

Our crew—including the crew chief and medic—had to clean our chopper after every mission, when possible. Sometime there was so much blood on the floors that we had to wash off the deck with buckets of water. We had to clean out blood that seeped into the floor panels.

Return to LZ Uplift

In late October 1967, I was flying out of LZ Uplift again with an entirely new crew. Randy Brewer, our crew chief, had just arrived from the real world and was an FNG. We became good friends and are still friends to this day. Our medic was a guy named Tom; he was a great guy and a good medic. The pilots' names aren't worth mentioning. Early one morning, sometime after midnight, a helicopter went down in flames in an unsecured area on the side of the mountain. There were no ground units in the area. Medevac never refused a mission. Our crew flew in, the pilot found an area at the base of the mountain to land and told the medic to go in and look for survivors. I couldn't let him go into the jungle by himself so I grabbed my rifle to follow. I thought the crew chief would stay with the aircraft for security purposes, but when I looked back he was about fifty yards behind me. We searched the area, but it was pitch dark, and we couldn't locate any survivors. We were returning to the helicopter when it took off and left us behind. We remained at the crash site all night. Sometime during the night, we separated and lost track of each other in the dark. The wreckage was still burning and had set fire to a log. I took cover in a shaded area not far from the burning log so I could see and not be seen. At daybreak I saw that the burning log was a crewmember from the crashed helicopter. He was a black male, thirty to thirty-five years old, with a gold wedding band on his finger. He was a major, and he had burned to death while crawling away from the wreckage. Half his face was gone, and the fire had burned through his skull, exposing his brains.

I thought about his family back home and how upsetting it would be for them to hear about his death. Once help arrived, and our cowardly pilots returned, I escorted the army major's body back to the AO and graves registration. This was a sad and personal situation. To this day, one of my many dreams is of him. In the dream I am crawling through the elephant grass and run across his body. I am still unable to cope with burn victims without thinking of him.

LZ English

Around June 6, 1967, LZ English was blown up when the VC lobbed mortars into the fuel depot. Corky Walsh, a close friend and my crew chief when I flew out of An Khe during operation Pershing in early January 1968, was in the shower when his bunker took a direct hit. Base camp assumed he was dead because his dog tags were recovered from the rubble. Hours later, however, he was found trapped in the bunker with shrapnel wounds to both legs, and only a towel around his waist.

The unit received a new pilot. I can't remember his real name but we called him Sam the Sham, the Chicken Man. We quickly found out he was a retread that his previous unit wanted to get rid of. This guy was short and chubby with a pencil thin mustache. He flew from the right seat, which was the same side of the helicopter where I sat. As a gunner, I had to assist him when he got into the right seat of the helicopter and pull an armor plate forward that shielded him from enemy fire, and then secure his door. One morning he showed up wearing a parachute.

I asked him, "What's that?"

He gave me a puzzled look and said, "A parachute."

"Why?" I said.

Sam the Sham said, "So I could bail out if we go down."

"It isn't going to do you any good," I said.

He wanted to know why, so I told him: "Because I'll shoot your ass before you can get out the door." Nothing else was said until we returned from our "milk run" that morning.

After we landed, shut down, and secured our helicopter, Medevac 458, Sam the Sham requested to talk with our platoon leader, Major Goodman. Also present, standing around the helicopter, was our crew chief Randy Brewer and our medic. Sam the Sham told Major Goodman that I had threatened to shoot him. Major Goodman asked him why I would want to shoot him. Sam the Sham explained the conversation we earlier had between us and asked what the major was going to do about it. Major Goodman said, "You had better take that parachute off before he shoots you." Nothing else was said. Major Goodman walked off, and Sam the Sham was transferred out a few days later, after he burned down the mess tent trying to bake a pizza after midnight.

Bong Song Plains

We had an urgent message that an ARVN (Army of the Republic of Vietnam) unit was being overrun by the enemy and was retreating. We only had two medevac aircraft left on site to respond to the call. They had "beau coup" wounded, mostly ARVN, along with some American advisors. We were the second medevac to arrive on scene. The most serious of the wounded Americans were loaded on the first aircraft. We loaded close to eleven ARVN on our aircraft, which was about the maximum load we could carry back to the aid station.

After unloading both medevacs, we returned for the walking wounded and any Americans still left. We arrived for our second load about the time the first medevac was pulling out again. You could tell they were overloaded by their takeoff. They were gaining altitude when they started receiving heavy enemy fire. I could see their gunners returning fire. When we landed, we loaded more ARVN and avoided their flight pattern when we took off. We returned to the aid station and unloaded our wounded. When we returned for a third trip we found that the other medevac had sustained substantial damage and was grounded. On this, our final trip, I noticed that the ARVN had pulled back even farther. As the enemy continued to move closer, the ARVN panicked. They dropped their weapons and ran. When the remaining walking wounded and the last two American advisors climbed on board, our pilot tried lifting off but was unable to do so because of the weight. ARVN soldiers were trying to board our aircraft in an attempt to leave the area before they were completely overrun. By now everything had turned into one big cluster fuck, and we, and we had to forcibly push them off the aircraft in order to leave the ground. Even as we lifted off, we had ARVN clinging to the skids. The pilot had to maneuver the aircraft to shake them, and we were instructed to shoot them off the skids if we had to. All of them either fell or jumped as we pulled out from the area. We made it back safely to return another day. Even though I felt sorry for those guys, I had no respect for them. My impression of them was that they wanted us to fight their war for them and that the majority were cowards.

LZ Betty

LZ Betty was located near the city of Phan Phiet, which is an old French town on the coast. We flew medevac missions into what we called Marlboro Country. One day we picked up a pregnant female Viet Cong, who squirted breast milk into our medic's face when he tried to help her. The medic was mad, and she was ready to give birth. He crossed her legs and sat on them until we arrived at the aid station. Upon arrival at LZ Betty, she gave birth to a healthy baby. My crew chief, Bill Hastings, and I didn't approve of what the medic did, but there wasn't a thing either of us could do. I think he got in trouble over it, but no one said anything to us about it. After that, the medic rotated out back to the real world.

I spent approximately forty-five days at LZ Betty. This was the longest time I had spent at any given LZ. We got to fly low level over the ocean to test-fire our weapons, and we flew a lot of backlogs to hospitals in the bigger cities. We were never able to get out of the chopper. We would land and the stretcher-bearers would take the wounded into the hospitals. About halfway through our time at LZ Betty, our aircraft went in for maintenance, and we got to go into town to relax. About five or six of us went to Phan Phiet, where I was taken to a "hutchie" place for the first time. Bill Hastings treated me to a live female Vietnamese Tour Guide. Afterward, we were in the courtyard of this nice French town that had red brick sidewalks and a well centered in the courtyard. One of our medics said, "I wonder what it would sound like if I fired my Thompson into the well." He then proceeded to fire his weapon into the well. We all felt the sound was awesome. At this point, things really started going downhill. The Vietnamese Police came out of the woodwork blowing their whistles, and the MPs (military police) rolled in with their sirens blaring and lights flashing. We took off running through the village with the Vietnamese hot on our heels. We ran through the streets, alleys, and houses where civilians were eating dinner or doing whatever else they did. We finally lost our pursuers and went to a bar, where I was introduced to alcohol. My buddy Bill Hastings and another guy left us and returned to LZ Betty as the excitement was too much for them. I started drinking screwdrivers, and they went down pretty smooth. They didn't seem to have much kick, so I ordered doubles and then triples. After a hardy meal, consisting of a water buffalo burger and fries, I started getting a little dizzy and was feeling the effects of the alcohol. This bar had a ceiling fan, and the more I watched it, the dizzier I got. I aimed my rifle at it, and shot the fan to pieces. The bar owner and employees were screaming at me so my buddies took the rifle away from me and rushed me out the door before the police arrived. I was put in a rickshaw. I remember being happy, waving at everybody, and singing as he pulled me through the streets.

The MPs were waiting for me at the gate. I was so drunk; I didn't realize that I was in trouble. They locked me up in a conex container, with windows cut out and bars, until my aircraft commander, Marty Walker, came and got me. He drove me back to the unit and told Bill that I was his gunner and to take care of me. Bill told me later, Marty wasn't mad at me, just laughing because I was a funny drunk. Once I was inside the tent, I puked my guts out. Bill cleaned up my mess and washed me up, like a mother hen. My wife and I are still very close friends with him and his wife.

The next morning, I was hung-over big time but still had to fly. The other two crews returned to An Khe. I walked into the mess tent for breakfast with the other crewmembers but had to leave quickly because the food made me nauseated. I waited at the aircraft, checking my weapons. When everyone else showed up, Mr. Walker said, "Well, was it worth it?" I responded saying, "I had a good time. I got laid and drunk for the first time and can't wait to do it again."

We had to fly a milk run that morning, and I thought the fresh air and flying would make me feel better. But, I was wrong. I was hanging out of the aircraft, puking again, which was a mistake. My vomit blew back in the door, all over me. Thinking back, that was a funny experience, and all of us laugh about it now.

LZ Baldy

Around Christmas 1967, we were flying out of LZ Baldy. I remember them spraying mosquito repellant during our Christmas dinner, which they managed to get on us, and some of us had to dump our food out. We had a call in the middle of the night regarding a cavalry (grunt) unit with casualties. When we arrived, two walking wounded were put aboard along with three or four KIA (killed in action). Before we took off, two runts escorted a soldier to our chopper and placed him in the seat next to me. He appeared to be in shock. The platoon sergeant asked me to watch him closely. I asked him why and he responded, "He was on guard duty when a patrol was coming in." He quickly added, "He panicked, opened fire on them with an M60 machine gun." He sat next to me all the way in. I couldn't help but feel sorry for him, having to live the rest of his life knowing he had killed three or four soldiers from his platoon. I suspected that he fell asleep while on guard duty and, startled by the noise of the others coming in, opened fire.

An Khe

After Christmas at LZ Baldy I somehow ended up back at base camp in An Khe. I was assigned to fly with Crew Chief Corky Walsh on Medevac 454. Corky was a short timer and I mean short. He was down to about three or four days left in country before he went home, back to the real world.

On January 2, 1968, we flew many missions out of our home base in what I believe was Operation Pershing. That morning started off fine until the battalion commander showed up and wanted to fly with us on our first mission. He wasn't a very popular man, and he also was a career soldier who wanted to be promoted. Flying missions was one way he could accomplish this goal. I'm not saying he was "yellow," but he was over cautious and lacked common sense.

The first thing the colonel did was to order us to take out the window from the doors on the crew chief and door gunner's side of the chopper. He also ordered the doors to be closed. This was idiotic and dangerous. This action made it impossible to maneuver our mounted M60s, which meant that we wouldn't be able to lay down a field of fire. Furthermore, it was dangerous being in a Huey with the doors shut during a hostile action. To say the least, Corky was pissed off at the colonel. Corky was cussing and told me that he was going to throw the colonel off the medevac. Corky also indicated that he signed for Medevac 454, which meant the chopper belonged to him and not the colonel. Corky ranted and raved so much that morning that I stayed out of his way.

Corky was one of those southern boys, born in Virginia. He had moved to Eugene, Oregon as a child, but he still had a southern drawl. He was usually calm and collected and never lost his temper, but that morning I only nodded my head in agreement with him. Corky had developed what we referred to as a "short timer's attitude."

Regardless of the circumstances, our first mission that morning went well. We made it in and out of a hot LZ without anyone getting hurt. We figured that the gooks didn't shoot at us on that trip because they were rolling over with laughter when they saw we were flying, like a bunch of fools, with our doors closed.

When we returned to base camp and the casualties were off-loaded, Corky began screaming at the colonel and cussing him out. He was so loud that you could hear him over the sound of the turbine engines. The next thing I knew, Corky was telling me to leave the fucking doors open and that he had thrown the dipshit off the Huey. Our trips back out to the field were successful.

We were back at base camp, and Corky was getting ready to go home. I remember telling him, "Send me your address from LBJ so I can write you." Corky went home and he was never disciplined over the incident with the colonel. I never saw Corky again until we were reunited in Denver, Colorado, in June 2002. We have since stayed in touch with each other and have become very close friends. In fact, he was my best man on November 11, 2009, when my wife Holly and I renewed our wedding vows.

As a combat veteran you develop a bond with friends you served with that is unexplainable.

A Shau Valley

Before every mission, I quickly learned to trust in God. As we took off, I would say this same prayer every time, "Dear God, get us in and out without anyone being shot, hurt, or killed. Amen." On April 3, we were flying out of LZ Stud, which was located in the A Shau Valley. The A Shau was called The Valley of Death by some of the soldiers. As we pulled out early that morning flying a hoist mission, I said my little prayer. We hoisted four grunts from the top of a hill with no trees to give us cover. As we were hoisting up the last trooper, all hell broke loose. The enemy had us zeroed in. Gunfire hit our tail boom, hard, and spun us around. I noticed the grunt's gunner firing into the trees below us. We were still receiving fire, so I opened up with my M60, laying down a field of fire into the same area. I think I fired my whole can of ammunition, which carried approximately six hundred rounds. We were still hoisting a grunt up as we gained altitude. The grunt got the ride of his life, and I had to fire carefully because he was still under the chopper on my right side, flapping around in the wind. When the medic got him in the chopper, the grunt grabbed me and wouldn't let go. We began to lose power as we approached the medical aid station and had to make a hard landing. The crew chief counted over one hundred bullet holes that penetrated the chopper. Medevac 458 was towed out of there with all its equipment on board, including our machine guns.

Later in 2004 or 2005, I reunited with a guy named Dick H., who was one of the grunts we had hoisted up. He told me that he returned to the field and that the last grunt that we hoisted up had his helmet shot off his head. It had a nice bullet crease in it. I had to ask, "Was the round incoming or outgoing?"

My worst day in country was the next morning, April 4, 1968. It is a day I will never forget. Our crew had an early morning mission to Khe Sanh. We had to use the last chopper left at the LZ, which was Medevac 451. It belonged to my good buddy Bill Hastings, who took a lot of pride in maintaining his assigned aircraft. Bill was the only guy I knew who would put three coats of wax on his helicopter. He used to laugh and say, The wax makes it fly faster.

We flew out of LZ Stud before sunrise, and due to a low ceiling we flew treetop level, following landmarks along the Quang Tri River on our way to Khe Sanh combat base. Our mission was to medevac a marine. It was a little nippy that morning with the cold wind blowing in our face.

There was nothing like flying at treetop level, hands on your M60s, ready for a firefight.

Years later I spoke with Lt. Fenstermacher, who flew from the right seat (same side of the chopper I was on). He informed me that due to the low ceiling, we took a wrong turn and flew into a box canyon with cliffs and hills on both sides of us. As we rounded a bend in the river, I observed a grunt platoon that appeared to be running out to wave at us. I quickly realized that they were a regiment or larger of NVA, in green uniforms that looked similar to our uniforms from the helicopter.

On April 1, 1968, the attack phase of Operation Pegasus had started. Weather had delayed the attack. The First and Second Battalions, Seventh Calvary, had expanded to the area of LZ Mike. This was the route we were taking.

A lot of things can go through your mind quickly during a firefight, and unbeknown to us we had just flown into an ambush. Several NVA soldiers were running to a machine gun, strategically placed on the side of a steep hill. They opened fire on us, and you could hear the thud of the rounds piercing the metal of the helicopter. Their machine gunners started at the front of the helicopter and they walked those rounds to the tail. Lt. Fenstermacher yelled out that he had been hit. Rounds had come up through the glass, on the right side near his foot pedals, and he was shot twice. He was bleeding profusely from the wound in his femur. I was busy on my side of the helicopter returning fire. I took the first machine gun out and yelled out over the intercom, "I got 'em for you." Our medic, Spec. 5 Tom Word, pulled the pilot's seat back and had him sprawled out on the floor trying to stop the bleeding. As we passed by the NVA gunner's location, I breathed a sigh of relief. But my vision was limited. From my gunner's seat I could not see that we had flown into a gauntlet of machine guns lined up on both sides of the mountain.

Warrant Officer Walker, our aircraft commander, was struggling with the controls from the left seat, attempting to gain control of the chopper. It is funny that I remember Mr. Walker calling in a Mayday and giving our location, just like in all the black and white WWII movies. As we started to lose altitude, our crew chief, Randy Brewer, yelled out that he had been shot. The NVA gunners had us, they were pouring in machine gun fire from both sides, and seemed like it would never stop. The firefight was so intense that I had to squeeze the trigger and hold on. I had spaced tracer rounds in my belt of ammo, every fifth round was a tracer. This made it easier for me to hit my target from the air. I finally ran out of ammo. I did have spare ammo, but you can't reload an M60 while in flight, especially when you are going down.

There were NVA soldiers everywhere. We were still in their gauntlet. I saw the ghost that morning. Several years later I reunited with Randy Brewer. He said he saw the ghost, too. I just knew that I was going to die that morning. The funny thing about the situation, I accepted the fact that I probably would die, and I was OK with it. In my mind I saw the NVA capture and torture me. I had heard a rumor that they chopped the heads off of captured GIs. I said a quick prayer: "Dear God, make it quick." Then I thought about my mom and dad at home and how it will affect them. At this point, I got mad and remembered my survival training.

We were in deep shit, and it kept getting deeper. One pilot was badly shot up, and the medic was on the floor trying to save the pilot's life. The medic, Spec. 5 Word, was so covered in blood he looked like he'd been shot. Rounds had also come up through the bottom of the aircraft and wounded Randy Brewer, our crew chief. The bullet had entered through his right buttock and stopped about one inch from his spine. He was also in bad shape.

Mr. Walker was struggling with the aircraft. As we lost altitude, we almost took a header into the side of a cliff. If we had hit the cliff, we probably would have exploded with no survivors. I kept thinking, we might go down, but I will not give up. I swore I would fight to the death and kill as many of them as I could. Because I couldn't fire my M60, I resorted to my rifle and sidearm. I always carried a bandolier of magazines just in case I needed them. I had twenty-and thirty-round magazines, and I set my M16 on full auto. I went through at least two magazines in the aircraft. When we hit the ground, I had reloaded. I was sitting in the right gunner's seat, and up popped a gook firing at me with a bolt-action rifle. I heard the round whiz by my head and hit the firewall behind me. He pulled the bolt back to reload, but by this time I had my rifle aimed at center mass. He froze and stared at me. I hesitated. I had never had to kill anyone that close and face-to-face. He was a young man about my age. He was wearing an NVA uniform and one of their funny-looking helmets. As I watched him down the barrel of my gun sights I knew that I had him. He looked at me and his brown eyes got big. He started to slide his bolt forward. I pulled my trigger. I hit him center mass and walked my bullets up to his head and watched his head explode like a watermelon.

I jumped out of the aircraft and thought about running. But where would I go? Mr. Walker was trapped in the aircraft, and I needed to get him out. Randy was shot, and Word was still trying to save Lt. Fenstermacher's life. I'm glad I stayed. I couldn't have lived with myself otherwise.

We heard some noise on the left side of our aircraft. Lo and behold, it was the cavalry, either the 1/7 or 2/7, running down a hill to our rescue.

It took two medics to stop Lt. Fenstermacher's bleeding. I opened the door and slid the armor plate back so Mr. Walker could get out. I then helped Randy and tried to patch up his butt cheek and stop his bleeding, which wasn't too bad. Mr. Walker used the ground unit's radio to report back to the Fifteenth Medical Battalion. Since we didn't have any medevacs left, he got a hold of a slick to transport our wounded. In two days we went through two medevacs, numbers 458 and 451.

Other than Mr. Walker, I never saw the rest of our crew again until 2008 when I reunited with Randy Brewer in Biloxi, Mississippi, at the Fifteenth Medical Battalion Reunion for Medevac and the support people on the ground. It was the fortieth anniversary of the day we were shot down.

After the firefight, I was totally exhausted. I sat on a tree stump and thought about what had happened. I thought about the NVA I killed. It felt good that I got him before he got me. Years later I still see his face and big brown eyes in my dreams.

I don't like to talk about killing the enemy, nor in fact do I take any pride in killing. Killing the enemy is something that is very personal to me, and when asked by someone, How many people have you killed? I won't answer the questions. No one ever has asked. How many people have you saved by medevacing them to a field hospital? People that ask these questions are not combat veterans, let alone Vietnam veterans. I only speak of it now because, number one, it is therapy, and, number two, people need to know what went on and that 99.9 percent of us were not kill happy. It wasn't something we liked doing; it was something we were forced to do. This is our opportunity to tell our story, the truth, for future generations to come. I am only going to mention this one time: Randy and I left behind beaucoup NVA bodies.

When I went back a few days later with another crew to retrieve our equipment and guns off our medevac, I realized God had blessed us that morning. I stopped counting the bullet holes in the aircraft after I reached one hundred. What got to me was the amount of bullet holes on the right side of the helicopter, where I had been sitting. There were numerous bullet holes in the firewall behind me, and a trail of holes in the deck showed where bullets had walked across my feet without hitting me. Out of all those rounds fired at us by their machine gunners, only one round hit me. That round had struck the center of my chicken plate. It never penetrated my skin.

LZ Stallion, May 1968

Another morning we flew out of LZ Stallion to perform a hoist mission in thick fog. We arrived and could see nothing. Our pilot's name was Tom Purcell, and he was all of nineteen years old. He was the aircraft commander, and he wouldn't give up until after we'd hoisted up the wounded soldier, even when the RTO on the ground told him to come back after the fog lifted. Mr. Purcell was bound and determined to get this guy out and to an aid station. There were tall trees on the side of this mountain, which we couldn't see. The crew chief and I had to hang out the door and let the pilot know when our blades were clipping the trees. The platoon leader was telling us to pull out before we crashed, but Mr. Purcell wouldn't give up. Finally we got the guy out. I see Tom as a hero who wouldn't give up until he had completed his mission. He was the type of person who stood by our motto, adopted in 1968: So others may live.

Tom was killed the following week. He was in the process of landing the aircraft while on a mission to pick up soldiers wounded in a firefight. Just as he was setting the aircraft down, he was shot in the head by a sniper. No one realized that he was shot until the medevac was loaded up, and the pilot, in the right side, noticed that he was slightly slumped over. He was rushed back to the aid station along with the others, but it was too late. He was pronounced dead. All this happened while I was on R&R (rest and recuperation). A friend of mine named Murray Gibbs had replaced me as the gunner on the chopper.

I felt kind of bad that I wasn't there at the end, but who knows how and when something is going to happen.

Camp Evans

I flew medevac missions up until the last week before I went home from Camp Evans. My last mission was a hoist mission off a mountainside. The medic was my friend, Tom, who I mentioned earlier in this chapter. We received enemy fire on the right side, where I was located. I heard and felt three thuds hit the helicopter. We made it out safely with the wounded soldier and returned to Camp Evans with one bullet in the door and two in the tail.

The next morning, Tom said that he refused to fly with me anymore. "Nothing personal," he added. I was a short timer, soon to go home, and I would bring them bad luck. I always felt the same way, and I was happy to sit around and do nothing for my last couple of days. But my ears had been bothering me a lot and I started getting bad earaches, which they prescribed medication, that didn't help at all.

I was finally starting to get worn down. Crewmembers were being shot or killed on missions at a rate of 90 percent. Many had received more than one Purple Heart. While they were in the hospital recovering, I kept on flying. By the end of my tour, my ears had begun to bother me. I was prescribed medication (it didn't work) for painful earaches. But despite being in numerous firefights, I was never wounded.

Note

While in Vietnam, I saw some beautiful scenery that included mountains and jungles with deer and a lion of two. We picked up not only wounded soldiers but also civilians. One family we tried to evacuate wouldn't leave without their pig and chickens, which was a funny site, trying to get the animals into the chopper. We also had to medevac a K-9 from the field. On another occasion, we transported some nuns and orphans. We flew out to sea and landed on a hospital ship with a wounded soldier who needed emergency surgery. On that mission, the navy fed us, and the food was much better than the C-rations we usually ate. On another mission, we flew into a place that I think was called Phu Cat. It belonged to the air force, and their food was even better than the navy's. We had fresh milk for the first time, all we could drink, steak, and even desert. All the cake or pie we wanted.

Another thing I would like to comment on is that, unlike some, I never felt any hatred toward the Vietnamese people and I never disrespected them.

Going Home: June 1968

The following week, I was back home and feeling a little out of my element. I didn't know what to do with myself. After all, the previous week people were shooting at me.

In Vietnam, everybody talks about going home, back to the real world. However, I returned home and quickly found out that the real world wasn't the same as it was when I left for Vietnam. When I landed at San Francisco

Airport I was greeted with hostility—while still inside the terminal—by some raggedy-ass hippies. If that wasn't enough, a group of female protesters wanted to know if I had "killed any innocent civilians or children today." I can't explain the hurt and the sadness I felt that morning.

My own dad asked me some very disturbing questions about my actions in Vietnam. He also said, "You realize that you weren't in real war." This troubled me because I wanted my dad and WWII vets to be proud of me. I always felt he belittled my service, and that I wasn't good enough. He wanted to know "how much dope I smoked in Vietnam." My unit flew mede-vac missions 24/7. Our motto was, *so that others my live.* If you smoked dope you were transferred out. But he kept up the interrogation: "Did you kill anyone?" he asked me. To me that was a very personal question.

In my first week home, I learned quickly to keep my mouth shut about Vietnam. No one cared or understood what we had gone through, so I clammed up. Friends I had before Vietnam were no longer friends. A lot of them had deferments or had turned into bums or druggies.

My dad insisted that I find a job. However, I wanted to go to college and get a better education. I enrolled at Sacramento City College. That was a joke. A lot of the students there were anti-Vietnam. So were some of the instructors. I dropped out, drank beer, and partied until it got old.

My life turned around when I found the love of my life, Holly Lee Hayden, who loved me for who I was and not what I was. She told me that she knew she would marry me on the first night we met. Back then she called me her "hunk of burning love," and she still does. We were married on Veterans Day, 1969.

No one would hire me for a decent job with benefits and good pay. During interviews at Yolo County and UC Davis, I was basically informed that because of my experiences in Vietnam, they didn't want to chance hiring me at the present time. What they didn't come out and say was that they didn't want to hire a "deranged Vietnam veteran who might be a druggie and go off on others." This was a bunch of BS.

I did finally get hired (to do dirty odd jobs) in the yard at Speckles Sugar. Here, too, I had to work with UCD students who opposed the Vietnam War and everything else. The older men, who had worked there for years, were all either WWII or Korean War vets. They laughed and joked when they threw me to the wolves, thinking it was funny that I had to work with draft dodgers and college students. I wasn't considered a real veteran in their eyes. They constantly told me I hadn't been in a real war, which pissed me off to no end.

One of my biggest disappointments over the years has been that my heroes, the WW II and Korean War vets, turned their backs on us. To this day, I have no respect for any of them. Even family members have been cruel. They believe the untrue myths about Vietnam and what vets did over there. I can't stand the military fakers and wannabes who now call them-selves *Vietnam-era vets.* The people who fit these categories are the same people who turned their backs on us after we came home.

Because of these issues and more that I haven't commented on, I will never turn my back on or disrespect any veteran that follows me.

Medevac helicopter with an M60 machine gun at the ready

Crew of Medevac 458: left to right
Lt. Dave Fenstermacher, pilot right seat; WO2 Marty Walker (RIP), aircraft commander; SP4 Jim Calibro, door gunner; SP5 Bill Ward, medic; Randy Brewer, crew chief

Jim Calibro points to a .51 caliber bullet hole in tail boom of Medevac 458 at LZ Stud on April 3, 1968.

CHAPTER FIVE

FLIGHTS FOR LIFE: MORE FROM MEDEVAC

Corky Walsh
Crew Chief-Spec. 5
US Army
Medevac 6616454
First Air Cav
1967–1968

What happened on December 31, 1966? Well, all I remember is being in Oakland Army Terminal and getting a butt load of shots for my trip to Vietnam.

The first place you end up is in Anchorage, Alaska, for a fuel stop. You zip away from there and stop to refuel again in Japan. Then you step off the plane at Bien Hoa in South Vietnam. The first thing that hits you is the stench: rotting vegetation, jet fuel, gunpowder, and sweat. About then you wonder: "Just what in the hell am I doing here?" When your named is called, you go to a Caribou sitting on the runway, and off you fly to An Khe in the central highlands of Vietnam.

If anyone says that they weren't scared and didn't feel anything, they are full of crap.

I was assigned to the First Air Cavalry Division. I ended up at Fifteenth Medical Battalion Air Ambulance Platoon, better known as Medevac.

One of the most memorable moments was on June 6, 1967, in LZ English at six o'clock in the evening. I stripped down to take a shower, hung my dog tags on a nail (a no-no) and proceeded to take a shower. Just as I got soap in my hair, Charlie dropped in a mortar onto the ammo depot. "Well, shit," I said as the first case of 105 rounds exploded. I leapt out of the shower, soap in hair, towel around me, and dove into the bunker. We sat there all night listening to 175, 155, 105, mortars, M60, and, every other round you could think of, going off. We heard fuel bladders blow and four of our helicopters explode. I can remember looking over at Dan Korte and seeing blood running out of his ears from the explosions. We were all praying to God that we would live through this.

They came in with armored personnel carriers (APCs) around one o'clock in the afternoon to get us out of the bunkers. A total of nineteen hundred tons of ammunition blew up that night. They sent us back to An Khe, and I stepped off the bird and met Bob McKinley who said, "You're dead!" I looked at him funny and said, "What do you mean?" He told me they found my dog tags blown clear across the runway at LZ English and that I had been listed as a KIA.

From there I went to LZ Uplift, where they assigned me a Delta Model with forty-seven bullet holes in her. When they sent her back to the world to be rebuilt, I received another D-Model. I went back to LZ English, where they gave me a FNG, Jim Calibro, as my new door gunner. Our first meeting was at the chopper on the ready line (location of choppers ready for flight). When the FNG started talking, he bumped the butterflies on the M60, and, of course the gun went off. It put two rounds between his feet. All I said was, "That's what it does when you pull those little levers. And, by the way, you now have to clean the gun."

The thing about flying Medevac is you are on call 24/7, and you become calloused to the everyday flights to get the wounded. It is not that we didn't have feelings or we didn't care, we just had to shut everything out and do our jobs because those wounded boys were counting on us for help. Thinking about it too much would affect you and your job, as well as the four other crewmembers on the aircraft. We relied on the pilot, medic, and door gunner—the same as they relied on the crew chief—to perform their duties so we all could return safely from the mission.

One of my last encounters with Jim Calibro was down south at LZ Phan Phiet. We all went to town—Jim, Bill Hastings, Delbert Fox, and myself. We had a few Bombdy Bas (local beer) and a couple of bottles of Tiger Piss. Jim was not feeling so good so we headed back to camp. Well, Delbert Fox was feeling his Wheaties, as Jim was, so up the street we went, and Delbert asked, "Have any of you guys heard a Thompson shoot?" In the middle of the street was a city well. He poked the Thompson over the side and cut loose. It was one of the loudest bursts from a machine gun I had heard lately. Of course, here came the MPs, blue lights revolving, whistles blowing, and me yelling, "Come on, you dumb asses! Let's get the hell out of here!" I am now dragging three drunks through hootches, running here and there, and finally getting back to the road about a quarter-mile from the shooting spree. I told the guys that if the MPs stopped us they should shut up and let me do the talking. But we made it back to camp, and no one mentioned the night before.

One of the last flights I had with Jimmy was out in Marlboro Country, out of Phan Phiet, where we had a hoist mission. I was telling the pilot, "Take her right, take her right," when this shaky voice came over the radio. It was Jim asking, "How much room do you have over there because I am in the trees." Jim was trying to let the pilot know his side of the chopper was almost in the trees. "That was the last time our paths crossed until forty years later at a medevac reunion in Denver, Colorado.

I went back to An Khe for maintenance on my new bird, a UH-1H, before I took off for three weeks in Kontum, Dak To, and Dak Sut in the central highlands. After that, it was back to Bon Son and LZ English for more fighting with the 22nd NVA Division. Once, we decided just to see how high a UH-1H could go. Know what? You lose lift at eleven thousand feet. You also enter the flight path of the F4U fighter aircraft. We had two come up on us as we were ripping along at 150 knots. Their noses were up in the air, their air brakes out; they were about to stall out and asked us what the hell we were doing up in their air space. The pilot answered said, "We just wanted to see what you jet jockeys did up here."

You remember the good times and try to shut out the bad ones. But it is impossible. I remember when one of our medevac choppers went down in September. The crew was Mr. Rose, Mr. Kuhns, the pilot, Larry Lantz (crew chief), Golf (the medic), and Sonny Glavebrook (the door gunner). It hits hard because we all know each other. You have flown with one another and you are a family. They say you don't want to make too many friends in war, but when you eat, sleep, fly, and just bullshit one another, how do you not become friends?

I want to say that I have never regretted going to Vietnam and that I am a proud to have flown in Medevac. I also made friends over there, and we get together every year at our reunion. We all turn nineteen or twenty years old again, and we will savor our friendship until the end of time. I am proud of the men and women that serve our country today. They are our heroes. Do not let them be treated the way this country treated us when we came home from Nam.

Jim Calibro and fellow Medevac crewmembers resting at a landing zone

CHAPTER FIVE CONTINUED:

MORE HELICOPTER ESCAPADES

Randell J. "Randy" Brewer
Crew Chief-Spec. 5
Medevac 458578
Air Ambulance Platoon
Hq & Sup Co.
First Cavalry Division (Airmobile)
October 1967–October 1968

I entered the army on March 27, 1967, and went through basic training at Fort Benning, Georgia. Upon graduation, I entered rotary wing aircraft training at Fort Rucker, Alabama. On arriving in the Republic of Vietnam (RVN), I was assigned to the Air Ambulance Platoon, Fifteenth Medical Battalion, based at An Khe. Our platoon leader, Major Doris Goodman assigned me as a crew chief of Medevac 458. The crew chief is the mechanic who keeps the aircraft flyable and doubles as the left door gunner. In 1966, our First Cavalry commanding general, Major General John J. Tolsen, said he was tired of his medevacs being shot up and armed them with M60 machine guns on the left and right sides. The gunner on the right side and the crew chief on the left cleared the aircraft (looked for obstacles the chopper could hit) for the pilots, so that they wouldn't hit anything on either side. They also cleared the main rotor so that it didn't strike tree branches, etc. The crew chief was basically the flight engineer responsible for maintenance and in charge of the crew when the aircraft was flying.

I was sent first for a short time to LZ Uplift and Two Bits and then to LZ English in the Bong Son Valley at the village of Bong Son. It was there that my aircraft was hit by ground fire directly through the tail rotor drive shaft. It was here that I was exposed to my first KIA and WIA, a captain and SFC who had walked into a booby-trapped 105 mm howitzer round. Captain Jacob Mast (a master pilot) asked on returning if I was OK. I was really shaken up but managed to say, "I think so." He grabbed me by my shoulders and smiled saying, "OK, you better check your aircraft out then."

We had a few minor missions, but nothing major, and I spent Christmas at LZ English. On returning to An Khe for regular maintenance, I found out the First Cav was moving north to Camp Evans, which was north of the old imperial capital of Hue. Because it was still in maintenance, my aircraft was the last to leave.

Camp Evans was much different than our wooden hootches in An Khe. We lived in tents and had only the very basic of life's necessities. All went well until January 31, 1968. My aircraft was at Red Beach in Da Nang for field maintenance, and Major Goodman decided that he and I would take the aircraft back to Camp Evans. For some unknown reason, we were unaware that the Tet Offensive had started. We hit heavy rains, and he decided to land at a small fixed-wing airstrip in Hue. We had no idea, but the North Vietnamese Army (NVA) had overrun the city. As we dipped beneath the clouds, I was in the right pilot seat, and I saw the yellow star of the NVA and enemy soldiers everywhere. I didn't know if I keyed the mike, but I was screaming so loud that the pilot couldn't have helped hearing me. He had seen them, too, and pulled back into the clouds before they had a chance to shoot at us. Thus began a month and a half of pure hell as the marines, First Cav and 101st Airborne began the fight to recover Hue. It was rainy and cold the entire time. I was assigned to Medevac 447, with Roger Badersneider (RIP) as aircraft commander, Captain Clarence Cooper as copilot, myself as crew chief, Murray Gibbs as gunner, and Terry Baldwin as the medic. When we made it through the entire campaign without taking a hit, I nicknamed Medevac 447 the Teflon Medevac.

On March 27, we were sent to LZ Stud. We were just two aircraft with no ground troops to cover us, so we set up a perimeter with the M60s off the aircraft. For three days we built revetments for the aircraft and ourselves, and slept on the ground at night. This was in preparation for the First Cavalry Division to relieve the marines at the embattled LZ at Khe Sanh, which had been under continuous siege by the NVA for months. On April 3, my aircraft, Medevac 458, was badly shot up by a Chinese Communist (Chicom) .51 caliber machine gun. The other aircraft, Medevac 451, was undamaged, but the crew chief had to go to base camp for some reason. So it was decided that our crew—CWO Martin Walker, Copilot David Fenstermacher, myself as crew chief, Jim Calibro as gunner, and Bill Word as the medic—would be transferred to Medevac 451. Using the other team's flight gear and machine guns, we set out to rescue the wounded marines that we had failed to pick up when we were machine-gunned the day before. As we topped a plateau all hell broke loose. I heard Jim firing. Lt. Fenstermacher was hit twice, in both thighs, and I was hit directly on the left side at belt level. There was nothing for me to shoot at on my side, but I heard Jim Calibro over the intercom say, "I got him for you, Lt. Fenstermacher." Then Jim's machine gun jammed, and he started shooting every M16 he could get his hands on, his and the pilots.

Walker managed to horse the aircraft around in a 180. There was blood all over the right windshield; every warning light on the console was on, including the master caution light, whose warning was screaming in our ears. We had no engine, no hydraulics (like power steering on a car), and the transmission light was on. As we did the 180-degree turn, the enemy came into my sights. But Jim seemed to have taken them all out. I wasn't taking any chances and shot them again. Mr. Walker managed to autorotate into a tiny 105 mm howitzer firebase with no hydraulics and almost landed on a howitzer. Medic Word had pulled Lt. Fenstermacher's seat back and was trying to control the bleeding. Jim told me forty years later that he expected the NVA to come charging in and hack us all to death with machetes.

Another aircraft that was behind us landed and took Lt. Fenstermacher and Word back to our hospital at LZ Stud. Jim was trying to put one of those ridiculous, one-foot-square field bandages on my butt but was laughing so hard he never got it on. He did manage to say, "You got shot in the ass!" So I became known as Magnet Ass after that. A few minutes later, another aircraft picked up the rest of us and took us to LZ Stud. Lt. Fenstermacher had already been evacuated to a hospital, and I was sent to Qui Nhon Hospital to have the bullet removed from my pelvic bone. Lt. Fenstermacher made it. I stayed in the hospital for a week and returned to Red Beach where the maintenance officer tried to make me stay in maintenance because my time in country was getting short. I hated maintenance and the maintenance officer equally. My aircraft was ready to fly, and Major Goodman refused to make me stay, so we took Medevac 458 back to Camp Evans.

I got back to Camp Evans just in time for the assault into the A Shau Valley (the valley of the shadow of death). The NVA had Russian trucks, roads, radar-controlled antiaircraft guns, and spider holes (slang for a hole in the ground concealing a sniper, not quite as big as a fox-hole) everywhere. After five days, my aircraft was shot to pieces again. When I got back to Camp Evans, Major Goodman asked if I had been on R&R. "No, never thought about it," was my answer. This was a Tuesday, and he said, "I've got a plane going out of here on Friday to Bangkok, and I want you on it." He quickly added, "You're grounded until then." So I went to Bangkok. He even loaned me five hundred dollars in green backs for the trip. I only spent three hundred and paid him back the rest. On returning, I found out that my Medevac 458 was totaled and had been sent back to the states, so I was given a new aircraft, Medevac 578. They tried to keep it in base camp because I only had a month left before returning to the States. However, Medevac 578 was sent to LZ Jane, and I went with it and stayed there until my last two days in country.

On returning home, most of my friends were gone, and the ones who were still around didn't want to hear about Vietnam. I was more or less shunned. I was sent to Fort Stewart, GA., to work on old aircraft from Vietnam in the open and freezing cold. I decided to volunteer to go back to Vietnam and Medevac. The army screwed me as usual, and I was sent to the Forty-eighth Assault Helicopter Company, which was worse than stateside. Formations, spit-shined boots, wooden barracks, NCO club with slot machines, air conditioning, even a movie theater. I hated it. All we did was resupply the Republic of Korea (ROK) Army with water, Korean C-rations, and ammo six days a week, 6:30 a.m. until dusk. The aircraft were old with 2500 hours on them. They were falling apart. It was the pits. Agent Orange was also sprayed out of my aircraft around the ROK Army's firebases, and I was drenched in the stuff. Bored and disappointed out of my gourd. I didn't feel like I was doing anything, a total letdown.

I began to have back troubles in the early 1990s. By 1997 my spine was completely gone, wasn't even showing on the X-ray. They put steel rods in my back and rated me 100 percent disabled. I have to take Lortab and time-release morphine for the pain and can't do much of anything. My legacy from the Forty-eighth Assault Helicopter Company, who thought they were the toughest of the tough. They had no idea. In 1971, they were sent north to insert Army of the Republic of Vietnam (ARVN) troops along the DMZ to combat the NVA. The ARVN chickened out and tried to jump back on the aircraft and the unit lost over 50 percent of their aircraft. So much for being tough. You can see what happens to them on the Military Channel in a documentary named *Lam Fong 719*. Glad I was gone by then. Clear Left, Medevac 458/578, Randy Brewer

Assault into A Shau Valley was conducted in late April or early May 1968. Pictured is Randy Brewer at Camp Evans, sitting on a Russian 37 mm antiaircraft gun captured in the A Shau Valley.

CWOII Martin Walker (RIP), aircraft commander, and CWO Tom Grove are shown checking bullet holes in Medevac 458 on April 3, 1968, at LZ Stud.

CHAPTER SIX

LIFE ON THE BROWN WATER

Alan Friel
SN E3
US Navy—Brown Water
LSMR 536
1967–1969

I was born in Calusa County located in Northern of California but basically spent my whole life in Oakdale, California. When I joined the in navy 1967 under a special two-year program, I wasn't even thinking about the possibility of going to Vietnam. I reported to Modesto for transport to the intake center located in Fresno. A group of us were loaded onto a bus for the ride to basic training in San Diego, California.

Prior to departing Fresno, a group of us loaded up booze for the ride. We drank and partied all the way, until we pulled into the base, where we suddenly became serious. I found out right away what military life was going to be like. With a few choice words we were ordered off the bus, put into a not-so-military-looking formation, and marched off into what was going to be a challenging couple of years. After boot camp, I received orders for deployment to the war. They sent me for a month of special training to prepare me for duty in Vietnam.

I spent two years in Vietnam working on rivers—what the navy called "brown water." It was called brown water because it wasn't blue like the ocean. One of my jobs was loading barges with rockets for our forces upriver, but most days were spent on patrol ships. Our job on these patrols was to locate and fire upon suspected Viet Cong villages. The villagers were located by spotter planes, who would radio the location of the village to us. We fired recoilless weapons and rockets into the villages. However, because we were destroying their refuges, the Viet Cong were constantly ambushing the patrol, trying to stop us before we reached the village. I am going to do my best to remember, but it is hard pulling up memories that have been buried for so long.

I had hooked up with a fellow sailor named Toby (can't remember how to spell his last name), and we became best friends. We served the whole two years together in Vietnam. One afternoon we were summoned to load a barge with five thousand rockets. We had been loading for about three hours when the Viet Cong began shelling us with mortars. The commander ordered us to abandon the barge and swim to the other side of the cove. A barge, loaded with rockets, wasn't the place to be with explosives falling from the sky. We were all shook up, but everyone made it to the other side. The commander called for air support, and to our relief, it arrived and wiped the enemy out. We returned to the dock area to resume loading when someone shouted, "Look!"

We looked to the entrance of the cove and saw a bunch of junks and sampans (both are small boats) floating towards us. The Viet Cong onboard immediately opened fire on us. We repelled them with heavy machine gun fire. Afterwards, it was back to work as usual except for Toby. Toby turned to me and said, "I am not loading any rockets today or tomorrow." I answered back, "Well, you can't get out of it!" He quickly shot back at me, "Watch!" He walked over to a small fan and stuck his finger in it. Moments later he was off to sickbay. No Loading!

Another incident occurred on one evening when some members of the unit and I were sitting on the dock throwing concussion grenades into the water. We were just joking and wasting time, when all of a sudden three bodies floated to the top of the water. The best we could figure was that we must have spoiled an attempted underwater attack against the dock area. Luck does sometimes play a roll.

Toby and I rotated home together, and he flew to Michigan, where he lived. On the flight home, I will never forget what I pulled off. As I boarded the plane I noticed one seat open, but it was between two officers. I just knew they were saving the seat for something, but I told myself that the seat was mine. I walked up to the pair of officers and told them that I was taking that seat, and without waiting for an answer, I sat down.

After arriving home, I shortly received some distressing news. It seemed that Toby had taken a helicopter from the airport where he landed, and the helicopter had crashed, killing him. I thought to myself, Here he survived two years in Vietnam just to die in the states on his way home.

CHAPTER SEVEN

VIETNAM, AS I SEE IT

Roland H. Froman III
HM1-Hospitalman First Class Petty Officer, Retired
RN, BSHS (Bachelor of Science Health Services)
US Navy attached to the US Marine Corps
First Battalion, Third Marine Division, Ninth MAB
June 1967-July 1968; RVN
Oct. 1973-May 1974; USS Ranger, Vietnam waters
May 1974-Nov. 1975; USS Midway, Vietnam evacuation

Well, the year was 1965, and I was just a dumb farm boy that had dropped out of high school to help Dad on the dairy. The top hits included, "My Girl" by the Temptations, "Help Me Rhonda" by the Beach Boys, "Hang on Sloopy" by the McCoys, "I Know a Place" by Petula Clark, and others. Life seemed easy and carefree. Once in a while, you heard about Vietnam on the news, but I knew little about what was happening over there.

It was the year I would turn eighteen, the magical year that you had to register for the draft. As it grew closer to my birthday (November 26), I began to hear more about this "conflict in Vietnam." People were concerned about the fighting going on across the ocean. I just kept working on the dairy. Shortly after my birthday, on December 28 to be exact, I was "getting in the cows." They were knee deep in manure, and I had to wash them down. Then the milkers (my father was one of the milkers) began to put the machines on the cows. I remember that one of the machines came off. This is a big problem because, if one is off and stays off to long, the lines will lose the vacuum, causing all the other machines to fall off. I quickly reached for the machine to replace it, when the cow kicked me across the barn. When I recovered and finally stood up, I realized that I was holding on to what was left of the machine. I threw the machine down and left the barn. Later that morning, I went down to see the navy recruiter (I didn't want to go to war in the army, or God forbid, the marines). I asked the recruiter, "How fast can you get me in the navy." He immediately replied, "Can you believe, we have an immediate opening, and I can get you in today."

I was transported to the military induction center located in Oakland, California. I was sworn in, had my physical, and was ushered onto a plane bound for San Diego, California, where I was to go through basic training. I arrived at the US Naval Training Center on December 30, 1965, at three o'clock in the morning. We went through a mandatory indoctrination and finally were allowed to go to bed at four thirty. I thought to myself, Finally, I get some rest. Yeah, right! The next thing I know, I hear this horrendous banging of a trashcan and someone yelling, "Reveille," a word I had never heard before. It was five o'clock—only thirty minutes of rest! I would soon come to hate the word. I guessed that I wasn't moving fast enough because someone lifted the foot of my bunk up and dropped it, jarring me from my head to my toes. The next thing I heard was, "Get out of the rack, maggot." It was then I realized I was in the navy.

When in boot camp, there comes a day when you go in front of a board to request the school you would like to go to. However, before that day arrived, I became ill and spent three days in sick bay. Upon my release from sick bay, I was assigned to a company from Texas. My new company had an ideal number. Its number was 013, which indicated it was the thirteenth company to start training that year (1966). While I was in sick bay, I noticed that the corpsmen did not have to work very hard. I thought these guys have it made. When the day finally came for me to go in front of the board, I asked to go to corpsman school even though I had been designated as an airman. I was granted my wish and upon graduation from boot camp on March 24, 1966, I was off to Hospital Corpsman School.

After spending fourteen days on leave, I reported to Hospital Corpsman School at Balboa Hospital in San Diego. One of the first things I noticed was a plaque that honored the corpsman (about thirty) that had been killed in the "Vietnam Conflict." When I inquired about this, I found out that the US Marines do not have non-combatant troops. Instead they use navy corpsmen. I realized that my plan to stay out of the marines had gone by the wayside.

I graduated from corpsman school in October 1966 and received orders sending me to Naval Hospital Camp Pendleton, California. I was assigned to the hospital's EENT & Dental floor but spent my duty days in the ER. Soon I received orders to the Field Medical Service School at Camp Pendleton. This school had an Advanced First Aid program that included field sanitation and training with the gear we would have to use in Vietnam, including the military .45 caliber pistol and other weapons. There were other courses at the school, but these give you the gist of it. Upon graduation, our drill instructor had a surprise us. He said, "I want you to know why I was so hard on you." He read his orders and said, "I am going with you." However, to my surprise, my orders were sending me to Camp Hanson, Okinawa.

When I arrived at Camp Hanson, I was assigned to the immunization line, which included giving shots to troops headed to Vietnam. I remember once a very short marine (about five foot four) was getting his shots when, behind him, a very large marine (about six foot four) saw him receive the injection and passed out at the sight. Anyway, after about four weeks, I was the senior corpsman on the shot line. The chief petty officer called me in to his office and told me to ask for volunteers for duty in Vietnam. I was getting so bored around the base, I told him to put me on the top of the list. So I was off to Vietnam.

I was flown to Da Nang Airbase, where they reviewed my orders and determined that I was to be assigned to the First Battalion, Third Marine, Ninth MAB. I arrived during the middle of Operation Bear Bite and was placed in the field with only my stateside fatigues and standard boots. The battalion was in Thian Quang Tri and Ting Thua Thien, which was about forty clicks (kilometers) south of the DMZ (demilitarized zone). This was known as the Street without Joy area. The battalion had spent seventy-two hours probing and destroying unoccupied enemy positions. I was given a canteen but had no other gear, but snipers and a stuck marine tank were the only casualties on this operation. C Company, where I was originally delivered, landed at LZ Startling without contact. The unit located bunkers and punji pits and destroyed them. Small arms fire was received with no casualties. Incoming resupply helicopters took sniper fire. C Company sent out patrols to engage the enemy. I was not sent on this particular patrol. There had been two firefights fought on the fourth, but I didn't report until the fifth, when the battalion was airlifted to the Fourth Marines area, where finally I received my gear. During this operation, the BLT (battalion landing team) received no casualties but reported two confirmed VC killed in action (KIA), and nine probable VC KIA, along with nine captured VC. I was then assigned to Company A.

On June 7, Operation Colgate began with Company A being airlifted into LZs Eagle and Hawk. Two VC were captured hiding in the water and four were engaged with the assist UH-1 Helicopters. On the eleventh, the battalion was airlifted to Phu Bai, and then trucked to the Fourth Marine area. This move was uneventful.

On June 11, Operation Cumberland began with Company A and Company B being airlifted into an area seven miles east of Phu Bai. The first day we made heavy contact with an intense enemy force. However, the last four days were light contact. 1/3 sustained three KIA and twenty-nine WIA while inflicting twenty-four confirmed VC KIA, and fifteen probable VC KIA and fifty-eight captured VC. Later a village chief indicated the enemy had suffered 125–150 KIA the first day of the operation.

1/3 had control and command of the operation and was assisted by H/2/26 and K/3/26. An armed chopper reported seeing two VC in the area. Our squad was sent to locate them and immediately came under small arms fire. This was the first time that I had come under fire. I remember being exhilarated. I thought I couldn't be killed. We sustained nine to twelve rounds of 60 mm mortar fire. We requested air, artillery, and 81 mm mortar-fire support. There was an estimated one company of enemy soldiers in the area, and they were well dug in. Company B moved up in support. I was busy answering the call "Corpsman up!" and treating the wounded. Two were already KIA upon my arrival at their location. There were twelve WIA and one ARVN-WIA. Company C sustained one KIA and one WIA. My entire time in Vietnam, I lost only one individual who was alive when I got to him. The autopsy reported the bullet passed through one lung and the heart.

On June 13, Operation Choctaw began in Tinh Quang Tri and Tih Thien provinces. Units deployed from Fourth Marines Headquarters, BLT 1/3, 1/4, 2/4, and 3/12 Artillery. Involvement initially consisted of several smaller unit missions and commitments assigned to the Fourth Marines in the Three River Area. Company A discovered fifty well-camouflaged punji traps, both foot- and man-size. Two men fell into one man-size trap with one WIA. In another case, on June 16, one marine stepped on a landmine causing two WIA. We also received five rounds of 60 mm mortar into the LZ as three helicopters were landing, causing no damage. Two WIA were treated and medevaced to an aid station. We had only light contact. In total the BLT sustained no KIA and seventeen WIA while inflicting nine confirmed VC KIA, twenty probable VC KIA, and capturing fifteen VC.

On June 25, Operation Maryland began in Phau Thien province. Units from the Fourth Marine Headquarters, BLT 1/3, had a search and destroy mission. My platoon had little to do with this operation. BLT 1/3 killed seven Communists, took three prisoners, and salvaged almost nine tons of rice at a cost of three marines wounded (not in my platoon). We then returned aboard ship for rest and to restore our gear. However, I will never forget the morning of July 3, 1967. After less than two days on the ship, we were called back ashore. I felt like a wet rag squeezed and left to dry. I drug myself aboard the vessel that would take me ashore. In the beginning of Operation Bear Claw, in the wake of Operation Buffalo, the area of concern was Con Thien, just south of the DMZ. Battalions 1/9 and 3/9 were ambushed and units from the Third Marine Headquarters 3/3, 3/4, 2/9, SLF-A (BLT 1/3), SLF-B (BLT 2/3), Ninth Marine Headquarters were called in to assist. It was discovered that major elements of the 304 B, NVA Battalion, and Ninetieth NVA Regiment were in the area. 1/9 conducted sweeps north of Con Thien and made *heavy* contact. They encountered two battalions of the NVA Ninetieth Regiment and got into trouble, a situation that later got them the name "the walking dead." On July 3, Battalion 1/3 was committed to assist them. The first wave of helicopters landed 2,500 meters south of the designated LZ. While we were linking up with 3/9 on the right flank, I received my first wound, shrapnel from an exploded grenade. Luckily, I only received one fragment, but it was right between the eyes. The wound was not serious, and the battalion surgeon would later make it look like it had never happened. But, it hit with such force that it caused my nose to bleed heavily. The two-day beard combined with the blood made me look like a disaster. Water was scarce, and I could not clean it up, so it looked even worse as it dried. This was my first Purple Heart, and I now knew that I could be hit, and that if I could be hit, I could be killed. But this only scared me for a short time—there were too many wounded to care for.

The calls kept coming in: *Corpsman up, corpsman up!* By the time we linked up with 3/9 on the right flank, the fighting had waned. A UH-34 helicopter was down in C Company area, and a CH53 lifted it out two days later.

The morning of July 5 started with a mortar barrage on Company A and C. Two corpsmen in another platoon were blown up (they had been in the same foxhole and received a direct hit). The commanding officer of that platoon went off. He grabbed pieces of the corpsman, yelling, "This is why corpsmen should never be together." Others in that platoon were injured, and since they were now without a corpsman I would have to cross an open field in order to get to them. Feeling it was my duty, I started across the field to the other platoon. Arriving in their area, I began to patch the wounded and prepared them for medevac. The platoon members who were not wounded transported them to the LZ for pick up. Back in my own platoon area, another 155 artillery barrage began.

After a short time it appeared that the artillery rounds were going over us into the next trench line. I heard the call, *Corpsman up!* I was tired, but I responded. The call came from my platoon staff sergeant (S.Sgt.). When I got to his position he asked, "Do you have any aspirin?" About that time I heard a tremendous crash and something knocked me down. I stayed down and crawled into the S.Sgt.'s foxhole. After the barrage was over, I got up and went down the trench line to see if anyone was wounded. One of the squad's sergeants stopped me and said, "Doc, look at your leg." I looked and found my entire trousers were wet with blood from mid-thigh down. I examined my leg and found the wound. I stuffed it with gauze and cotton and wrapped my leg with a battle dressing. I thought to myself that it would hold. Meanwhile the calls—*Corpsman up!* — Continually could be heard. By then, only two of the eight corpsmen assigned to the company—the senior corpsman and I—were still in the field. I couldn't leave him.

Refusing to take a medevac for myself, I continued to care for the wounded of both platoons. I tried to care for everyone I could. I remember that the commanding officer of another unit must have called an air strike on his own area because from a distance I could see them crying, *Why me?* This still haunts me in my dreams because I could do nothing for them. I continued to care for the wounded for the next three days. The senior corpsman finally told me that I must medevac myself on the next flight. He told me that if I evacuated myself, he would write me up for the Silver Star, but if I didn't follow his order he would write me up for disobeying an order. I told him, "I can't leave you alone. You'll have to write me up for disobeying the order." However, when the next flight came in, first off the chopper were five replacement corpsmen. When I saw the replacements, whatever was keeping me going evaporated, and I agreed to the evacuation. I didn't have the strength to walk to the chopper, so I was carried.

I received the Silver Star Medal issued by President Johnson and endorsed by OVH Krulak, Lieutenant General, US Marine Corps, Commanding General, Fleet Marine Force, Pacific. It reads:

> For conspicuous gallantry and intrepidity in action while serving
> as a corpsman with Company A, First Battalion, Third Marines

Ninth Amphibious Brigade, in connection with operations against the enemy in the Republic of Vietnam from July 4–6, 1967, during Operation Buffalo. Company A sustained numerous casualties from heavy rocket, artillery, mortar, and enemy ground attacks. With complete disregard for his own safety, Hospital man FROMAN, fearlessly moved from one fighting position to another to administer first aid to the wounded of his platoon. Although constantly exposed to enemy fire, he then moved across the fire swept area to administer first aid to casualties of another platoon. While he was painfully wounded in the leg by mortar fragments, he steadfastly refused medical evacuation and he calmly and proficiently continued to provide medical assistance throughout the battle. On one occasion, when he and a wounded patient were attacked by enemy soldiers, Hospital Man FROMAN picked up a rifle and fired it at the advancing enemy, forcing the hostile soldiers to withdraw, undoubtedly saving the life of the wounded marine. Throughout the engagement, he unhesitatingly reacted to every call for medical assistance until the seriousness of his own wound necessitated his subsequent evacuation. His decisive and courageous actions, at great personal risk, were an inspiration to all who observed him. By his courage, outstanding professionalism and selfless devotion to duty, Hospital Man FROMAN, upheld the highest traditions of the Marine Corps and the United States Naval Service.

I also received my second Purple Heart. I never finished the operation.

I spent the next month in sickbay on the USS Okinawa. The wound in my leg was cleaned, debrided (the damaged tissue cut away to enable healing), and sewn up three times. However, each time the wound was sewn up it became infected. I asked the doctor to leave it open. I would care for it myself and let it heal by second intention (healing from the inside out). We were in Subic Bay when the wound finally healed. The doctor initially wouldn't let me go on liberty, but finally he gave in and let me go. I had a good time on liberty, but as the ship was getting underway, back to Vietnam, the doctor wanted to send me back to the United States. I told him that I wanted to finish my tour of duty. He finally agreed, but informed me should I receive another Purple Heart that I would be sent home.

Upon my return to Vietnam, I was assigned to Company C instead of going back to Company A. I had missed Operation Hickory II, Operation Kingfisher, and Operation Beacon Guide, but was back in time for Operation Beacon Gate. On August 7 1967, First Battalion, Third Marines, started Operation Beacon Gate by landing southeast of Hoi An along the coastal boundary of Quang Nam and Quang Tin provinces. Company C didn't land with the above units but remained on the USS Duluth and later landed along the coast at Blue Beach. The landings were conducted by both helicopter and amphibious assault craft. Intelligence reported elements of V25 Local Force Battalion and other VC units were in the area of operations.

During the southerly sweep, the marines endured continuous sniper fire. The UH-1E helicopter was used to suppress the snipers, and numerous VC were detained. While traveling through the underbrush, the sergeant in front of me turned to say, "Watch out for that booby trap." As he did, he stepped into another hole onto a barbed screwdriver attached to a block of wood. We had to dig the block of wood out of the ground and lift his foot out with the screwdriver sticking through the foot. Then we had to wrap the screwdriver and the foot together to keep it from pulling on the foot. I said, "This is a rotten thing to have happen on your birthday." He replied, "No, it is the best thing that could have happened." He quickly added, "This is my ticket home, a million dollar wound." He left on a medevac to the ship, and I never saw him again.

On August 9, 1967, Company C came under heavy sniper fire receiving two WIA. We also spotted two VC on the perimeter, and we exchanged small arms fire. During this operation, BLT 1/3 sustained one KIA and twelve WIA while inflicting twelve confirmed VC/KIA and four probable VC/KIAs. The battalion also took twenty-six VC/POWs.

August 11, 1967 saw the beginning if Operation Cochise with BLT 1/3 conducting a helicopter-borne assault from the area of Beacon Gate into an LZ approximately seven miles to the east of Que Son. The following units were involved: First Marine Division Headquarters, Task Force X-Ray, BLT 1/3, 1/5, 3/5, and the 2/11 Artillery. Company C, BLT 1/3 was sent to set up blocking positions in support of sweeping units of the Fifth Marines who were attacking to the east. BLT 1/3 was put under operational control of Task Force X-Ray. The battalion was put at LZ Grouse, where it came under sniper fire.

On August 16, during a sweep with elements of the Fifth Marines, the battalion made heavy contact with an NVA unit of undetermined size. This NVA unit was in a defensive posture and employed small arms and automatic weapons. The battalion made extensive use of artillery and fixed-wing air strikes, but the NVA unit escaped from the area under the cover of darkness. The remaining of time spent on Phase One consisted of a search and destroy operation to the east with enemy contact limited to occasional sniper fire. At the LZ, B Battalion 1/5 turned over a captured NVA officer to Company C. This officer led us to a cache of two tons of rice. One detainee escaped from the perimeter of Company C, and when he couldn't be caught, he was shot.

Phase II of Operation Cochise began on August 19 with BLT 1/3 conducting a heliborne assault into the Hiep Duc area to conduct search and destroy operations. The BLT continued to sweep from Hiep Duc to Que Son, uncovering rice caches and twenty two-pound sticks of TNT in a tunnel, which was later destroyed.

Phase III of Operation Cochise commenced on August 25 with BLT 1/3 continuing with search and destroy operations. This phase was characterized by light contact with snipers. The operation was terminated on August

27 with the arrival of BLT 1/3 at Que Son. On August 28, the BLT was carried by helicopter from Que Son to Chu Lai and was back-loaded aboard ships.

On September 1, BLT 1/3 landed in Thau Thien Province for a southerly sweep of the by now familiar Street without Joy. The only resistance we encountered was snipers and booby traps. Company C landed at LZ Sparrow and lost one marine to a booby trap. Five marines were wounded on the second day, and on the fifth day, a short round caused a marine to be wounded when he tripped a booby trap. We conducted a foot movement southwardly to the Camp Evans area. We were slowed by finding over thirty-five tons of rice. About twenty tons were evacuated, and the remainder was destroyed. During this time my platoon was detached, by night, to an ARVN camp about fifty kilometers from the rest of the battalion. We had to travel through the night, crossing rice paddies and a sandy area. It was hard travel but we made it. When we arrived, we were given an area to sit in, and once settled in I began to catch a nap. This, however, was cut short by the call, *Doc up!* I was escorted into the building where I was told that one of the ARVN soldiers had been caught in an ambush and had severe shrapnel wounds to his scalp. They had the appropriate equipment, so I washed and set up my field station in order to begin work. Five hours later I finished removing the shrapnel and sewing up the wound. He would live to fight again. After I had finished an E-8 army medic said, "You navy doctors sure do fine work." I was shocked by this statement. I replied, "I am not a doctor: I am an E-3 hospital corpsman." He then said, "I believe, if you wanted to change services, that I can get you a warrant grade promotion." Not knowing at the time that in an army unit the E-8 in charge did not necessarily have to be a medic, I said, "If an E-8 in the army does not know more about medicine than you, I don't want to be in the army." Shortly after that we rejoined our company and I heard no more about it.

During Operation Shelbyville, I returned to Company C, which was now in Quang Nam, four miles southeast of Dai Loc. On September 22, BLT 1/3 swept the operational area in an easterly direction. Sniper fire was the only enemy response. On September 20, we entered a village and found seventeen Vietnamese women and children, most of whom were wounded. They explained to us that the Viet Cong had removed them from their bunker so they could use it, and when the area was hit with air strikes the villagers had no cover. They told us that five of their friends had been killed. We medicated and treated them. We received significant contact on September 26 from a VC company. Air and artillery were called in, and a number of the VC Company were killed. On 28 September 1967, Company C marched to Liberty Bridge for loading back aboard ship for an extensive rehabilitation effort.

During the month of September 1967, BLT 1/3 participated in four operations. We sustained six KIAs and 107 WIAs. We inflicted twenty-six VC KIAs (confirmed), nineteen VC KIAs (probable), and captured a total of 111 VC/POWs for the month.

During the first nine days of October 1967, while BLT 1/3 was in rehab, SLF Bravo participated in Operation Kingfisher. On October 10, the First Marines, having moved to Quang Tan Province from Da Nang, initiated Operation Medina as part of a comprehensive plan to eliminate enemy base areas. The Hai Lang Forest contained the Communist Base Area 101, elements of the Fifth and Sixth NVA Regiments who operated around the region.

SLF Alpha's mission in Operation Medina was to serve as a blocking force for the First Marines on the eastern edge of the operational area. BLT 1/3 made its helicopter move to assigned blocking positions on October 10, under the code name Bastion Hill. At approximately 0400 hours (about 4:00 a.m.), Company C was overrun, sustaining heavy of casualties including the commanding officer who was WIA and the executive officer who was KIA. During fierce action between Company C and a company of NVA, a wounded marine in the next trench line called out, *Corpsman up!* I started across the open field when a machine gun opened up on me. I dropped to the ground and waited for the gun to begin firing in another direction. As soon as it did, I got up and began running for the trench again. This time I made it to the trench and found a man down who was not breathing but had a pulse. I began artificial respiration but soon noticed he had also lost his pulse. I called for a chopper with a request for a doctor and continued CPR until the chopper arrived. There was no doctor on the chopper, but there was a corpsman. We loaded the soldier on the chopper, and the corpsman took over the CPR as they flew away. (This was the one man that I got to while he was still alive, but he later died because he had a bullet through the lung and heart). But there was no time to quit because the calls of *Corpsman up* kept filling the air. By the time I got back, my platoon said, "When we saw you fall, we thought you were dead. When you got up again, we thought we were watching the dead rise." The battalion involvement was scattered firefights, incoming mortar rounds, and booby traps. Company C again was attacked by a forty to fifty-man NVA force. An LP received an incoming satchel charge. Other elements of the company received grenades and additional satchel charges. On October 14, we observed seven VC dressed in helmets and flak jackets moving towards our area, and 81mm mortars were called in. During the fight, a green cluster (flare that was fired up in the air, and there were no friendly troops in the area. On October 17, twelve to fifteen VC were spotted through a Starlight scope, and 60 mm mortars were fired at them. On October 19, operations started with a heliborne assault into the area.

Immediately after Medina, BLT 1/3 moved south to new blocking positions west of Route 1 and the railroad between Hai Lang and Phong Bien to participate in Operation Liberty II/Fremont. October 20–23, operational control of BLT 1/3 passed from First Marines to the Fourth Marines. We were being transported to the new blocking position in six Trucks. At one point, when the trucks were stopped, we heard the sound of an M79 launcher go *Bloop*. Next, our M79 man said, "That went straight up." We scrambled out of the truck and tried to hide under it. However, the round landed about a hundred feet out in the field next to the road. Boy, did we feel dumb.

Operation Liberty II/Fremont was intended to prevent the Communists from disrupting the South Vietnamese National Assembly Elections. During the three days, squad and fire team patrols encountered the enemy. By this time, I no longer carried a Unit One (a corpsman field kit) but a demolition bag with my supplies in it. I didn't wear my corpsman insignia or navy rating insignia but instead wore a pair of marine corporal insignia to camouflage the fact that I was a corpsman. However for some reason, sick Vietnamese still came up to me saying, *boxy* (the word for corpsman). I treated the ones I could.

After Operation Liberty II/Fremont, we were trucked to Camp Evans for assignment. One of the logistical considerations during this period was to get the marines of 1/3 ponchos and liners. The monsoon had come to Vietnam. From October to November 4, Operation Granite took place in the provinces of Tinh Thua, Thien-Hai, Lang Forest. Again 1-4 and BLT 1/3 were under the Fourth Marines operational control. There was a two-battalion sweep into Communist Base 114. The enemy constantly harassed BLT, staying within a few hundred meters and making nightly probes. A friendly-fire strike wounded two marines; a short 60 mm Mortar wounded one, and an artillery round wounded the other. The operation appeared jinxed. Base camp 114 was never located, and the BLT returned to Camp Evans.

Operation Kentucky ran from November 6–16 in the Quang Tri-Ton Thien area known as Leatherneck Square. Company C was airlifted through sniper and mortar rounds into Cam Lo. On November 10, Company C moved out into the field to act as a blocking force for the Ninth Marines. On November 12, Company C walked into C3 then moved to Dong Ha by helicopter.

Next was Operation Kentucky V in providence Quang Tri, between Ton Thien and Gio Linh at A-3 Base. We called it Hill Three, and BLT provided security at the new fire base. As marine engineers and navy Seabees built the bunkers and command post, it rained almost constantly and our fox holes filled with water. The weather was cold and miserable. We received incoming artillery three times a day. Rain and mud were the words of the day. Company C, on patrol south of A-3, walked into a minefield. After this, we were ordered OPCON to the First AMTRAC BN at C-4 complex. On the seventeenth, Company C went to fire base C-4 and had a major battle with the enemy, north of C-4. A number of friendly casualties were burned with friendly napalm from friendly aircraft.

BLT 1/3 participated in three operations during the month of November. We sustained four KIAs and seventeen WIAs while inflicting twenty-five VC/NVA KIAs (confirmed), twenty-three VC/NVA KIAs (probable), and captured two POWs.

It was about this time that we were told that a number of corpsmen were to be transferred to Quang Tri and then to Phu Bai Medical Battalion R/T. The battalion was coming off float. I was returned to the A-3 base and required to give a report to the new senior corpsman, while the other corpsmen were loaded for transport back. I remember that they kidded me about having to stay behind for reports. However, as the chopper lifted off and got about fifty feet in the air, it exploded into a large ball of fire. I believe it took a hit from enemy fire. All the corpsmen on that craft were killed. Sometimes I wonder: Why them and not me?

After that I was at Quang Tri base for a time. The food was good, and I got some needed dental care. When I arrived at the medical battalion, I was issued new clothing (my old ones were close to rags) and new boots (the old ones were rough and had no black on them). I was also assigned a hootch and a cot. This was like luxury for me. We even had a hootch lady to do the cleaning. I was assigned to the medical supply. I dressed in my new clothes and boots and left my old boots by my cot and threw away my old clothes. After moving supplies all day—with a break for lunch at the chow hall (this was a new and wonderful thing)—I came back to my hootch, and to my surprise the old boots were almost like new, so shiny they could almost be worn to an inspection. I hadn't thought it could be done. I asked the other men in my hootch, and they said, "Well, you left them at the foot of the cot." This apparently was where you left your boots when you wanted the hootch lady to shine them. I was told that for this service it would cost me five dollars a month and that she also washed and ironed our uniforms. I thought I was in heaven.

The days ran into each other. We filled request orders for supplies during the day. We even got hold of a freezer for storing ice cream—there was a place that made it just a short distance from where we kept the oxygen tanks. Then Tet (the Vietnamese holiday) was upon us. Unknown to us, in the days leading up to Tet, hundreds of Viet Cong had infiltrated the city, mingling with the throngs of pilgrims pouring in to Hue. They easily moved their weapons and ammunition into the bustling city by concealing them in the wagons and trucks carrying the food and wares intended for the celebration of Tet.

In the dark, quiet morning hours of January 31, the Viet Cong unpacked their weapons, donned their uniforms, and headed to positions across Hue. There they linked up with crack VC assault troops and the People's Army of Vietnam (PAVN), who were closing in on the city. They assembled at the Citadel gates, ready to lead their comrades to the key targets.

At 3:40 a.m., a rocket and mortar barrage from the mountains to the west signaled the assault troops to launch their attack. By daybreak, the lighting strike was over, and the invaders controlled the city unleashing a harsh new reality over the stunned city. As PAVN and VC troops roamed freely consolidating and reinforcing their gains. Political officers set about rounding up South Vietnamese and foreigners unfortunate enough to be on their "Special List." Marching up and down the Citadel's narrow streets, the Cadre called out the names on their list over loud speakers, ordering them to report to a local school. Those not reporting voluntarily would be hunted down.

What happened to those rounded up no one would know until the battle ended. Even then, the facts surrounding their fate would be the topic of angry debate among Americans—a debate that still endures four decades later.

The action unfolding at Hue on the morning of January 31, 1967 was only one part of a ferocious coordinated attack stunning in its scope and execution. An estimated eighty thousand North Vietnamese and Viet Cong troops simultaneously struck three quarters of South Vietnam's provincial capitals and most of its main cities. They achieved total surprise in most objective areas, as they did in Hue, where the longest and bloodiest battle of the Tet Offensive was just getting started. One of the most venerated places in Vietnam, Hue in 1968 had a population of 140,000, making it South Vietnam's third largest city. In reality, Hue is two cities divided by the Song Huong, or Perfume River, with two thirds of the city's population living north of the river within the walls of the old city (known as the Citadel). The Citadel was once the home of the Vietnamese Emperors, who had ruled the central portion of present-day Vietnam. The three-square-mile Citadel is surrounded by walls forty feet thick and rising to thirty feet in height, forming a square about a mile and a half long on each side. The three walls not bordering the Perfume River are encircled by a zigzag moat that is ninety feet wide at many points and up to twelve feet deep.

Inside the Citadel are block after block of row houses, apartment buildings, villas, shops, parks, and an all-weather airstrip. Tucked within the old walled city is yet another fortified enclave, the Imperial Palace, where the emperors held court until the French took control of Vietnam in 1883. Situated at the south end of the citadel, the palace is essentially a square with twenty-three-foot-high and 2,300-foot-long walls. As one observer put it, the Citadel was a "Camera-toting tourist's dream." But in February 1968, it would prove to be "a rifle-toting infantryman's nightmare."

South of the Perfume River and linked to the Citadel by the Nguyen Hoang Bridge is the modern part of Hue. With about half the footprint of the Citadel, it housed about a third of the city's population in 1968. Here was the city's hospital, the provisional prison, the Catholic Cathedral, the US Consulate, Hue University, and the newer residential district. As Vietnam's traditional culture and intellectual center, Hue had been treated almost as an open city by the Viet Cong and the North Vietnamese and thus was spared much of the war's death and destruction. The only military presence in the city was the fortified army of the Republic Of Vietnam (ARVN) First Infantry Division, headquartered at the northeast corner of the Citadel. The only combat element in the city was the division's reconnaissance company, the elite HHC and BAO Company, known as the Black Panthers. The rest of the division's subordinate units were arrayed outside the city. Maintaining security inside Hue was primarily the responsibility of the National Police.

The only US military presence in Hue on January 31, 1967, was the Military Assistance Command Vietnam (MACV) compound, located about a block and a half south of the Nguyen Hoang Bridge on the eastern edge of the modern sector. The compound housed about two hundred US Army, Marine Corps, and Australian officers and men who served as advisors to the First ARVN Division. The nearest US combat forces were at Phu Bai Marine Base, eight miles south on Route 1, home of the Task Force X-ray, a forward headquarters of the First Marine Division that was made up of two marine regimental headquarters and three marine battalions. Communists forces in the Hue region numbered eight thousand and consisted of ten battalions including two PAVN regiments. These were highly trained regular North Vietnamese units, the Sixth Viet Cong Main Force Battalion, which included the Twelfth and Hue City's Sapper Battalions.

While very adept at fighting in jungles and rice paddies, the PAVN and the VC troops required training for fighting in urban areas. While the soldiers trained for the battle ahead, VC intelligence officers prepared a list of "Cruel Tyrants and Reactionary Elements" to be rounded up in Hue during the early hours of the attack. On this list were most of the South Vietnamese government officials, military officers, and politicians, as well as American civilians and other foreigners. After capturing these individuals, they were to be evacuated to the jungle outside the city, where they would be held to account for their crimes against the Vietnamese people.

The Battle of Hue started on January 31, 1967, and continued for twenty-five days until American and South Vietnamese forces retook the city from Communists forces on February 24, 1968. The epic battle for Hue left much of the ancient city a pile of rubble as 40 percent of its buildings were destroyed, leaving some 116,000 civilians homeless. Among the population, 5,800 civilians were reported killed or missing.

While the battle in Hue ensued, I remained at Phu Bai. I worked loading medical supplies to those in battle at Hue and other northern areas. I was often called out during the night to fill an emergency order of medical supplies. Others were running medevac to Hue. The OR and treatment areas were working around the clock. We frequently received incoming mortar rounds, and I began to sleep in the bunker so I could get more sleep.

When the battle in Hue finally ended, life for me became again as it was when I first arrived at the medical battalion. There were no major battles while I finished my tour of duty.

I returned to the United States in June 1968. On the way back, I arrived in Da Nang a day before my scheduled flight. I shared a berth with a couple of sergeants who were stationed in Da Nang. That night a mortar attack hit on the other side of the airfield. The sergeants ran for their bunker. I just sat there finishing my beer. It was to far away for me to worry about.

When I returned to CONUS (continental United States), my mother picked me up at the airport in Oakland, California. At that time she lived in San Leandro, California. I spent my leave with my parents, and my fiancée from Oregon came to visit us. We went on a camping trip. When I took her home to Oregon in my 1962 Buick LeSabre, we enjoyed a visit with her parents, and then I returned to report in for duty at NAS in Alameda, California. However, a few weeks later I got a Dear John letter. My fiancé said that she had never dated anyone but me, and that before she got married she needed to date other people. We had met at a carnival where I worked before I joined the navy. She was sixteen years old then, and she was almost nineteen years old now. She had written to me every day when I was in Vietnam.

A few days later, I had duty in the ER, and a young dependent daughter (the daughter of a serviceman) came in with a finger cut. The MD was busy with a cardiac emergency, so I was assigned to prepare her for sutures. I cleaned the wound, but every time I got the bleeding stopped she would wiggle her finger and get it bleeding again. This continued until the doctor was ready to suture her finger. Later I called her for a date, and we were married on March 16, 1969. I reenlisted in December 1969 and then received orders to Aviation Medicine School, Pensacola, Florida. While we were waiting for school to start, we went to see my wife's real father in Jacksonville, Florida. He was a retired ABE1 (Aviation Boatswain Mate Equipment, First Class Petty Officer) The first day we were at his place, we got up and had a six-pack of beer for breakfast and then commenced to do some real drinking. I thought to myself, this man is an alcoholic. Ten years later, I caught myself doing the same thing.

After my first tour of duty in Vietnam, I learned that it was not a good thing to wear my uniform on liberty. People would call you all sorts of names—baby killers was one—so instead I wore civilian clothing. I also learned it was not good to talk about my experience in Vietnam because people would blame me for the war. The fact that I kept those things that bothered me pent up inside tended to make it hard to sleep. The scar on my left leg had healed, but there was nerve damage. I often had leg cramps that made me wake up screaming in pain. But my leg was not the only reason I woke up screaming. I had dreams of Vietnam.

The story I have told you, so far, is the operational story with a few items I added from my memory. However, that story doesn't tell you about the hot weather. Or that no matter how hot it was, at times but yet you had to wear a flak jacket and a heavy helmet to keep from being injured. It doesn't tell you of crossing rivers and then having to stop to get the leeches off. It doesn't tell you of having wet feet all the time and the need to care for your feet. It doesn't tell you of walking through rice paddies or jungle watching for punji sticks or land mines. I did not tell you that you even had to watch out for small children who would drop a hand grenade at your feet. You never knew who to trust because the North Vietnamese and South Vietnamese looked alike. Then there were the snakes, the bugs, and the mosquitoes that seemed as big as a chopper and were constantly around.

There was also the monsoon rain, which lasted for days and left nowhere to sleep because there was mud everywhere. You ended up sleeping in your poncho in a mud puddle, hoping your body would warm the puddle. I did tell you about the snipers, rockets, and mortars, but I didn't tell you about the fear that they caused. I found that sleeping in a graveyard was one of the best places to sleep because the VC would not mortar their cemeteries.

I didn't tell you about seeing your friends killed by enemy fire, or another friend blown apart by a mortar or artillery round. I didn't tell you about always knowing that the friend you joked with today might not be there tomorrow or seeing the pain of your comrades when they were wounded. I didn't tell you that, when you were patching them up, you had to tell them that everything would be OK, while you trying to hide from them that parts of their body were missing. Being the doc made it your responsibility to care for them and to see that they got back to the states in the best condition possible.

Many a night I dreamed of these events. I almost felt like I was living them over. My wife tried to comfort me, but that made it difficult on her so I tried not to tell her about it. I have had times when I took it out on my wife, and she didn't understand why. To my astonishment she has stayed with me these forty-two years. I had trouble making and keeping friends, and after a time I no longer wanted friends. I could not understand why. Nor could I understand why I no longer enjoyed things that others enjoy. At times I felt that I would have been better off had I been one of those killed. Then I wondered why I hadn't been.

However, I remained in the navy. I finished Aviation Medicine School and was transferred to VF-121 (Top Gun) as the senior corpsman. I was a HM2 by this time. At first I worked in the aviation medicine department at the dispensary. However, I was transferred to sick bay and placed in charge when I became HM1. But then it was time to go back to sea duty.

I received orders to VA 113 (notice the number again), whose homeport was at Lemoore Naval Air Station. My wife was pregnant, and once I had gotten her situated in navy housing on base, I reported for duty. The first thing the officer of the day asked me was, "Are your sea bags packed?" I asked in reply, "Why?" He replied, "We are embarking on the USS Ranger in one week." In the meantime I was assigned to the dispensary. I don't remember what I did there, but it didn't seem like a week. I was assigned to the medical department of the ship and placed in charge of aviation medicine. The ship sailed for Vietnam. We were stationed off the coast of Vietnam, but it didn't seem like we were in a war zone. My first daughter was born in February. We did air operations, and I performed the required physicals. I was also in charge of the eye lane and ran eye exams and ordered glasses. There was a request for volunteers to go on a forward deployed ship to be home ported in Yokosuka, Japan. I volunteered for the assignment, and the USS Ranger finished the cruise and returned to Alameda.

I had received my orders to be home ported in Yokosuka, Japan, while aboard the USS Midway. VA93 would be the squadron I was attached to. We said farewell to the Bay Area on September 11, 1973, and we arrived in Japan on October 5, 1973. We had not been told one fact: that we wouldn't be allowed to remain in port longer than twenty days. Soon we were in the waters off Vietnam flying flight operations. My wife arrived in Japan about six months later, when housing became available. For a time, we lived in navy housing in Kenagowa because I had accepted E-5 housing to get my wife there faster. Later, we lived in Nagi Heights, which was a nice two-story two-bedroom with maid quarters. I continued in aviation medicine until the evacuation from Vietnam began in April 1975, when I was put in charge of medical supply. I reenlisted in April 1975, and we received word to go back into the waters off Vietnam and assist in the final evacuation.

I remember a few things about the final evacuation. We were landing a number of helicopters that had everything taken out of them except what was required to fly. This was to make room for people who were desperately trying to get out of Vietnam. In one case, we had an aircraft fly over seeking permission to land. He was told to ditch the plane in the water, and he would be picked up. On another pass, he dropped a rock with a note on it which said "Wife and five children on board". The Midway pushed five of those stripped helicopters into the water to make room on the flight deck so the plane could land. The pilot was a major in the South Vietnamese Air Force, and he made aviation history by being the first pilot to land on a carrier without a tail hook to catch the arresting gear or a safety net. Altogether, we had over twice as many refugees as we had crew, about ten thousand people total. On another occasion, a few days later, we had a boat pull up and request to board. We unloaded over thirty people, and their boat sank as we took the last one on board.

When I had reenlisted, I had requested Independent Duty School. I received my orders and left the ship in January 1976, right after my son was born in Yokosuka Naval Hospital, Japan. The School was at Naval Hospital, Balboa San Diego, California. While I was at the school, my brother Irwin died in September 1976, so when I graduated I requested duty anywhere on the West Coast to be close to family. However, I received orders to Navy and Marine Reserve Center, Richmond, Virginia. Upon completion of shore duty, I received orders to the medical battalion, Camp Lejeune, in North Carolina. But by the completion of my enlistment, I was beginning to have trouble with PTSD. I was not allowed to reenlist and was discharged from the navy on April 13, 1981.

I never received any information on my VA benefits, or any other benefits for that matter. After a time, there was something about Agent Orange, so I went to get the free physical that they suggested I have done. A short time later, I received a letter that said my exposure to Agent Orange had been determined to be service-connected, but that I was 0 percent disabled. I did not know what that meant until I had a heart attack in May 2010. A friend of my wife's twin told us that cardiac problems had been determined to be related to Agent Orange, and that I should apply for benefits.

When we went to apply for benefits, the interviewer said that I should apply for PTSD benefits also. I applied and was evaluated for both PTSD and cardiac problems. Shortly after we received notification that I was 50% percent disabled R/T PTSD. Guidelines had not yet been established for the cardiac problems. However, in November of 2010, I was notified that the disability for my heart condition was 100 percent. I am now a 100 percent disabled veteran and retired.

I am glad that the military and VA are now disseminating the information on VA benefits to all veterans. However, if they had done this at the time of my release, life may have been different.

* Due to PTSD, I am unable to remember dates and names well, so I had to consult the following sources in order to write the above:

"1/3 in Vietnam," compiled by Don Bumgarner and Ron Asher (C Company).

"First Battalion, Third Marines," Wikipedia. January 25, 2011

Roland H. Froman III, US Navy Enlistment Service Record.

Wilbanks, James. "Tet: What really happened at Hue." Historynet.com. January 25, 2011.

CHAPTER EIGHT

SEA DUTY TO COMBINED ACTION FORCE

Cpl. William A. Bayha
Corporal
USMC, 2425185
Quang Tri Province
Fourth Combined Action Group
Squad Leader, CAP, 4,3,4
III Marine Amphibious Force
1968–1970

I was born into a family of agriculture heritage and strong moral values. Military service not an option but a responsibility met with pride. My father was a WWII pilot, and other family members served in the army, air force, and navy, including the construction battalion, Seabees. All branches were represented in my family except the United States Marine Corps.

One of my high school agriculture teachers had served in the USMC in WWII. He was my best role model, always squared away. I decided early on that I would serve in the Marine Corps. My plans were to finish college, enlist in officer candidate school (OCS), and become an officer. The Vietnam War draft quickly changed my plans. I was able to complete an associate of arts degree, but my bachelor of science would have to wait. It was clear that neither of my two brothers had any intention of serving, so I decided to volunteer for the USMC.

From the time I hit the yellow footprints at Marine Corps Recruit Depot (MCRD) in San Diego, California, my life changed forever. I quickly realized my boot camp platoon was on a motivation/disciplinary agenda. Most of the recruits had problem backgrounds. Some fought the program through boot camp, but by the time boot camp was completed, they were eager to complete infantry training to become hard-charging marines.

One day, I was pulled from my infantry training company by an order to report to the commanding officer (CO) of my company. In the past I had seen people ordered to report to the CO for less than favorable reasons. By the time I reached his office, I was scared to death, shaking like a leaf.

After knocking on the door, I heard the response from within: "Who is there?"

"Recruit William Bayha reporting as ordered, sir," I said.

When he told me to enter, I did, shut the door, approached his desk, planted my feet, stood at attention, and saluted, saying, "Reporting as ordered, sir."

"At ease, recruit," he said very calmly. When he lowered the tone of his voice, I immediately felt more like a human being. I could actually see a set of sincere eyes glaring at me.

"Recruit Bayha," he said, "You realize that you have some real challenges ahead in the months to come."

"Sir, yes sir!" I replied.

"Relax recruit," he said. He continued, "I have a once in a life time offer for you. Your background check is complete and you qualify for duty requiring a special clearance. I will be straight up, Recruit Bayha. Your odds for survival will increase greatly if you first extend your enlistment one year. I can offer you sea duty. You can give me an answer now or you have twenty-four hours."

"Sir, I accept your offer, sir," I said.

"That is a very smart decision, Recruit Bayha," he replied.

"Yes sir," I answered back.

He quickly said, "After you graduate and become a marine, you will receive orders to Sea School and then assigned to a navy ship for duty." He added, "That will be all, Recruit Bayha."

"Sir, yes, sir," I said and did an about face and exited his office.

On that day, after returning to my infantry training company, I realized I had made a very wise decision. I graduated with my company and received orders to report to MCRD, San Diego, for Sea School. Upon graduation from Sea School, I received orders to report to the USS Hornet, located in San Diego, scheduled to leave dry dock for the West Pacific (WESTPAC) cruise to Yankee Station, in Vietnam.

Reporting aboard the USS Hornet for duty felt like being processed into a state prison. This being my first duty station, and holding the rank of private, I quickly realized I was the lowest form of life. Being a private in the USMC was bad enough, but joining a strong rank and file command in such small quarters would be a challenge, at best. After reporting aboard, going through the staff, then the noncommissioned officers (NCO) above me, and then reporting to the marine detachment commanding officer for my "Welcome aboard" briefing, I was assigned to my locker and rack (bed).

I soon learned that any respect from higher-ranking NCOs had to be earned. Bad attitudes didn't belong aboard ship and would get you a trip to the first sergeant's office. I quickly decided, as was suggested by my former high school AG teacher (a retired marine commanding officer), not to fight the program but to make the best of a bad situation.

As time went on, and we set sail for our WESTPAC cruise, I was shown the ropes and molded into a seagoing marine. I spent my shift on the mess deck, working with the officers' chef. After cleaning the meat grinder and finding cockroaches, I imagined what was crawling about the enlisted mess deck. Returning to my regular duties, I was a little apprehensive at mealtime, but grabbed a metal tray and lined up for chow.

Another duty was handling prisoners confined to the ship's brig. I had to chase them through the ship for work details, escort them to and from chow, to the head, to chapel, to the dental and medical ward, and so on. While I served aboard the USS Hornet, we had only one marine sentenced to the brig for bad behavior. For some reason, I was the lucky brig chaser assigned to guard this individual on work details. I noticed him becoming more aggravated, depressed, and violent with each day he was incarcerated. One day I was ordered to escort him to the fantail of the ship. This area is located at the extreme rear of the ship, just above the four big propellers that push the ship. When the ship is underway, the propellers create an extreme amount of churning water. I was within arm's length of him when, without warning, he tried to jump the rail above the churning wake. I grabbed his legs just as his head was about to hit the water. If I had not caught him, it surely would have been his last jump. After this incident, I tied a rope around his waist. His attempt to take his own life scared me to death. Not only because of the tragic loss of a life. I could picture trying to explain the marine detachment commanding officer how this prisoner got away from me. They would probably still be piping daylight to me. The prisoner challenged me several other times after this incident, but you can be sure I had him like a dog on a leash!

Probably the worst mess I was involved in aboard ship was the shell back initiation (February 23, 1969). When a ship crosses the equator (Realm of Neptunus Rex), and crewmembers aboard ship are crossing for the first time, the tradition is for the seasoned sailors (shell backs) to initiate the green sailors (pollywogs). As you can imagine, this is a great time for the sailors to get revenge on the marines. After being dragged through garbage and dunked in a urinal, among other things, I was hung by my feet over the edge of the flight deck.

During the initiation, one of the senior staff NCOs decided he would hide out and avoid all the torturous ceremonies of the initiation. At the onset of the initiation process, I was on duty at the ship's brig, which was located across from the print shop. I observed this sergeant entering the print shop in order to hide. I decided before we changed guard that I would go in and invade his hiding place. This was a bad idea. When I entered the room and found him, I quickly saw that he was not going to join the initiation. He locked and loaded a .45 caliber weapon and pointed it at me. "See you later," I said, and that was the end of that idea. I was very happy to see the shell back initiation end.

As a seagoing marine, I felt very fortunate that I was able to visit seaports in many countries during the 1968–1969 WESTPAC cruise. Some of these include, Pearl Harbor, Hawaii; Yokuskia, Japan; Hong Kong, China; Sasado, Japan; Subic Bay, Philippines; and Singapore.

One duty aboard ship that nobody ever volunteered for was Man the Rail. This is a navy tradition that when a ship enters a port, a formation of marines in dress blues lines the bow (in drill formation with rifles). This means standing at parade rest with the butt of the rifle on deck and barrel cocked forward. The position might be held for an hour or until the ship was secure at the dock. I can remember my hands going numb in cold weather. We used an old trick, handed down by the old salts. We would borrow a larger jacket and line it with newspaper to block out the cold.

On April 16, 1969, the USS Hornet received orders for North Korea due to the fact that a US plane had been shot down. It was C-121 with troops on board. Cold weather gear was handed out, and the biggest convoy since the Korean War was deployed with the USS Hornet leading the way.

On April 18 we ran patrols in the Yellow Sea under battle alert conditions with planes on deck loaded with rockets. The conditions were very cold. Aircraft were launched to ward off a North Korean PT boat. The USS Enterprise was also in the convoy and launched aircraft. On April 27 we were taken off station.

During battle alert conditions, my station was as a member of the 5-inch/38-inch gun crew. My job was projectile loader; my position was at the gun breach. After the projectile was lifted off the fuse setter, I loaded the breach with the fifty-pound projectile after the powder charge had been loaded. Then the breach would close, and the gun would be ready to fire. I remember we were experiencing severe weather conditions, with water inside the gun tub from the sea swells splashing up to our position just below the flight deck.

On June 5, 1969, the USS Hornet was designated as the prime recovery ship (PRS) for the Apollo Eleven recovery mission.

Between June 21 and 25, while at Long Beach Harbor, we loaded various support equipment for the recovery mission. We departed Long Beach and headed for San Diego, where we loaded more support equipment for the mission. On July 1 we left San Diego and headed for Pearl Harbor.

We commenced a training program for the Apollo Operation. On July 7 we began our at-sea training, which included using a heavy crane as the pick-up vehicle. We practiced recovery of the astronauts and had a debriefing concerning the practice mission. On July 8 we practiced a night recovery. On July 9 we entered Pearl Harbor, and on July 11 NASA and the media personnel arrived on board ship.

On July 12 a press conference was held as we headed for the mid-Pacific line. Press conferences were held twice daily until we returned to Pearl Harbor. We crossed the equator on July 15 for the second time, and since I had already become a shell back, I was home free.

On July 19 we practiced for the arrival of President Nixon. On July 23 final preparations for the Apollo Eleven recovery were made. Admiral McCain (John McCain's father) was welcomed aboard the USS Hornet. The recovery station was adjusted north due to adverse weather conditions. On July 24 we were on station for the recovery mission. At this time, President Nixon arrived aboard the ship. After Apollo Eleven splash landed, divers reached the capsule and installed the flotation device. The command module was then brought aboard by USS Hornet and Apollo recovery teams. The astronauts were brought aboard by helicopter and were placed in a decontamination chamber. Once the astronauts were in the chamber, President Nixon addressed them. After leaving the mobile quarantine facility (MQF), the president was escorted to the flight deck by navy command and marine detachment security personnel. On the flight deck, the president greeted the flight crew. Then he entered Marine One (the presidential helicopter) and departed from the ship. He was on board a total of three hours.

The duties of the marine detachment of which I was a part of during the Apollo Eleven recovery operation were to provide very precise security for the astronauts and protect the president while he was aboard the ship. In addition, after the president departed, it was the responsibility and duty of the marine detachment to guard the astronauts while they were confined in the decontamination chamber en route back to Pearl Harbor. During this time, we had an excellent opportunity to talk with the astronauts as we provided twenty-four-hour security at their location in hangar bay two.

The crew who served on the USS Hornet, CVS-12 during the 1968–1969 WESTPAC cruise, which included the Vietnam patrol in the Tonkin Gulf (Yankee Station) off the coast of North Vietnam and the patrol in the Yellow Sea off the coast of North Korea in battle alert conditions, were awarded the following: Meritorious Unit Commendation USN, Armed Forces Expeditionary, National Defense Service, Vietnam Service, and the Republic of Vietnam Campaign Medals.

In September 1969, I volunteered for ground forces. I wanted to experience the regular marine infantry for which I was originally trained. I received orders to report to headquarters, Fourth Combined Action Group, III Marine Amphibious Force, in Da Nang, South Vietnam. In October another marine and I reported for duty to the III Marine Amphibious Force. We were immediately scheduled to Vietnamese Language School. My fellow marine from USS Hornet began to experience some health problems and within two weeks was sent back to the United States and eventually discharged.

After I completed the language school, I was assigned to my first field unit and was transported by air to the Fourth Combined Action Group Headquarters, Quang Tri Combat Base. I was assigned as a squad leader with the Combined Action Platoon (CAP) 4,3,4 Quang Tri province.

The function of the combined action group was to train assigned/attached South Vietnamese troops and to protect the South Vietnamese villages/hamlets from unfriendly forces. Each CAP consisted of the USMC squad (one leader, corpsman, radioman, four fire teams of three marines each) and the South Vietnamese squad (one leader, who was a sergeant, and approximately twenty-five South Vietnamese troops).

The South Vietnamese sergeant, Sergeant Dam, and I worked very closely together. I not only was the USMC squad leader for the CAP 4,3,4, but the senior NCO responsible for the supervision, training, and coordination of United States and South Vietnamese Forces. Sgt. Dam and I discussed each day's strategy/tactics/ambushes. We worked to improve communications in the combined operation between the marines and the South Vietnamese troops. Most of our operations, such as ambushes, were conducted in the hours of darkness. We rested and slept during daylight hours.

Each day our CAP always relocated to a different village/hamlet to avoid being located by unfriendly forces. Each day camp security watch/patrol was rotated between troops made up of combined teams of South Vietnamese troops and marines. Sgt. Dam and I always teamed up together to best use the time to plan/execute the next day's maneuvers.

One day at about 1400 hours (2:00 p.m.), as I remember, Sgt. Dam and I were taking our turn on security watch when a senior citizen from the village approached us. The villager was crying and appeared to be suffering from shock when he told us a young person from the village, a female approximately twelve years old, had been discovered dead just outside the village.

Sgt. Dam and I were taken to the location, approximately a hundred yards from the village, and found the site empty of any other villagers. The scene was very gruesome and stressful to observe. The young female had been severely beaten and her hands and legs tied together. But most shocking was that her head had been removed from her body. We found the head twenty to thirty feet away. When Sgt. Dam retrieved the head we discovered the victim to be a well-known citizen, very much respected and liked by the other villagers as well as the troops of the combined force. I personally had become very close to this young girl. She had given me a small hand-made friendship gift—a necklace that she had made herself. She said it was in appreciation for the security work accomplished by the CAP 4,3,4. This killing of such an innocent child has affected me to this day. I cannot get through a day without thinking about this incident. I feel partially responsible and think that maybe I could have prevented this from happening to her. However, for whatever reason, she had left the safety of the village, and none of us had realized that she was gone. I continue to suffer nightmares and flashbacks in which I see the severely mutilated body of this child.

Sgt. Dam, after communicating with the head of the village, advised me that the family of the child requested to remove the remains for religious reasons. I agreed. As I recall, we began immediately to investigate the scene to determine whether friendly or unfriendly forces were responsible for this killing. Sgt. Dam and I organized a search patrol of the area to secure the village perimeter. We included the villagers as much as possible in this investigation. We wanted to ensure they knew we were covering nothing up.

The victim appeared to have been dragged approximately 150 feet after being killed. The evidence—footprints and materials used—indicated unfriendly forces had been responsible. The girl probably had been killed for the hospitality she showed the USMC and South Vietnamese forces. In the interest of protecting her fellow villagers, she had provided friendly forces with information when enemy forces approached the village. Somehow this young girl slipped by the CAP's security perimeter, and for this reason I will always feel responsible and guilty for her death.

In memory of this sweet young girl, I wrote the following dedication to honor her bravery and service to our country as well as to her family and her country.

Dedication

Forty-one years late, I would like to honor a true fallen hero. She was a patriot in every sense of the word. This hero could see a future of freedom and peace. She loved her country as well as her beloved marines, whom she so bravely served.

This hero paid the ultimate price, unselfishly sacrificed her life, knowing well the dangers. Through her unselfish devotion, and in honor of her country, she placed herself in harm's way. This hero became victim to unfriendly forces, voluntarily helping her fellow citizens and the United States Marine Corps she so dearly loved and respected for their gallant bravery as she had told me many times. She thanked me and the CAP marines for helping keep her family safe as well as the other South Vietnamese citizens. She gave me a friendship necklace, which I put away and have not seen for over forty years. After all these years having passed, I still hold this hero in my memories. I still feel guilty and partially responsible for the young hero falling victim to unfriendly forces, the Ugly face of War.

Even though I know I could not have prevented this cruel act of hate and revenge, and even though I know that I can never do so, I would like to put this tragic memory of war to rest forever. I would like to remember only the loving, innocent child of twelve years old, an innocent who my fellow marines and I had learned to love and respect.

May God bless this lovely child who gave the ultimate price, her life. May her soul rest in peace.

In order to maintain a successful friendship with the South Vietnamese citizens, I soon learned that you had to show respect toward their native customs and life styles. Every village and hamlet we entered, we would first have to earn the welcome and respect of the village chief. We would never disrespect their property in any way. Often times we questioned some of the individual citizens attempting to find out if they were Viet Cong sympathizers or actually Viet Cong. Many citizens were afraid to expose non-village members for fear of retaliation. I also learned to always respect their hospitality and to share a meal with them, even though the menu was very questionable. We would often times stuff something less than edible into our fatigues while pretending to eat it. Some of the rice was so sticky you could hardly eat it, but I would sometimes eat it later on ambush as a snack.

One morning at around 1000 hours (10:00 a.m), I was setting up a temporary security watch program at a new location when I sensed something was not normal. A dead silence fell over the perimeter of the village. I, as well as my fellow platoon members, knew that there must be unfriendly forces already in or near the village. No citizens came to greet us, as was the normal routine. One senior citizen at the edge of the village cast his eyes towards the west side, which was to my right. I walked approximately twenty more feet, and I could see what appeared to be a Viet Cong with an AK-47 in hand. He was behind a female resident of the village. At this time, my finger on the trigger, I quickly came to a stop. I was too frozen even to communicate with my fellow troops. I had Sgt. Dam on my right and a fellow marine on my left. I could see that the Viet Cong was as shocked as we were. With citizens located between us, my worst fear would be an exchange of weapon fire.

We very cautiously held our location, approximately fifty feet from the Viet Cong, trying to show that we intended no exchange of gunfire. Sgt. Dam stated in a firm voice in Vietnamese that we would not enter the village.

Our platoon exited the village, which was located near a large rice-growing area. We traveled approximately one mile and strategically changed direction and set up an ambush. We were very fortunate that the Viet Cong didn't panic and open fire. This would have caused irreversible damage to our relationship with the citizens of the village and could easily have resulted in death or injuries to the villagers. We had no idea the size of the unfriendly forces that were located in the village. We set up the ambush on a rice paddy bank. Our position allowed us to cover two different routes the Viet Cong might travel. We hoped they didn't leave the village the same way we suspected they had come in.

We stayed two days in the position before we decided that we had made a big mistake. At sunset on day two, my point man, who was approximately five hundred feet in front of me, motioned that we had unfriendly forces approaching. From my location it appeared to be about thirty Viet Cong. At that point we were losing daylight quickly. Our ambush engaged the Viet Cong, and after about five minutes we realized that we had executed—luckily—a flawless ambush and a good kill zone.

Of the hundreds of ambushes and patrols conducted during my tour of duty as a platoon leader, the above-described ambush always stands out in my mind. Two days earlier, when my combined action platoon came face to face with unfriendly forces in the village, the outcome could have ended in a disaster. But my platoon hadn't panicked. In consequence, no civilians were caught in the crossfire. The teamwork and the mutual respect the two teams showed each other paid off.

The mission of the combined action forces was to eliminate unfriendly forces from demanding (stealing) food and supplies from the South Vietnamese citizens. This was accomplished by showing our presence and intercepting (ambushing) enemy forces before they could enter or leave a hamlet or village. We took pains to keep innocent citizens out of harm's way. I personally didn't want to see the special bond that developed between my platoon and the locals come to an end.

In August of 1970, the Fourth Combined Action Group, Quang Tri, South Vietnam, was disbanded. This order to terminate the combined forces came with no warning. My squad of marines as well as the South Vietnamese forces was in shock. I had a feeling that we were abandoning a very successful program. As much as I welcomed the thought of returning to the United States, our mission was not yet completed. As soon as the Combined

Action Group Forces were gone, I felt all that our combined expertise had accomplished would be lost. The unfriendly forces were eager to cross the border and invade, but the South Vietnamese forces were not yet ready to assume the security role developed and practiced by the Combined Action Group unit.

Returning home was difficult for me. I was very happy to be on US soil and to reunite with my wife, family, and friends. But I had developed very mixed feelings concerning my Vietnam experience. I felt no closure. I felt then and still continue to feel until this day that the mission of the Combined Action Group was not completed. When my unit was disbanded, we left many citizens who trusted and depended on us in jeopardy.

After arriving home, I felt like I had done something wrong for serving in Vietnam. All I heard was, "Why are we over there?" or "Why did you volunteer for ground forces?" I also found that people questioned how my service in Vietnam might affect my behavior—particularly on job applications and during employment interviews.

The Vietnam veterans, as a rule, were not welcomed home and never received the respect given to the veterans of WWI, WWII, and the Korean War.

Vietnam combat veterans were expected to become productive citizens without any transitional counseling. I was told by my last commanding officer, "Don't think about your combat experiences. Don't talk about them, and you will be OK. Keep your anger inside, you will learn to live with it."

I often ask myself, Why was I one of the lucky ones to return home? I have always suffered from survivor's guilt. I think of all my fellow marines, soldiers, sailors, and air force veterans who never returned home to family and friends. May God bless the POWs and MIAs of the war.

I bid farewell to my fellow servicemen, soldiers, and marines, warriors who left their home, the United States, to serve their country in a place called Vietnam.

Semper Fi!

William "Wild Bill" Bayha on duty at the guard shack aboard the USS
Hornet CVS 12, July, 1969

The Apollo capsule on the flight deck of the USS Hornet CVS 12 after being recovered from the ocean, July 1969

CHAPTER NINE

MY JOURNEY TO THE PROMISED LAND

Rufino "Joe" Centeno
Spec. 4
US Army
Troop C
First Squadron, Fourth Calvary (Search & Destroy)
First Infantry Division (Big Red One)
1968–1969

I was born in Texas in 1947. I had three brothers and four sisters. We were a poor and a very hard-working family, but we were happy. We had many fun times together out in the fields, but work came first. I had very wonderful parents who taught me good morals and how to follow the golden rule, — Do unto others as you would have them do unto you.

When I was eighteen years old, I signed up for the draft. My older brother had joined the army and did his time in Germany. In September of 1967 I was drafted, and it was my turn. I wasn't as lucky as my brother. I went to Oakland, California, and from there to boot camp in Fort Lewis, Washington. My advanced individual training (AIT) was in Fort Knox, Kentucky. I thought that afterward I would get a thirty-day leave so I could go see my family, but I had thought wrong. The next day, March 4, 1968, I was on a plane destined to the Promised Land of Vietnam. The guys on the plane, as well as me, were very quiet. We were young kids, eighteen and nineteen years old, and we had no idea what was going to happen when we landed. The only nice thing that I can say is that the plane was a beautiful United Airlines 747, what I later would refer to as The Freedom Bird.

As the plane was descending into Bien Hoa, we all had a sinking feeling: "What would happen to us next?"

When we exited the plane, the army personnel directed us to the processing center. I was assigned to the First Infantry Division (Big Red One), Troop C, First Squadron, Fourth Calvary, and our first duty was to burn human waste. We did this for about a week, and then we were assigned to the field. They designated me as scout observer. This is the person who goes out first to find the enemy and comes back with news of the enemy's strength and location coordinates.

In March of 1968, as we departed Bien Hoa to go to the field in our armored tank, the tank in front of ours hit a mine. This was my first taste of things to come.

I was on patrol searching for the enemy when we heard them coming and had to lie down in a pile of leaves. As we lay there, trying not to be seen, a snake about eight inches in diameter slithered over my chest. I could not move or make a sound for fear of being located and killed. I was so scared! I thought this was my last day on earth. This happened sometime in April of 1968 in the central highlands of Vietnam.

The next day we were patrolling the area known as The Iron Triangle when we got our first big taste of what war was all about. We were hit by a sneak attack. Bombs came in from all sides, and we didn't know which way to turn. We covered each other's back and the radio telephone operator called in for help. As scout leader, I told him, whatever happens, to make sure to protect his phone. We lost six good men that day. Air support came in, and the enemy retreated (or so we thought). Afterward we recovered the bodies of our buddies and loaded them in the medevac chopper along with the wounded. While loading the wounded, one of the door gunners was hit with enemy fire and I had to step in and cover his position. When everyone was on board, the chopper took off and we rested for a bit. We moved back to our perimeter and I split the guys into twosomes. This was my first experience at war.

I recall another time when we set a perimeter of armored tanks around us. I remember this because it was close to my birthday at the end of May 1968. After three other soldiers and I had gone on reconnaissance, I came back with information that we were going to be hit that night. I slept for a few hours and took the night watch to be sure we didn't miss anything. I had night vision, and sure enough I saw them coming. I signaled my men, we engaged in battle, and all hell broke loose. We lost two good men, and they lost over one hundred men.

So this is the life I came to expect. I used to pray, "Please, God, keep me and my buddies safe for another day." I felt a great responsibility because I was chosen as scout leader, and I didn't want to let them down. I was so scared, but I was determined to make it back. I just couldn't let them win. I hated what I had to do, and prayed it would just end.

During the Tet Offensive, I was moved to the Fourth Infantry Division, Troop C, Second Squadron, First Cavalry. During my time there, we were moved to Pleiku in the central highlands. We covered areas that were being sprayed for vegetation with Agent Orange. We knew nothing about Agent Orange and the fact it would lead to health problems. That first day we set camp and unexpectedly we were hit, Big Time! We lost thirty-five good men with the enemy losing 150. I was so happy to see the air support, Cobras, Hueys, and artillery support. They made it look like a hundred Fourth of July celebrations. The fighting lasted six hours. I don't know how many M50 calibers I had to replace because they became so hot from firing. I was replacing an M50 barrel when the tank next to me took a direct hit. I was thrown off my tank and hit my head and was knocked out for a time. I woke up and went back at it.

My next experience happened sometime soon after I transferred in June 1968. I was on patrol at around 8:00 a.m. when my radio telephone operator was shot in the leg. When I saw him go down, I told him, "Don't Move." I always carried some rope on my belt loop and I threw him the rope and told him to tie it around his waist. I and another soldier pulled him to safety. Thank God it was only a graze on his leg. It bothers me that I can't remember his name, but I know he was from Kentucky. I am grateful for all the men I served with. I am just so sorry that I can't remember any names, but I am so grateful for all of their support. All of these men deserve our gratitude and praise. They did a hell of a job.

Many times we had to fight in hand-to-hand combat. I recently remembered an experience where I had the enemy down and was preparing to tie his hands and take him as a prisoner, when I heard footsteps behind me. I grabbed the prisoner and spun around and the oncoming enemy soldier stabbed him instead of me. I reached around and found my .45 caliber pistol and took care of business. As I recall, I think that was late in August 1968.

Days rolled into months. We had to deal with the monsoon rains in the jungle. We also had to deal with the bugs, the snakes, and the heat. All while fighting the enemy (the Viet Cong) and never knowing who they were. They might be a child with a booby trap. It was hell for nineteen and twenty year olds in a foreign place. Every day you wondered, "Is this my day to die?"

We would walk miles in the jungle searching for signs of the enemy. I remember one day, maybe in October of 1968. I am ashamed to say that I can't remember my buddy's name, but we were walking, and he was in front of me a little to the left, when he stepped on a land mine. I was thrown back and hit in the knee with pieces of metal from the mine. When I got up, my buddy was lying there with the bottom part of him gone. We had just talked that morning about never knowing when it would be our turn, we were swearing to tell our families we loved them, and now I was picking up his body parts to load into the plane. It haunts me to this day that I can't remember his name.

These are only a fraction of the things I saw and experienced in Vietnam. I had so many great buddies. The day they brought us out of the field, I was processed out in Cam Rahn Bay, and the Freedom Bird was there to take us to the USA. As I sat in the seat in that plane, looked out to where I had spent the last year, and felt a great sense of loss and guilt. I had come as a boy, and I returned as a man who had served his country well, but I felt so much guilt at leaving my buddies behind.

When I was being processed out, my company commander, Captain John Abrams, asked me if I wanted to stay in the army. He said he would send me to officer candidate school (OCS). I was so moved by the offer, which meant he felt I had done a good job, but I knew it meant I would have to return to Vietnam. I couldn't imagine going back. It was especially an honor because the captain's dad was the commander of US Armed Forces in Vietnam, replacing General Westmoreland.

There is so much more to tell, but I will close now by saying, I was proud to be in the army but not proud of what I had to do. Coming home was a whole other story. I joined the army a happy, young man, and I came back from Vietnam a lost soul. I returned from Vietnam on March 4, 1969. I am grateful I made it home, but I am so sorry to have left my buddies behind. They were all good men who served their country well.

I am proud to be an American soldier, and I respect the service of any veteran.

In honor of all my buddies who I left behind.

I would also like to thank my wife, Louise. She is a proud American who met a man who had seen the horrors of war, and she looked past the strange ways and odd behaviors and took care of me. I would also like to thank all the air support I received while in Vietnam. All the divisions who gave us support when we were being hit. Just to name a few: 25th Infantry, Cu Chi; 173rd Airborne, La Khe; 101st Airborne, An Khe; and all the artillery units and the Marine Division Support. Without them, I would not be here. Thank you my friends, and may God bless you.

CHAPTER TEN

NOTES FROM A VIETNAM VETERAN

Phillip Schmitt
Sergeant
US Air Force
389th Tactical Fighter Squadron
Da Nang March 1968–March 1969
Phu Cat March 1969–October 1969

A s a young man I had a deep sense of honor and country. This comes from my family; we all served our country. My father volunteered for the OSS during World War II, and as a result, spent seventeen months as a prisoner of war. I was in my sixties before I started to understand how these experiences affected him. My war experiences had a profound effect on me. The difference between us was, my father never knew about having a problem, and I was lucky enough to receive help.

My father was very strict and always insisted that I spend my evenings in my room studying, with no TV and little family interaction. I could only listen to the radio with headphones. This isolation would have a tremendous effect on me later in life. I went to work early in my youth and was active in theater in school. This gave me a sense of liberty. I didn't have a bad child-hood, but there was a lack of continuity with family. As with all families, there were good times too.

My senior year was the most difficult because of the restrictions I lived with at home. I felt like a prisoner and could not communicate with my parents. About four months before my graduation, we had Armed Forces Day at school. I had a disability, but I applied to the army and navy. When I was turned down, I went to the air force recruiter, and they were more open to my application. After getting letters from my doctor, I was able to take the entrance exam. I scored very high and was admitted to the air force. Even though I was eighteen years old, I still had to have my parents' signature. This presented a problem with my father. He wanted me to go to college. I told him that I wasn't ready for college, and after some heated discussion, and my telling him that I would join after graduation, he finally agreed to sign.

I was in the service for three months before graduation. Upon graduation, I departed for basic training.

For me basic training was pretty easy. It was a lot like the scouts, with people telling me what time to get up and eat. Each day was full of activity. But about two weeks into basic, I developed a knee problem and they wanted to give me a medical discharge. When I told them I didn't want out, they put me in a cast, and I was sent to supply for six weeks while I recouped. Working in supply, I learned a lot about how things worked, and this knowledge served me well throughout my service. After I healed, I was sent back to a training flight and finished my basic training. During this time I was introduced to weapons systems for aircraft. It was presented in such a way that most of us were chomping at the bit to get signed on. I was the first to volunteer, and in October of 1966 I was sent to Lowery Air Force Base in Denver, Colorado. After receiving my secret clearance, I was advanced to weapons training. After six months, I was sent home on leave.

Being home after almost a year's absence was very interesting. I was still under the house rules and had to be home at certain times and so on. I was glad when my leave was up, and I went on to my duty base. In hindsight, I should have handled the situation differently. There were rules and restrictions which made me feel like I was back in high school. Instead I took the easy way out. I didn't express my feelings and clammed up. Taking the easy way out would become a bad habit for me.

I arrived at Homestead Air Base in April of 1967 to start my weapons training on the F-4 Phantom Aircraft. By October of 1967, I was eligible to volunteer for Vietnam duty, and I did. I had prepared my mom for this by telling her that there was a good chance I would go because of my job choice. When my orders came in I called my folks, and I asked Mom to put Dad on the extension. When he got on the phone, I told him I had orders. Mom asked where and I told her, "Da Nang, Vietnam." There was first silence on the phone, and then I heard a click. I asked Mom if she was OK. She said, "Dad had hung up." Mom and I talked, and I assured her that I would be on a base and not in the field. I was surprised that my news would affect my dad so much. I didn't understand, at the time, and when I came home on leave in February 1968 we didn't talk about it. When I shipped out for Nam in March 1968, my dad acted like I was going on vacation. I just didn't get it.

I went to Norton Air Base in San Bernardino, California, for transport to Vietnam, and I have to tell you that I was very nervous. The Tet Offensive had started and Da Nang had been hit real hard. I'm not a coward, but I was beginning to realize that this was some serious shit.

Our first stop was Hawaii, we had to stay on the plane—bummer. We then flew eleven hours to Guam, and again we had to stay on the plane. We finally arrived at Da Nang Air Base, and when they opened the doors we felt the blast of hot, humid foul-smelling air. They hustled us off the plane to a covered area, like a long pole barn. We picked up our bags and were loaded onto a bus and driven to Camp Da Nang, where we were assigned to a barracks. We were taken to a briefing and informed about base rules. After chow, we went to the barracks and were left on our own. That night's sleep eluded me. With all the sounds of jet and flight line noise, I was too excited about what was coming the next day. Day one was over.

We were up at six in the morning, sent to chow, then assembled on the flight line for crew assignment. We had a long day of training, and it was very hot. Our flight was building a dayroom behind the barracks, and everyone was helping during their time off. I went out there to get a beer when one of the guys asked me if I would help. We were using blowtorches to lightly burn the plywood walls. Talk about hot, I was frying. One of the guys handed me a glass of cold liquor, it tasted good, and I downed it. A few minutes later I was handed another glass, and I did the same thing. I didn't know that I wasn't expected to drink it. Pretty soon I was feeling a little funny. I was seeing double, and my head was spinning. The room was built four feet off the ground and didn't have steps yet. I stepped out the door, and down I went. I was having a little trouble walking, so I went on hands and knees to the barracks. I pulled myself up the bunker wall and had trouble with the door. I rubbed up against the door to find the knob, got into the barracks, and walked into every center post in the room, getting to my bed. I must have passed out on the bunk because the next thing I remember was three guys giving me a shower. Apparently, they pull this on new guys, something like an initiation—except I drank the glass dry. It was a large tumbler with six shots of four different liquors. Later I was told that after I collapsed on my bunk, I started getting sick. This was not a good idea with the temperature in the barracks at 100-degrees. I was lying on the bunk repeatedly saying, "Oh God, I wish I was dead." After the shower, they put me on my bunk and left me. At six in the morning, my sergeant was trying to wake me but I was out of it. With the threat of an Article 15, I got up and had the worst day of my life.

Since Tet was in full swing, we were put through certification quickly so we could be of some help. The next thirty days were the most intense I had experienced in my life. Kagh Sanh was in full swing. We were flying missions around the clock. Our crews were working twelve-hour shifts, seven days a week, and sometimes we would pull thirty-six hours straight. I have to admit that I felt very alive and believed I was doing something that was very important. I had a real sense of pride in the knowledge that I was helping to save lives. After the Tet Offensive, we would go back to regular duty, twelve on, twelve off, and one day a week off. During the Tet Offensive, the base was attacked several times. My first attack happened about ten days after I got there. We were so busy that I hadn't had much time to wonder what I would do when this happened. I had just gotten back to the barracks at around one o'clock when all hell broke loose. A couple of rockets hit the flight line behind our barracks. For me, everything after that was a blur. According to the guys who survived my quick exit from the barracks, it kind of went like this.

Our barracks was two stories: open bays, with support posts down the center. When the rockets hit, I made a beeline down the center of the barracks, hitting every post on the way. I went through the screen door and ran over six to eight people on my way to the bunker. The first thing I remember was sitting in the bunker, breathing hard, and seeing only two other people there. I waited a few minutes and then exited the bunker to find a few people pissed off at me and the rest laughing. I soon realized that most attacks at Da Nang were one or two rockets, and it was over before you could respond. Most guys continued what they were doing, and if things got close, they sat on the floor. After a month, I was an old hand.

There were attacks directed at the base about every eight to ten days and most were two or three rockets. One night it became more personal. Jerry and I were at the end of the runway to de-arm the F-4s when they returned from their mission. We sat on benches in front of a bunker, waiting for our birds, when all of a sudden the sandbags of the bunker were on us. A rocket went through the roof of the bunker and went off inside. I don't remember hearing the rocket but I sure felt the blast. I couldn't hear for a while and later found that I lost most of my hearing in my left ear. I didn't let on, but this shook me up pretty good.

The months clicked by, and I decided to extend my tour. I made sergeant and in December of 1968 was able to take a thirty-day leave. At this point I had been in country for nine months. I flew back to the States and walked into culture shock. We had heard about some of the problems in the States, but I wasn't ready for the outright hate and hostility people showed us. Two of my service friends were on leave at the same time, so we hooked up and spent time together. We stayed pretty much to ourselves and didn't mingle with other people. Our haircuts telegraphed our connection to the military. Most places we went weren't a problem, but some people had comments for us. I got tired of being called a baby killer. One night I was at a club when a guy shot his mouth off and I closed it for him. My civilian friend got me out of there before there was more trouble. When my leave was over a few days later, I was ready to get back to the Nam. I actually felt safer there than I did in San Francisco.

I got back to Nam in January 1969. I was off weapons crew and moved into a job suitable for my rank. I went to work in weapons debriefing and target scoring. In March, I was transferred to Pho Cat Air base. I worked there until October. This last six months were very tough. I had several close calls and my nerves were on edge. I wasn't so sure the unit was doing the right thing. As I reviewed our strike films, I developed doubts that our mission was sound. When my time was up, I was glad to get out of there.

But being back in the States was a short-lived joy. After we got off the plane in Seattle, we were debriefed and changed into civilian clothing "for our safety." We were transported to the airport on buses and caught our planes home. While on the plane, I was talking to some people to find out what was happening. There were a lot of demonstrations against the Vietnam War and a lot of hatred toward us. This really pissed me off. When I got to San Francisco airport, I changed into my uniform. I must have had a look of don't mess with me on my face, because nobody said a word to me. I spent two weeks at home and went to my next duty station. I was discharged in December of 1969.

I went to school and worked. I didn't associate with other veterans, and because of my schedule I didn't have much of a social life. I lived at home with my parents. This was very awkward at first because my dad still wanted to set the rules. We had words about this, and he pretty much left me alone after that. I withdrew and kept to myself. Again, because of my schedule, I wasn't home much. I had no idea how my service in Vietnam had affected me. I was short tempered and my drinking had increased. I did OK in school but I wasn't excited about it. I finished two years of college with an AA in business and took a job that became the first of many I would hold over the next thirty-five years (specifically, twenty-one jobs in thirty-five years). I didn't do well with bosses. I got married at twenty-nine years of age and was lucky enough to have a wife who would put up with my shit. By the time I was fifty-nine years old I was an alcoholic, and my wife was ready to leave me when on November 22, 2006, I had a stroke.

Talk about a life changer. After I got out of the hospital I could no longer work. I started drinking more than ever and my wife was again getting ready to leave me. I knew I had to do something. By this time I was in the VA system for my medical needs. I was service-connected disabled because of my experiences in Vietnam. I decided that I needed to stop drinking, and I quit cold turkey. This was a bad idea because I had bad dreams and couldn't sleep. My temper got worse and I was experiencing more panic attacks. My VA doctor sent me to the Mental Health Department, and I was given medication to help me with my problems. This helped but wasn't the answer. Like most things I did in my life, I took the easy way out. Within a short time I was almost as bad as before. I was quickly going downhill. I was told about the Vet Center in my town but as usual I didn't pursue it until I hit rock bottom.

I finally went to the Vet Center and was lucky enough to get to see a counselor right away. Within ten minutes I was bawling like a baby. This guy was able to get in my head, and I couldn't stop him. We sat and talked for three hours. I started going every week, and he also suggested that I get into an alcohol program, which I did and still go to. It wasn't easy. There were a lot of ups and downs. I was diagnosed with PTSD and now, with three years of therapy, I am able to have a more normal life. I also do volunteer work with veterans to help them the way people helped me. I am now sixty-three years old and have a better understanding about who I am. I also have a better understanding about who my father was. I am not cured, but I can at least deal with my life in a better way.

Over the last three years the Modesto Vet Center has guided me toward a better life, but they didn't do it alone. One of the experiences that had a big effect on me was when I entered group therapy. Realizing that there were others with similar problems and listening to them helped me. The Modesto Vet Center offered programs for vets with PTSD and I decided to try one. I went on a trip called Rivers of Recovery, a therapeutic fishing program, and this was a game changer. There were six vets on each trip. I didn't know any of them, but within a day we were like old friends. We traveled together, ate together, and fished together. We are fast friends and communicate with each other on a regular basis. Most of my life, I lived in isolation and had few friends. Now I have more people in my life, and my wife and I are doing much better. This is good!

In reviewing my life, I have come to the realization that we have little control over life's challenges, but we can decide how we will deal with them. Developing a better understanding of who I am has given me the tools to deal with life's everyday problems. I never forget that the monkey is still on my back and I will have my ups and downs. It is my belief that my Vet Center counselor did save my life. My advice to the reader is, If you know a veteran who is hurting inside, and you want to help, contact the VA and a Vet Center. Let the professionals handle the situation. They have outreach people who are trained for this.

To all my fellow vets, be well.

A special thanks to Steve Lawson, Team Leader, Modesto Vet Center, Modesto, California.

CHAPTER ELEVEN

THE RELUCTANT GRUNT: A DRAFTEE TURNED WARRIOR

Mark Tury
Spec. 4
US Army
Charlie Company, First Platoon
2/501st Infantry
101 Airborne Division, Screaming Eagles
1968–1969

On June 19, 1969, we had just come off an extended operation in the mountains around the A Shau Valley when word came down to saddle up for an extraction to FSB Tomahawk. Outstanding! A mini R&R where we would be pulling perimeter guard duty at a small firebase, located along Highway 1, within sight of the South China Sea.

The operation had stretched over sixty-two days, during which we lived on LRRP rations and never had a shower. It was a continuous cycle of jungle patrol and night ambushes. We recorded fourteen enemy KIA and no losses in the First Platoon. We had to get out within the hour, so the C-4 and blasting caps were given to those of us who were familiar with the explosive and its use. We had to prepare an area so the helicopters could land. We downed sixteen trees in less than thirty minutes and fifteen minutes later we heard the unmistakable sound of a half dozen slicks (helicopters) inbound to pick us up. Charlie had certainly heard the LZ prep and could be moving in soon. Perimeter positions were established, and everyone was tense. Inbound choppers were a natural magnet for Charlie. But the extraction went off without a hitch, and a collective sigh of relief could be heard as we lifted out of the jungle. The thirty-minute ride to the firebase lulled us all into a hazy, surreal state of mind. Bodies were drained of energy and situational awareness was nonexistent. The prevailing mindset was fixed on food and sleep.

As the UH-1H began to flare into the LZ, everyone was suddenly energized and tense, which was a typical response after participating in numerous combat assaults. After the last bird landed, we formed up and were given bunker assignments. First order was to check ammo and grenades and clean weapons in preparation for the night's watch. After completing this task, we wandered down to the makeshift mess hall where there was warm food in insulated containers. At this point, anything was better than LRRP rations. We would enjoy a cold shower with Ivory soap in the morning.

I watched the sun set into the mountains west of our position. It was as if the sun disappeared right into our extraction point, the point we had occupied only a few hours earlier. The slight breeze off the South China Sea was refreshing as I sat atop my bunker. It was too hot to stay inside. I made an easy target for any would be sniper, but I still felt safe in an area where little enemy activity had been reported. What I didn't know was that FSB Tomahawk was an ill-conceived firebase.

The hill across Highway 1 and directly east of my bunker was higher than the highest point on the firebase. At the west end of the firebase, a finger ran up to another hill that was also higher than any point on the firebase. Directly in front of my bunker, a steep incline offered a blind expanse fifteen meters in front of the bunker's firing position.

Now, I am a simple grunt. Sure, I am a squad leader. I can handle myself in the bush; But firebase construction? That is done by a higher pay grade than mine, E-5. This place didn't feel right, and I was to find out, thirty years later, that Tomahawk was indeed a poorly designed firebase. De-classified after-action reports are available on the Internet, and my research proved that my suspicion about this place was right on.

I piled a couple of sandbags on top of my bunker to make a nice backrest. I sat atop my position, my M16 across my lap and the selector switch on A (for rain). This is habit. In the bush, one did not carry his weapon on S (safety). In the larger firebases, LZ Sally or Camp Eagle, you were not even supposed to have a magazine in your weapon unless you were on perimeter guard. We never followed that rule. We were in the bush most of the time anyway and simply would not remove the magazine unless we were cleaning our weapon. Officers and REMFs would not hassle the grunts. I remember walking to the PX at Camp Eagle (101st Airborne Division headquarters) and catching a glimpse of a baseball cap with two stars on it. Now, I had seen a two-star general up close before, but I realized I had just passed the division commander and hadn't rendered a hand salute. General Zais didn't say one word, but I think I noticed a slight grin. I was filthy; I mean smelly, dirty, unshaven, boots un-bloused, and steel pot unstrapped on my head. Nobody seemed to mess with a grunt just out of the bush.

Feeling perfectly relaxed and enjoying the breeze, M16 cuddled close, I could not believe the bone chilling *thump* that came from the eastern slope of the hill directly across from me. No way! My mind yelled. Then another and another thump were heard, and after the third thump the first mortar exploded on the helipad directly behind me, destroying a three-quarter-ton truck. I dove into the bunker as the second mortar exploded near the CP. The third or maybe the fourth mortar landed directly on top of my bunker. Bunker construction withheld the blast, but I was concerned about another hit. I directed two of my fellow soldiers, Becker and Wilson, to lay down a field of fire towards the side of the hill where the mortars were coming from. I moved to the small entrance of the bunker to take a position outside where the visibility was better. But I realized that better visibility for me also meant better visibility for the enemy because I was now outside the bunker. Whoever saw the other guy first would have the better odds. As I moved my head out of the opening to get a better view, I heard the distinct sound of a high-velocity bullet passing in close proximity to my head. The sound is a *pop* not a *swish*—due to the fact that the bullet is traveling faster than the speed of sound. Breaking the sound barrier, jets have an accompanying boom. Likewise, high velocity bullets have a pop when moving in close proximity to one's head. It's a very discomforting sound.

The mortar barrage continued for a few minutes, with sporadic incoming automatic weapons fire spraying the perimeter. This is not looking good, I thought to myself. I stayed inside the bunker with Becker and Wilson and tossed a couple of grenades down the slope in front of the bunker. Experience had taught me that most firebase attacks, with mortar and automatic weapons fire, will be accompanied by a sapper attack.

Now, sappers are interesting characters. They possess the patience of Job. They were in the wire, moving ever so slowly and very stealthily, and they would take several hours to move a few meters. On the incline in front of my bunker, they were impossible to detect. Each one carried three or four satchel charges (explosives). They didn't carry AKs, just the stuff to blow you up. The sappers were backed up by NVA regulars who for the most part were fearless.

The mortar barrage ended, and now was the time to really start worrying. Just as soon as the barrage stopped, the sappers made their move. We were all inside our bunkers, which was right where they wanted us. I didn't see the charge land just inside the entrance opening to our bunker. I did see a glow that resembled a cigarette and asked Becker, "What's that?" He didn't have time to respond. The explosion was deafening. Bits and pieces of wood and steel lacerated all three of us, but Becker was the worse. The concussion from the explosion rendered us partially and temporarily deaf. I tied a makeshift tourniquet on Becker's leg as McDuff fired out the front of the bunker. I grabbed my M16 and started toward the front of the bunker to assist McDuff when I caught some movement out of the corner of my eye. I spun around to acquire what I thought was a target coming through the entrance of the bunker. My M16 was on auto with my finger on the trigger. I paused as I waited for decent exposure of my target. In a microsecond my finger pressure released ever so slightly, as I noticed the figure coming through the entrance was huge, black, shirtless, and bloodied. Platoon Sergeant Lawrence stood six foot six and weighed about 260 pounds. No way could this intruder be a gook. Sergeant Lawrence, an old school airborne ranger, yelled for anyone who could walk and shoot to get their ass out of the bunker and to follow him. He must have been talking to McDuff and me because Becker was disabled. I joined Sergeant Lawrence with my M16 and a couple of bandoliers of ammo and McDuff with his M60. We picked up five more troops and began the assault toward the west side of Tomahawk.

The west end was where the track 155s were dug in. Hence the name *firebase*. The guns provided much needed harassment and interdiction (H&I) for us grunts in the bush. They were on call to kill, maim, and otherwise demoralize the bad guys. Very handy to have when you need to open a large can of whoop ass, which was called in over the PRC-25.

Moving out on a dawn patrol after a night of H&I would on occasion provide a surrealistic landscape. The still-smoking craters and splintered trees decorated with body parts invariably provided fodder for some clown to polish his comedy routine. The nervous laughter was clearly was a façade to cover the intensity of emotion everyone felt during missions of this nature. A search and destroy mission was just like it sounds: You search out the enemy and destroy them. We were getting very good at it. So Charlie hated the 155s at Tomahawk and every other firebase in the region. His mission was to silence these guns. On June 19, 1969, he succeeded. I had no idea how successful Charlie's mission had been that night until thirty years later, when I accessed the after-action reports. An interesting sidebar to these reports was something called Lessons Learned; it is found at the bottom of all after-action reports. A bit more on that later.

We learned, rather quickly, that Charlie's target had been the guns. Jam some satchel charges down the 155s' barrels and render them inoperable. That side of the firebase took heavy casualties. Eyewitness accounts of the action from surrounding units in the area surprised me many years later. "I've never seen so many explosions and fire." "Green and red tracers were everywhere." "I can't believe anybody could survive that attack." Too many did not survive it. A book named *The Sons of Bardstown* illustrates this grim reality.

Seven of us from the bunkers surrounding the helipad moved into a skirmish line (this seemed to me to be a Civil War tactic) and started to move toward the 155s. I felt as if we were walking on a carpet of brass. The slightest movement in the shadows was all it took to begin firing on full automatic. My squad's gunner was a step behind me, and as he swung his M60 from the hip and fired, I could feel the muzzle blast buffeting my jungle fatigues. I dropped back a step to avoid losing a leg. An RTO took cover behind a fifty-five-gallon drum that was dug into the ground at an angle facing the wire on the perimeter. I advised him that if a tracer were to hit the barrel it could quite possibly burn him to a crisp. The barrel was a defensive device, half filled with a mixture of gasoline and some other substance, which produced a gelatinous mixture called Foogas. This mixture acted very much like napalm, which produced a similar result when detonated. The RTO moved away from the barrel.

The firing had diminished now and what was left of the NVA regulars had pulled out in an attempt to make their way to safety. However, two circling Cobras (helicopters) had other ideas. As I watched the beautiful red stream of tracers from the gunships tore into the retreating soldiers. I guessed (correctly) that not too many bad guys would escape the Cobras' wrath.

I found Roger on his hands and knees next to two obviously dead NVA. He tried to stand but fell back to the ground. I knew he was wounded but didn't realize that I was wounded, too. I grabbed his arm and pulled him up over my back in a fireman's carry. He groaned as I lifted him. I made my way back to the helipad where a rudimentary triage was underway. He groaned again and asked me to put him down so he could take a leak. He was standing now but had a funny look on his face as he turned to look at me. "Are you OK, man?" he asked. I replied, "Yeah, I'm good." He added, "You don't look so good." That is when I wiped my face to clear the sweat, only it wasn't sweat.

Adrenalin does funny things to one's body under extreme duress. I had no idea that the satchel charge that had rung my bell earlier in the engagement had also shredded part of my scalp, face, and neck. My face was completely covered in blood. I managed to get Roger, who had received a wound that went completely through his side, to the helipad, where a series of medevacs were inbound. Roger was loaded on the first one along with Becker, who by now was half asleep from a well-placed morphine injection. The Cobra began taking fire from the slope in front of my now destroyed bunker, but the Cobra silenced the shooter. Doc sent me out on the third medevac. Again, the slick took incoming. Sixty-Seventh Evac, Qui Nhon, was only ten minutes away. The engine seemed to quit as we descended onto the landing pad. The slick spun ninety degrees and we landed with a thump. Nobody was hurt, but the pilot was cussing up a storm. I never did find out what happened to the slick.

The toll taken that night on Tomahawk was the most devastating action of the entire war if you were from Bardstown, Kentucky. It was common practice to rotate National Guard units in country for a six-month tour of duty. These units provided much needed support in the areas of transportation, construction, and artillery. The guardsmen from Kentucky were due to rotate back in two weeks. That night all four 155s were knocked out with ten guardsmen killed and thirty wounded. All of these guardsmen were from Bardstown, Kentucky. This action was covered in the book *The Sons of Bardstown*. My platoon was providing most of the perimeter guards. We suffered four KIA and thirteen WIA during the battle. Keep in mind we were an undermanned platoon (as usual) of eighteen personnel.

I found out later that this was not the first time Tomahawk had come under attack. Under the "Lessons Learned" from the after-action report, it was determined that the fire base was ill-conceived and poorly designed. This made it impossible to successfully defend under an attack by a hardened NVA regiment. That's right, an undermanned platoon plus some guardsmen against an NVA regiment. We did the best we could. Many soldiers were decorated from that action, some posthumously. I'm still in contact today with McDuff, the M60 gunner, and Kaepp, the CP RTO who called in the medevac and artillery. Many of us also were involved in hand-to-hand fighting. Both of my buddies and me do not understand to this day how we survived that night.

As I write this, it's been forty years, and it is as clear as if it happened last week. I have since traveled back to Vietnam, in 1999, to slay some dragons as it were. It was an incredible experience and I recommend that every combat veteran take a trip back to the country. It is a beautiful country with beautiful people. You will be welcomed with a smile and a bow along with a desire from the locals to make you feel comfortable. Even old enemies want to forgive and forget. It's still a Communist country, but it has excelled, much like Japan after WWII. Its resources and exports are the main source of income which is typical of any capitalistic country, a lot of luxury to be had at an incredible low cost.

After the Attack

My wounds were superficial. A few stitches and a couple of days, and I was released back to my unit. I was glad to get out of the hospital. I spent the next few days were at LZ Sally, where I moped around complaining about formations and boring repetitive procedures. In one formation we were told to look our best because General Zais was stopping by for a medal awards ceremony.

One at a time, the general would have us step forward to receive a Purple Heart, Silver Star, or Bronze Star with V device denoting valor. It didn't really mean much then, but it does now.

On June 26, 1969, the unit formed up at 0430 hours (4:30 a.m.) at LZ Sally. Everyone had a typical combat load of a ninety-pound rucksack and a clean weapon, which was locked and loaded. Where we were going didn't matter, the bush was the bush and that's where Charlie lived. I hate this shit, I thought, I gotta get out of here. How does that song go? "We gotta get out of this place, if it's the last thing we ever do."

The Shithook (CH-47 Chinook helicopter) landed and the gate dropped down and we climbed in. We lifted off and started banking to the northeast. Wonderful, we were headed back into the A Shau Valley. We set down at the base of Ap Bia Mountain. I cannot believe this; I thought to myself, we are back at this useless piece of real estate. About six weeks before our arrival at Ap Bia, better known as Hamburger Hill, the 3/187th, 101st Airborne, were involved in a major battle that gained national attention. The unit suffered heavy losses and finally called in reinforcements. My unit was sent to a finger on the northeast side of the mountain to act as a blocking force. We set up a one-platoon sized L-shaped ambush and waited. A huge kill zone was established. We sat and waited for several hours.

An LP (listening post) radioed in that eight NVA were moving quickly in your direction. The NVA troops were getting out as the 3/187th was making a final push to the top of Ap Bia Mountain. Usually quiet and careful in their movements, these guys were practically running. *Come to Papa!* It was over in thirty seconds. Three claymores fired nearly simultaneously and dropped five of them. An M60 and four M16s dropped the remaining three. Although the NVA were down, the weapons sprayed again and again. In those days, there was no such thing as overkill. *If they're dead, make 'um deader* was the plan and a good one at that. We rifled through their belongings looking for intelligence and collected the AKs (weapons). As usual, one of the bodies had an Ace of Spades (101st Airborne's calling card) placed half way into his breast pocket, visible to all who passed. The officers, major and above, frowned upon this, but usually looked the other way. The real hope in these situations is that no contact be made. We were not over there to kill the bad guys. *A bad guy is* a term I must stop using since, depending on who is reading this, it can apply to either side. We did not necessarily want to kill anyone. At least most of us thought that way. We were there to keep each other alive. When we had a successful ambush, it only meant we had more gear to carry until a log bird picked the stuff up and whisked it all away to be given to higher ups as souvenirs, signifying their tour of duty in harm's way. In this case, Harm's way means being in well-protected offices with air conditioning and hot and cold running water. Rank has it privileges!

We moved out of the area and found another location, a couple of clicks away, which seemed to be good for another ambush. This time it was the usual squad-size ambush. Daytime ambushes are freaky. You don't have the cover of darkness, and it is tough sitting in the heat of the day with bugs buzzing around your head, sweat dripping into your eyes, and your bladder telling you to take a leak.

This time we ended the ambush with what was called *no contact*. No contact was the typical end to most ambushes. Days of grueling workouts climbing mountains, hacking away at wait-a-minute vines and performing inspections for leeches—nasty little creatures that like to suck your blood and typically head toward the warm, moist area in your crotch. A guy in our platoon was once medevaced out after a leech attached itself to the head of his penis. Infection is a common problem in the jungle, and in this situation one does not chance an infection where amputation could be a possible result. I mentioned wait-a-minute vines. Picture treble fishhooks spaced every five inches on a vine with the strength of forty-pound test monofilament fishing line. When your jungle fatigues get snagged on these, one has to stop, carefully hold the vine, and remove it from your clothing. If you try to cut it with a machete, it would sink its hooks in deeper and puncture your skin, another opportunity for infection. Hence the name, "wait a minute." An infection in the jungle turns into something we call jungle rot. I've had it, and I don't recommend it. I had a case of this jungle rot in my left armpit. It continued to itch for several years after the initial healing, but hair would simply not grow there. To this day, I have less hair in my left armpit than the right armpit.

The uneventful ambush was terminated, and we saddled up for a pleasant five-click hump to a hill south of Ap Bia Mountain. A light drizzle was falling now and footing was getting a little precarious. We never hump at sling arms, where your weapon is over your shoulder, instead the weapon is always carried in your hands with the selector switch in the A position, which stands for rock and roll. This made it impossible to regain your balance if you slipped. To make matters worse, some thoughtful operations planner had decided that it would be great if we had a Starlight scope to assist us in night trail observation. Now, the technology for night vision was in its infancy in 1969. The scope was large by today's standards and needed a decent amount of ambient light from stars and moon. Also, it was packaged in an all-aluminum Zero Halliburton case and weighed about twenty pounds.

Now keep in mind we are in triple-canopy jungle, in overcast and rainy conditions, where at night one can barely see his hand in front of his face. No ambient light to speak of. The lucky person who got to carry the scope was the only one who had a decent stool to sit on. That was about the only use a starlight scope provided in the jungle. I can remember climbing up a slippery, muddy trail where I had to use a vine to pull myself up the slope. Only one hand could be used in this situation and it wasn't my gun hand. I grabbed the scope case by the handle and tossed it as hard as I could up the hill, and then I would grab the vine. This was repeated until I reached an easier part of the climb.

When the scope was first issued to our platoon, we were trained and lectured on its use and care. Do not drop the scope. Keep the scope clean. Avoid moisture and handle with care. This is an expensive, state of the art, piece of military hardware. Yeah, sure! I dropped the scope, got it dirty and wet, tossed it here and there, and sat on it. This "state of the art" piece of technology was totally useless in the jungle.

We reached our NDP (night defensive position) about two hours before nightfall. Three squads positioned around the top of a jungle-covered hill. Three-man positions allowed for a three-hour rest with an hour and a half watch. We dug in as best we could. It is very difficult to dig a position with roots everywhere. With the positions prepped, claymores set, and grenades within reach, we settled in for dinner.

We carried LRRP (long range recon patrol) rations to eat, which were dehydrated food in a plastic pouch. Just add hot water and enjoy. Now, the fuel tablets we were issued were to heat water in our canteen cup for the rations, coffee, or cocoa. It took forever for a fuel tab to heat a cup of water, so we burned C-4 explosives to heat our meals. We took the C-4 from inside the claymores we carried. Everyone was issued a claymore, and since a position only needed two claymores, there was always an extra we could harvest the explosives out of. All you had to do was pinch off a piece the size of your thumbnail, light it with a match, and your water would boil in a minute and a half. Once you had boiling water, you poured the water into the pouch containing chicken and rice (my favorite), closed the pouch, and waited five minutes for a gourmet meal.

The jungle at night is a quiet place. No birds (they sleep too), no screaming monkeys (though most ended up in Charlie's stew), an occasional tiger (very thin), and a rodent or two for the tigers dining pleasure.

Your eyes and ears strained for any sign of human presence. I was told that Charlie knew the jungle so well that he could smell the presence of Americans upwind of him. I don't doubt that, as we were pretty rank after a few days in the bush. You sat quietly, claymore detonators within easy reach, scanning your area of responsibility and then some, ears straining to hear any unusual sound and eyes seeking shadows on the move. We were trained to look off center in order to better gauge movement. At night, staring at something head on will not detect movement as easily as off-center focusing. Those were long nights with little, if any, sleep.

So here we were again at the base of Ap Bia. Bad memories, bad feeling; I hated this place. Why couldn't I have been a truck mechanic? That was what I had hoped to become—something I could use back in the world. What kind of job could a guy get whose sole training and purpose in the army was to kill other human beings? The cycle of ambushes and patrols started again.

This time we moved down the center of the valley, mountains to the left and mountains to the right. The valley was a main route on the Ho Chi Minh Trail. We shouldn't be on this trail, on any trail for that matter. There were booby traps and we were easy targets from the hills. What the hell was wrong with the Lt.? He had to be a West Point graduate. Platoon leaders didn't stay in the bush very long, maybe three to four months before they moved on to other jobs. I hated that because you never knew what you were in for when it came to leadership. OCS (officer candidate school) lieutenants were better in the field simply because they had not yet decided to make a career in the army. West Point grads, on the other hand, were dangerous. A green lieutenant, fresh from West Point, had nothing on his mind other than accumulating a body count. Their mission was to find Charlie, make contact, and get a medal, which usually came at the expense of us grunts. OCS grads would generally not seek out the enemy. People sometimes die when contact is made. I'm not saying they were afraid. Quite the contrary, they were cautious with other men's lives. But, when the shit hit the fan, they would be up front shooting and directing.

The platoon sergeant quietly told the lieutenant to get his men off the trail. The lieutenant replied, "Can't, Sarge, we gotta make good time in order to reach our objective before nightfall." The sergeant looked at him with disdain, like a father might look at his son who had just done something stupid. "Lieutenant, I'm moving the platoon off the trail and putting out flank guards. The Second Squad will perform a rear guard action to protect our butts and act as a flanking force in case of contact. We probably won't make your objective in the time allotted, but at least we'll make it." He continued, "You may precede down the trail if you like, sir, but I've been out here for over a year now and I don't recommend diddy bopping down a marked trail. With all due respect, sir, listen and learn. Things out her aren't quite like what they taught you in school." The lieutenant finally replied, "Move the men off the trail, Sergeant." The sergeant quickly answered, "Yes, sir."

Our objective was yet another hill to occupy for a night and set up ambushes. This went on for the next three days, setting up NDPs on a different hill each night. However, there was no contact, and the lieutenant was visibly discouraged.

Word came down for a six-kilometer hump to a clearing that was located west of our position. We were to move out the first thing in the morning.

This could mean only one of two things, extraction to Sally or a CA to new territory. We were never given you the full story until the last minute. We finally got the word as the slicks were approaching: We were going back to Sally! We would either be pulling perimeter guard duty or setting up local ambushes.

The slicks came in staggered formation on either side of the clearing. The clearing had room for three slicks and we were waiting with two men on one side and three men on the other side of the slick. The loading took only three to four seconds and we were airborne! We were flying in a formation at an altitude where Charlie couldn't touch us unless he had a .51 caliber crew-served gun. If that were to happen, a Cobra would be on site within a matter of minutes, and the gun along with the crew would be history. Charlie knew this.

LZ Sally meant a cold shower, warm food, and a bunk. This was luxury for a grunt. We got outfitted with fresh jungle fatigues and socks. A few of us would try to search out some of Mama San's OJs (opium joints). Mama San would squeeze the tobacco out of Kool cigarettes and replace it with pot soaked in opium. We were on stand down and knew we had the night to ourselves. An artillery unit had moved out of Sally and left us with a very nice bunker system to kick back in, get loaded, and listen to tunes. If you have seen the movie Platoon – the scene where the guys are in the bunker smoking pot and blowing smoke through a shotgun barrel—then you've seen an accurate picture of some of the grunts on stand down during the Vietnam War.

Unlike the all-volunteer troops of today, about 33 percent of the soldiers of the Vietnam era were drafted into service. The draft would take you unless you were lucky enough to have a college or medical deferment. This made for some reluctant warriors, which I certainly was. To get out of that place meant one thing, survive. Your odds were much better if someone had your back when the shit hit the fan. If you wanted your buddies to watch your back then you watched theirs. We became A Band of Brothers, just like the WWII series (and the same unit, 101st Airborne). If your buddy was in trouble, you did what it took to get him out of trouble. You know what needs to be done, and it fills you with fear. But you react anyway and do the job. That, in essence, is courage. Yes, the troops of that era may have been less motivated than the warriors of today, but it is well documented that Uncommon Valor was a Common Virtue. So some of us got loaded in a rear environment (dusted was one word for it), others got drunk. But in the bush we were always ready, seasoned, and deadly. So was Charlie.

Waking up, hung over and hungry, we made our way down to the mess tent. We gorged ourselves on bacon, pancakes, what they called scrambled eggs, and several cups of coffee. Next, we hit the showers again and hung out in the battalion headquarters area waiting for orders. It never took long. Charlie Company was ordered to set up a local ambush that night with First Platoon assigned to set up two kilometers west of Sally.

We moved out from Sally an hour before dusk. We headed for a tree line two kilometers west. We followed a rice paddy dike and passed a small cemetery used by local families. Vietnamese cemeteries are circular in design with a berm on the outermost circumference. Domes of dirt mark a burial site. These made a good defensive perimeter at night, as we didn't have to dig in our positions. As long as you were prone, you were out of sight. Some of the larger cemeteries allowed you sit up without giving much of a silhouette for the enemy to shoot at.

Moving off the paddy dike, we were now in an open field heading toward the tree line. It was dark now, with only the light of a crescent moon to move by. Specialist 4 Janosek was on point with the lieutenant walking slack. Lt. Jergans was an OCS grad and a good leader. Lieutenants usually didn't walk slack because it's too dangerous. However, the lieutenant wanted to be up front. He wanted to be first to observe any situation in order to better direct the platoon. I was number four in line and never really knew what happened until it was over.

Janosek was moving slowly when he stopped and held up a fist, which was the signal to stop. He took another two steps to better see what he thought was a small bush located twenty-five meters to his front. As soon as his mind realized the bush was actually a bi-pod with a human attached to it, it was too late. The ten-round burst hit him in the right arm and ripped through his canteen which was hanging on his web belt. The lieutenant was in a crouched position and a round punctured his torso between his neck and shoulder and exited midway down his back. A couple of us fired back at moving shadows, but they were gone before we could regroup. We set up a hasty perimeter and put some claymores out. A medevac chopper and a Cobra were on the way. The Cobra arrived on site first and ran defense while the medevac came in. The lieutenant and Janosek were on their way to the hospital. We backtracked to the cemetery and set up an NDP on 100 percent alert.

The scariest thing about setting up an ambush at night is the possibility of walking into an enemy ambush. We never found out if those shooting at us that night were NVA or ARVN. ARVNs were the Army of the Republic of Vietnam. These were the guys that we were over there to help and train. They were supposed to be on our side, or we on theirs, or something. Some ARVNs weren't too smart and could have mistaken us for NVA. However, this was unlikely. The ARVN were, for the most part, a nine-to-five army. To see them on night ops by themselves was unusual. However, there were some who were ARVN by day and VC by night.

Spending the night in a cemetery is spooky enough in and of itself. But if you add the element of superstitious comrades and little guys who want to kill you, you have a situation where it is easy to stay awake called extreme situational awareness.

Early the next morning we were headed back to Sally. We had no platoon leader so we would probably end up pulling bunker guard until we a received a replacement. That was OK by me. The great thing about bunker guard, in a large base like Sally, is during the day you have nothing to do. Get a haircut, go to the PX, work on your tan, or visit the creepy little tent next to the barber that was showing stag movies. Yup, that is what they were called before the term porno was popular. This kind of activity led to a few guys sneaking off Sally and heading for Hue. We were hauled around in bicycle-powered rickshaws that had a rain cover so that no one could see who was in the vehicle. Remember, Hue was off limits to the 101st, so we were constantly on the lookout for MPs.

The rickshaw drivers knew what we wanted and would take us to the apartment where the girls were. Two or three girls would share an apartment in order to split the cost. So there we were, three guys in an apartment with three girls, getting ready for some action. Suddenly a small boy comes running down the wooden deck yelling, "MP, MP!"

"Oh great," someone said. We had no way out except the way we came in, and the MPs were nearly at the door.

"Quick, into the shower room!" one of the girls said. The shower room was a large area completely lined with tile. A regular hinge doorway was the entrance. We moved into the shower and closed the door.

Moments later the MPs arrived and started questioning the girls. Not satisfied with their answers, they started looking around. Finally, they came to the shower room. The door opened, and the MPs smiled and one said, "Come on, let's go soldiers."

My heart sank. Now, what's going to happen? I thought to myself. I was pretty sure that not much was going to happen. What are they going to do to me, send me to Vietnam? I was behind the door as it was opened and couldn't be seen unless the MPs stepped in the room and looked around the door. Why they didn't, I don't know. I didn't move and waited to see if they would find me. They left with my two good buddies, and I lost whatever carnal desire I had. I just wanted to get back to Sally without being seen. For a dollar or two the young boy who had warned us about the MPs would arrange transportation back to the road leading into Sally. Once on the road I could jump on a deuce and a half and ride into Sally.

Whew! I got away with it. The guys I'd been with were punished by burning shit for two days. Shit-burning detail was the worst detail one could draw. The latrines were of a typical outhouse construction. One holler for officers and two to four hollers for enlisted. Under the seats were cut-down fifty-five-gallon drums. No sweet smelling chemicals were put in the drums. Just poop and pee. One would open the trap door and drag out the drums. Pour in diesel fuel and mix thoroughly with the excrement. Then you lit it off. To burn it completely, you had to stir it occasionally while it is burning. I made the mistake of walking by, giving them a thumbs-up, and smiling. They came after me swinging those stir sticks. I moved out swiftly.

First Platoon was called to a formation at 1600 hours (4:00 p.m.) that day. We had a new lieutenant. This guy was a West Pointer. We are in deep shit now, I thought to myself. He introduced himself and gave us his patriotic speech and his expectations. By this time in the war, many of us had come to the realization that this war was not in the best interest of our country. Some considered it downright immoral. I was one of those. My reluctance to participate was growing each day, and when I was subjected to the words spilling from the lieutenant's mouth, my heart beat faster and I felt my face flush red. This SOB didn't have a clue. Most of us had been out there for several months, killing, bleeding, and dying. We were fighting a more motivated enemy who seemed to have an endless supply of soldiers. The lieutenant either would come around very quickly, or he might get fragged or perhaps accidentally shot during a firefight. It wouldn't be the first time. Hopefully, the platoon sergeant could redirect the lieutenant's focus. Junior officers fresh out of West Point were dangerous and unpredictable when put in charge of seasoned combat vets.

I was worried. The formation was dismissed with instructions to form up at 0600 hours (6:00 a.m.) in front of the battalion headquarters. Since we weren't meeting on the helipad, this meant that we were doing local patrols out of Sally—a relatively safe operation since it happened on a daily basis. There was usually a company at Sally on a rotating basis. The purpose was to maintain a secure environment in the area and in the villages surrounding the large firebase. Daily patrols and night ambushes were the routine. The patrols also served to maintain a cordial relationship with the locals as they could be a good source of intelligence. We were often invited to sit and drink a cup of tea. This was a social imperative with the Vietnamese, and it would offend them if you refused. They were a beautiful people. But there was a problem there. There was no way of telling if they were VC or friendly. It was not unusual for a local farmer to smile and wave at you while working in the rice paddy and set an ambush for you that night. Crazy war!

First platoon was to patrol the tree line west of Sally, through an abandoned village, and back to Sally. About a ten-hour day, which was a breeze compared to climbing mountains day in and day out. We carried light combat loads, which consisted of ammo, water, and some C-rations. We had just received two new recruits with brand new jungle fatigues, web gear, and rifles. They stood out like a sore thumb. We came to the abandoned village while First and Second Squads worked the trees west of the village. The village was eerily quiet. Paranoia raised the hair on the back of my neck. Several weeks before, a squad from the Second/502nd had made contact in this village. A VC had popped up out of a spider hole and raked the squad with a burst from an AK-47. They suffered three wounded, one seriously injured. The VC dropped back in the hole and disappeared down a tunnel. Shoot and scoot, hit and run. They knew better than to face us in a firefight. The reason why was obvious as we walked through the village: The ground was pockmarked with the sweeping firepower of Snoopy's (small aircraft) with mini guns which were electronically operated eight-barreled Gatling guns capable of firing six thousand rounds per minute. The ground showed 7.62 mm impact holes every six inches along a fifty-meter-wide swath.

There was no escape from that monster, and the tunnel system was destroyed shortly after the 502nd's contact. But it was still a spooky place to be walking. The new guys (cherries) had gone through their water and were beginning to fade. We still had an hour-and-a-half hump back to Sally. I had been a cherry six months ago. Sweating profusely, failing to conserve my water, and scared to death. A cherry was a new guy not yet initiated in a face-to-face firefight, a virgin to combat, if you will. Although, if a cherry denoted a virgin to combat, what did that make me, a slut? But I digress.

When we got back to Sally, the cherries made a beeline to the water trailer and placed their mouths under the faucet. They chugged down as much water as they could until they had to stop to breathe. Taking a few deep breaths, they repeated the procedure and promptly threw up. Welcome to Vietnam! We then cleaned up, moved down to the mess tent, and had a sit-down dinner at table seven. That night we were on bunker guard again. Sally had occasional probes and rocket attacks by the enemy, but it was generally a safe place. Don't get me wrong: You could be killed in this place and some guys were killed there. However, compared to the A Shau Valley it was R&R (rest and relaxation). The routine of local patrols and bunker guard lasted for four days. The idea behind this was to acclimate the cherries and get the new lieutenant up to speed on platoon tactics in a real-time combat environment. This was ridiculous, of course. It takes weeks to figure out how to handle yourself in the bush—if the lieutenant lasted that long. New platoon leaders had a tendency to make fatal mistakes, which usually got someone else killed beside them. We could only hope we made no contact out in the bush until he learned what to do. Luckily, that was the case about 90 percent of the time. Typically we passed long periods of time performing tedious search and destroy missions and night ambushes, punctuated by the intense adrenaline-fueled fear and chaos of a firefight that lasted anywhere from thirty seconds to thirty minutes.

With R&R over, we were told to form up at the chopper pad at 0500 hours (5:00 a.m.). We were given rations and ammunition including a M72 LAW (light anti-tank weapon). Why we were given this weapon, I don't know. The slicks came in, and we loaded onto them. They took us to a location just south of the Song Bo River. The river was wide and rather swift moving. I thought, This could be an opportunity to do a little fishing. We humped along next to the river for several hours until we finally stopped for a lunch break. First Squad was assigned to pull flanking guard. Rucksacks off, we dug out our LRRP rations, heated up some water, and ate lunch. I was laying back on my rucksack, enjoying the rest when I looked up and saw Grafanini, my friend, playing with a hand grenade. Our eyes locked on each other, and he smiled toward the river while make a reeling motion with his hands. I said, "Hell, yes!" We both got up and walked over to the river edge. Graf pulled the pin on the grenade and tossed it upstream as far as he could. The explosion was muffled by the water, but a huge column of spray erupted. A few seconds later, some good size striper-looking fish floated to the surface. I grabbed one and Graf grabbed one and we took them back to the platoon. The lieutenant was furious. We calmly stood there while he read us the riot act. When finished, he asked for some sort of response. Now keep in mind that he is yelling at us in front of the whole platoon. Graf, a high school social studies teacher from New Orleans, put on his sheepish act and addressed the lieutenant: "Suh, with all dur respect, these here fish are for the village elders who already know we're coming. Ya see, suh, we been down this way before, and Papasan really appreciates the fresh fish." Graf continued, "We've done this before, suh, and got some good intel from the kids who speak pretty good English. It's kind of a snub if you don't bring the elders something to eat. We're just trying to make your job easier, suh." Graf quickly added, "Suh, they don't teach you this at the Point." The lieutenant was speechless. He stared at us for a moment and finally said, "Carry on." Graf and I looked at each other and said, "Carry on?" We laughed at the spit and polish of the lieutenant. I asked Graf, "What village elder?" Graf laughed and replied, "The one in my imagination." I said to Graf, "You know he'll figure it out." He answered, "I'm ready for it." We saddled up and, with fish in hand, continued down the Song Bo River.

After twenty minutes of walking, we came to a shallow point in the river. It was only about waist deep. The First Squad sent a guy across with only a weapon and some rope. He tied the rope off to a tree and we tied our end of the rope to a tree on our side. The platoon crossed the river using the rope to hold on to. The rope was necessary because with eighty to ninety pounds of gear on your back and the fast current of the river, you could drown if you fell in. After humping along for another thirty minutes, we took another break. "Smoke 'em if you got 'em," the platoon sergeant called out. After a few minutes had passed, the lieutenant strolled by asked Grafanini, "Where is the village elder? In fact, where is the village?" The lieutenant quickly added, "It ain't showing on my map." Graf explained, "Because we crossed the river we must have bypassed the village." Graf continued, "It was a very small village, suh, and it is not unusual for a small village not to show on a map. The mapmakers fly over and can't really see everything from the air, but it's there, suh, honest." The lieutenant couldn't argue with the logic. The maps were made from the air with updates coming from the input of officers on the ground. "Very well, Grafanini," the lieutenant remarked, and he turned and left. Graf looked at me and said, "Very well?" Again we chuckled at the lieutenant's barracks-soldier spit and polish. We buried the fish, not out of respect, but to fertilize the woods and keep Charlie from finding an easy meal. We continued our hump toward our objective, wherever that was. The platoon was making a large loop, and I suspected we would be crossing the Song Bo again in a day or two. I was thinking that this must be a shakedown operation to break the lieutenant in. I hoped we didn't make any contact.

Although we had made no contact yet, we did see a great light show. Spooky, a converted civilian twin-engine DC-7 (military designation C-47) armed with two electronic 7.62 mm Gatling guns, made lazy turns around a target, its twin guns pouring down their six thousand rounds a minute. This was an incredible amount of firepower. When viewed from the ground, all one sees is a long snake-like red stream, much like a laser, and the sound is a painful groan. Beautiful!

That night we set up an NDP in a smelly swampy area. At least we weren't out on an ambush. We did make contact, however, sort of: Lots of leeches and lots of mosquitoes. I didn't sleep very well. The repellant we used smelled awful but worked pretty well. Still some mosquitoes always got through.

The Second Squad, who had been out on an ambush mission, returned without making any contact. My thought was that Charlie knew exactly where we were but chose not to engage. I have no problem with this. Their returned signaled to everyone else that they had thirty minutes to eat, brush their teeth, and prepare for the 0600 hour (6:00 a.m.) start of the platoon's push back to Sally. We used the river water to fill our canteens and since we didn't have water purification pumps in those days, we used iodine tablets to purify the water. The bad thing about this was that the iodine left you with a bad taste in your mouth. Today's campers and backpackers have a myriad of small purification devices to ensure plenty of good water. I broke out a can of chopped ham and eggs and some crackers, and I heated up some water for coffee. When finish, I cleaned up the area. Shortly after I finished eating and cleaning up, I threw up. This was unusual for me. I was feeling a little tired and queasy. I felt a small headache coming on. I headed away from the unit to relieve myself and dispensed a pool of watery stool. Minor dysentery was not unusual for us, so I didn't pay much attention to the symptoms.

We finally got back to Sally and the normal routine of food, shower, and haircut. Next was a trip to supply for more socks and mosquito repellent, along with a run to the PX for miscellaneous stuff like razors and ballpoint pens. Finally, we pulled our regular perimeter bunker guard duty. The bunkers at Sally were large and comfortable, meaning they actually had wooden bunks to sleep on. We enjoyed all the comforts of home; all most. Two days of this daily routine allowed us to rest—and lose our edge.

Charlie didn't have this opportunity. He was hunkered down and getting stronger. Perfecting his bunker systems and building booby traps meant for the poor grunts moving around on the trails. He also was caching his weapons and food throughout the jungle, all the while gathering intel and re-supplying troops and medical supplies. Charlie had the edge.

I was still not feeling well. I still had diarrhea, along with a bit of fever and general lethargy.

Our next operation was on foot—no slicks. We would be doing local ambushes at night and patrols during the day. We headed for the hills directly west of Sally. It was a long hump, and we had to get there and set up before nightfall. The fever was making me lightheaded and I was getting weaker. We stopped for a break about five hundred meters from the base of the hill, and I told Doc (the medic) that I was having problems. He took my temperature and pulse and after a few questions about my symptoms made an educated guess—malaria.

Doc told the lieutenant that I needed to be medevaced back to Sally for further diagnosis. At that point I couldn't make it up the hill. The lieutenant refused and said if I was sick, I could go back to Sally tomorrow on the log (logistics) bird. I tried to make it up the hill but was lagging behind at the end of the column. A couple of buddies, Graf and Washington, came back to help. They took my rucksack and ammo. I struggled but finally made it up the hill. We (they) set up our position and settled into chow. I didn't eat, so I took the first watch, which ran from 1900–2100 (7:00 p.m.–9:00 p.m.). I got into bed but was too sweaty to sleep. The sweat turned into extreme shivering and then back to a soaking sweat. This went back and forth all night. I was unable to pull my 0100 hour (1:00 a.m.) guard watch. By 0600 hours (6:00 a.m.) everyone was awake and preparing to eat and getting ready for a 0730 hour (7:30 a.m.) departure. It was 0700 hours (7:00 a.m.). I was sitting cross legged on the ground with my M16 across my lap, looking down on the rice paddies below with a detached stare. Doc had checked my temperature thirty minutes ago, and it was 104. I was weak, sweaty, and oblivious to what was going on around me. My stare had settled on a water buffalo two thousand yards away. I was wondering if I could hit it if I took careful aim. Maybe I could see the bullet impact the rice paddy water and adjust from that.

About that time, the lieutenant walked up next to me and told me to police up the perimeter before the log bird came in. I didn't move. He repeated the order, but I still didn't move. He moved directly in front of me and in a loud, irritated voice; he repeated the command, "Tury! Get off your ass and police the perimeter! That's an order." I sat rock solid, staring at the water buffalo, calculating range and the wind. The only movement I made was with my right thumb. With my thumb on the selector, I pushed it to the second detent, which was *A* for automatic. The lieutenant freaked out and backed away from me, saying something about a court martial. I didn't understand what was happening. Why was he so pissed? Maybe he thought I was going to shoot him. I think maybe I was.

The log bird came in and, after off-loading supplies, I climbed in. Grafanini loaded my rucksack but kept my hundred-round belt of 7.62 - M60 ammo. Everyone carried the belt of M60 ammo. The gunner carried two hundred rounds; the assistant gunner also carried two hundred rounds. The remaining six squad members carried one hundred rounds each, which gave the gunner at least one thousand rounds of ammo. I was in an extreme shiver again and wasn't sure where I was or where I was going. One of the door gunners noticed my distress and told the pilot we had a problem. The copilot turned around and also noticed I was not well. The pilot was rerouted to 65th Evac Hospital and radioed ahead that they had a patient on board with malaria symptoms and that they were inbound to their location.

They were waiting for me when the slick touched down. I was put on a gurney and wheeled into the emergency room. A quick diagnosis of malaria and I was rubbed down with alcohol and had ice packs put in my armpits and crotch. Talk about the shrinkage factor. I couldn't have found my joystick if I had to. My temperature had risen to 107 degrees, and I was bordering on delirium. When my temperature came down to a manageable 104, I was put into a room with a television. Now this was cool. I could watch AFVN-TV (Armed Forces Vietnam Network). One of the doctors came by and asked what took so long to get medical help. I said, "West Point." The doctor didn't get it so I explained the difference between a West Point trained officer and an OCS graduate. "Ah ha, I see. You're absolutely right, you know," he said. I replied, "Yes sir, I know."

Later that night as I was lying back watching TV the orderly came by for my hourly temperature check. He gave the thermometer a funny look before shaking it and re-inserting it under my tongue. I was feeling comfortable, maybe a little warm, but not uncomfortable. He checked it again and called a nurse over. She looked at it, shook it, and put it back under my tongue. A couple of minutes later she pulled the thermometer out and squinted at it. She quickly moved away and began barking orders, instructing personnel what she wanted done. A moment later a fan was placed at the foot of my bed and the isopropyl alcohol was being applied to my body. Then the ice came, again, applied in the same locations. I thought to myself, where do they get all this ice in Vietnam? I know they can't find it at Sally. I told myself, Man that's cold down there! Shrinking, just like a turtle pulling its head back into its shell. Embarrassing!

I've told the story about my malaria in the past and everyone concurs: I've probably lost a few critical brain cells due to overheating which provides a good excuse for my occasional loss of grip with reality. However, my wife of thirty-five years doesn't buy it. She just thinks the cheese has slipped off my cracker. She's usually right.

After a week in the hospital, I found myself on my way back to my squad. Maybe someone else had taken over the squad, and I could do a mundane job at Sally for the rest of my tour. I had lost some weight and was still a little weak. I hoped at least I could hang out at Sally. Maybe burn shit, if I had to. Don't believe that an E-5 buck sergeant has never been assigned that duty. I would have to wait and see what happened.

Well guess what, one day later I was put on a loach (LOH: light observation helicopter) and headed for FSB (fire support base) Bastonge in the A Shau Valley. Great, only got one day at Sally. We flew through a storm and that little chopper was tossed all over the place. I really love flying, but this was one rare time when I couldn't wait to land.

It was rainy and muddy on Bastonge, but I found my squad occupying a couple of bunkers next to the quad 50s. Graf was waiting for me. "Sgt. Mr. Tury, are you done profiling? Did Ya have a nice R&R," he quipped. I answered, "Eat shit, Graf. Where is my bunk?" Graf showed me and I immediately tossed my rucksack on it and lay back on the wooden bunk. "Graf, you won't believe what that round-eye, blond nurse did to me," I said with a smile and waited for his response. Finally Graf said, "OK, Sgt. Mr. Tury, I give up. What did the round eye, blond nurse do to our wannabe warrior?" When I didn't respond, Graf remarked, "Look, Tury, you got a story or what?"

I finally asked Graf, "Have you ever been packed in ice?" He mumbled in reply, "Whaaa…, are you serious?" I said to him, "Like a turtle disappearing into its shell."

My tour of duty was over and I arrived at Bien Hoa to catch a plane home. I stood looking at the only 707 on the tarmac, hot, but not sweating. I was feeling a little anxiety. My pulse seemed to be quicker than usual for a twenty one year old in terrific physical shape. I had mixed feelings that it was finally over and sadness that I was leaving a bunch of guys that I would die for if need be, knowing they would do the same for me.

New guys getting off the jet looked at me with stares that said 'wow, look at the old guy with all those ribbons on his chest, 101st Abn!' I calculated in my head how many would actually see combat, maybe as many as one in ten. How many would die? There was no emotion, just letting my mind wander.

Arriving home there were no parades. No announcement in the paper about a returning vet. After a month of state side duty at Fort Hood, I cruised home in my Datsun SPL 2000. I received a hug from mom and a question, "What are your plans" she asked. I thought 'Plans?' I had no plans. Probably drink a lot of beer.

I didn't tell anyone where I had been or what I saw. I just tried to melt into society. I had never heard the term PTSD. I could not cope well in this new world whose main concern seemed to be what's for dinner and what's on TV. My first marriage collapsed after one year. She had no idea who I was although we knew each other in high school. I had no idea who I was.

PTSD was a big factor in my life for many years. My second wife (the love of my life) for thirty seven years knew there was a problem. She tenderly talked to me about PTSD and helped me seek help.

There was no crisis counseling, but I did hook up with an ex-marine who also happened to be the senior pastor at the church I was attending. We became very close and I confided in him about the anger I felt along with the events I was involved with in Vietnam.

A small group of trusted men came around and helped me deal with the anxiety that was now slowly disappearing. I began to understand that I wasn't some freak of nature and that what I was going through was normal for a guy who had been exposed to so many traumas. I had seen more trauma in one year than most people would ever experience in their lifetime.

It took several years but this turtle, this reluctant grunt, had finally and permanently come out of his shell. However, I still rarely speak about my experience in Vietnam unless it's to another combat veteran.

CHAPTER TWELVE
NATURAL PATRIOTS – WAR BROKE UP BAND, BUT MEMORIES REMAIN

Michael (Spanky) Thorington
Spec. 4
US Army
4/9, Twenty-Fifth Infantry Division (Manchu)
March 1967–March 1968

This story originally ran in the *Modesto Bee* on November 11, 2001 and written by Roger Hoskins, Bee Staff Writer. The story is published in this book with permission from the *Modesto Bee*.

The best measure of people's sacrifice in serving their country may not be in wars fought or wounds endured. For many the yardstick is what might have been.

Back in the early days of the British music invasion, circa 1963, four young men from the Modesto area formed a band called The Ratz and came within a few heartbeats of becoming the next big thing.

While their mop-top hair and Beatle boots became issues at school and at home, the band's popularity soared. They made the "A" list, or as close as you could come, touring with Chad and Jeremy, and also playing with Sonny and Cher and The Munsters.

The Ratz played almost exclusively outside Modesto. Ratz fan clubs formed, and concertgoers around the West Coast waved stuffed rats when the boys played.

The band's undisputed leader was Gary Grubb, then 18, of Ceres. He later changed his name to Gary Duncan and has played with Quicksilver Messenger Service for more than 30 thirty years.

The others were drummer Ray Rector, 18, of Modesto High School; bass player Paul Stewart, the eldest at 19, of Ceres; and rhythm guitarist Mike Thorington, then 16, who lived in Riverbank and attended Oakdale High School.

They opened for The Rolling Stones in San Jose, and a promoter signed them to open for The Beatles at Candlestick Park in San Francisco in 1966.

Capitol Records approached the band about a contract. And then the Vietnam War intervened.

Surviving Vietnam

Thorington is 54 now, living in Modesto and playing music again. He came home from Vietnam with two Purple Hearts and today is 80 percent disabled, walks with a limp and uses a cane.

In March of 1967, a mortar shell took off a large part of the muscle of his left leg. He did not suffer any broken bones, so the Army sent him back to the front lines. On March 2, 1968, just two weeks before he was due to come home, the enemy ambushed Thorington's company during the Tet offensive. Of 126 men in the company, 102 died. Thorington counts all of them as friends. "We were close because we kept each other alive."

The scars of that ambush stayed with him until he visited the portable Vietnam Veterans Memorial in 1986 in Tulsa, Okla. "I'm OK now," Thorington said. "Look at this." He offered a framed snapshot of a picture of the wall where his fallen comrades' names are engraved. A cross with a halo is in the middle of the picture. "The cross is there from when I took the picture. I didn't notice it as I was taking it, but when I saw the picture, I just got the feeling that everything is OK and they are all right."

The Generation Gap

Thorington played guitar and sang with the Ratz from the band's birth in 1963 until he was drafted in 1966. His musical odyssey began at age 7 in Iowa. "My parents gave me steel guitar lessons. My dad thought I'd play country. They made me play at school and in front of the PTA." He taught himself the regular guitar. "I'd watch my dad; that's how I learned to play. When I saw Elvis, I wanted to play rock 'n' roll. And then the Everly Brothers were on TV every week and it was all over. It was all rock 'n' roll from then on."

When Thorington moved to Riverbank in his teens, he lived where the Galaxy 12 theater stands now. Thorington recalled that his music opened up a generation gap between his father and him. But his dad always came through in the end. "I got a chance to play at a high school homecoming dance while I was still in junior high," he recalled. "But I needed a regular guitar. Dad asked if I was going to play country and I told him 'No.' But Dad took two weeks of take-home pay and bought me a Fender Stratocaster for $287. I'll never forget it. This was from a guy who hated rock 'n' roll." Thorington auditioned for the rest of The Ratz in late 1963. "I played a couple of songs for Gary and he jumped and said, "you're just what we're lookin' for.' "

The boys' long hair became a problem, at least for Thorington, who had a run-in with officials at Modesto High, where he went to summer school, and with his father. "The vice principal ...wanted me to cut my hair. He said it was a distraction and to stop wearing Beatle boots, too. "Hundreds of kids protested, and the compromise was the hair could stay and the boots would go. From then on, I wore tennis shoes and tucked in my hair."

But the battle over his hair would force him out of his home. "I had to move out, and I was sleeping on my girlfriend's living room couch," Thorington recalled.

A Father's Love

But just like when he needed a guitar, his father's love was stronger than his disdain for long hair. "During the Fourth of July Parade (in Modesto) I walked across the street right near where my dad was standing," Thorington said. "A cowboy behind me made a remark like 'look at that freak.'

"My dad turned around and pointed out a flower on his boot and then hit him. He knocked the guy through a plate-glass window. I didn't know it until my mom called that night. She said it was time to come home. My dad never mentioned my hair length again." Thorington's dad actually would sign contracts for the group and act as guardian when the band played Reno. The band went straight from the garage to bright lights.

"Jim Burkett was a big entertainer around here and had played with some of the big names. Chad and Jeremy were coming to Stockton, and Burkett was supposed to open but he had a chance to do a Beach Boys show, so he used us to substitute. "Chad and Jeremy heard us and liked us, so wherever they went, we went." Thorington said it was six months before many people around Modesto had even heard them. "We did one local show," he said, "and it was the only time we weren't in front of thousands."

A crowd of 25,000-plus awaited at Candlestick Park in the summer of 1966, for what would be The Beatles' last concert. The Ratz never got to open the show. The Ratz broke up—one more casualty of the Vietnam War.

Thorington said he believes the only remaining tape of The Ratz is in the possession of his ex-wife's mother. "Our last show was in the spring of 1966. Paul joined the Air Force because he would have been drafted. I was drafted because I was in a rock band instead of college."

Back to His Music

When he returned to America, things had changed. "When I left the music was 'I Wanna Hold Your Hand.' When I got back it was The Doors and all psychedelic. I didn't know what drugs were."

Within a year, Thorington had a reunion with Ratz band mate Gary Duncan. "I went to a Quicksilver show and Gary saw me. After the show he jumped down and asked how I liked it. I told him it was great, man. He was a star—on a record and on TV. He leaned over and whispered, 'But not as good as The Ratz, huh?' That made me feel so good."

Thorington put aside his music and would eventually drift to Tulsa in 1981. He would not pick up a guitar again until a teacher chided him at a reunion. "It was my 20th reunion in 1985. Mr. Thrasher stuck his hand out and said, 'I thought you were gonna be a rock 'n'roll star?' I made all these excuses, but I knew they were just that. It just started burning inside. When I moved back to Modesto in '88 I had to see if I had what it takes."

Since then Thorington has been in three bands. Now he plays base in the Steve Clifton Band. The group covers rock standards and plays some originals, like The Ratz once did.

Give Peace a Chance

Thorington's patriotic fervor never waned. "I'm extremely sensitive during the playing of the national anthem," he said. "It's like it's just for the boys (who died). It's my time to talk to them. I get annoyed when youngsters cut up during the anthem. I see the flag as a symbol of all those who've died for this country. I'm not patriotic for the government, but it's the whole people and the idea of freedom — what people around the world don't have. That's what's important to me."

Thorington said he hopes people will remember war's toll, and always give peace a chance first. "If we forget those who gave so much, we'll engage in more conflicts like Vietnam over and over again. I'd like to think as human beings, that that's behind us."

His own survival left him grieving. "It's very sad to realize what I represent. I mean me being alive. That means many others had to die. I don't just mean on our side, but their side too. It bothers me some that I'm alive because somebody else got killed."

He summed up his life and service briefly. "I've experienced a lot of things, more than many people. I could have been dead. I'm the luckiest man in the world."

CHAPTER THIRTEEN
INITIATION INTO COMBAT

Thomas "Tom" Thompson
US Army, Sgt. E-5
December 22, 1964–February 24, 1970
RVN - July 27, 1966–April 25, 1969
Purple Heart Recipient
Bronze Star with V Device Recipient
VSM, VCM, CIB Recipient

After hearing President Kennedy's Inaugural Speech in 1961, where he said "Ask not what your country can do for you, but what you can do for your country," I had thoughts about joining the army. With that thought in the back of my mind for a few years, I decided to forgo my senior year of high school to join the army and get my GED.

On December 22, 1964, I was sworn into the army at Fresno, California. After a two-week leave over the holidays, I reported to Fort Polk, Louisiana, for basic training. After two months of basic training, I reported to Fort Leonard Wood, Missouri, for Advanced Individual Training (AIT) in communications. After two months of AIT, I shipped out to Germany where I spent thirteen months before getting orders to go to Vietnam.

After a one-and-a-half month leave, I got to Vietnam in late July 1966, where I was assigned to the First Infantry Division. I spent one week at First Infantry Base Camp for orientation and zeroing my weapon at the firing range. Also, I tried to persuade the division sergeant major that my MOS (military occupational specialty) was communications, but he informed me that my primary MOS was infantry. Needless to say, I was promoted to ground pounder with little fanfare.

I was assigned to Company B, First Battalion, Twenty-Sixth Infantry Blue Spaders. Upon getting to my unit, I was informed that I would be in the headquarters platoon communications section. My duties consisted of being the company commander's radio telephone operator in the field and maintaining the radio when in base camp.

After three days with the unit, I had my first glimpse of combat. We were alerted mid-afternoon that another battalion had made contact with a superior VC (Viet Cong) force. We did a heliborne assault to reinforce the other battalion. As we were coming into the LZ (landing zone), we could see it was going to be a hot LZ. Rounds were kicking up water in the rice paddies. Jumping out of the helicopter over the rice paddy, I had my first confrontation with water buffalo dung as it was floating all over the paddy. After calling in artillery strikes and having gunships strafe the tree line where the VC were firing from, we started moving toward the other battalion. After we made contact with them, the VC decided to break off contact and lived to fight another day.

After everything settled down and we got the wounded and killed dusted off and the other battalion extracted, it was too late for our battalion to be extracted, so my company did a search and destroy mission. We set up a company ambush on a trail that went into a village known to have VC activity. At about three in the morning, twelve VC walked down the trail into our ambush site. The next morning we swept the area and found eight dead VC with their weapons. We also found blood trails going back into the village. Upon learning of this situation, the rest of the battalion moved up to our position. After the other three companies encircled the village, my company went in to search it. As it turned out, we found our four wounded VC and eight others hiding in spider holes. The rest of the villagers were considered VC sympathizers and were sent back to a repatriation area. That was my initiation into combat in Vietnam.

My unit participated in Operations Junction City and Junction City II from February 22, 1967, to April 1. During this time, we mainly conducted search and destroy missions. At one time, we did get a break by conducting perimeter security for an engineer company that was making an airstrip along Route 246, west of An Loc.

Late in the afternoon on March 30, after being delayed by bad weather, my unit made a heliborne assault into LZ George, near the Cambodian border. The next day the battalion recon platoon walked into a Viet Cong base camp and was engaged by small arms fire, killing the platoon leader and several others. My company was sent into the area to reinforce and withdraw the recon platoon. When we were about twenty meters from the recon platoon, the whole jungle lit up. We knew at that point we were in for one hell of a firefight. Four hours later, following sustained artillery fire and in-close air support, the Viet Cong force broke off the contact. After getting the killed and wounded medevaced, we returned to the battalion nighttime defensive position for what we believed would be a long and eventful night.

At 5:00 a.m. the next morning, our position received approximately two hundred mortar rounds followed by a ground attack. The battle lasted over three hours. The final count, after a sweep of the area, showed there were 609 Viet Cong killed and three prisoners taken. Friendly casualties were ten KIA and sixty-four WIA. This battle was known as the Battle of ApGu. After Operation Junction City and Junction City II, the Viet Cong could no longer regard War Zone C as a safe haven.

By this time, I had been in Vietnam for almost nine months. I realized that I would probably spend the rest of my tour at base camp, pulling perimeter guard. I decided to extend my tour for six months and to go to

Military Assistance Command Vietnam (MACV) as an advisor to the South Vietnamese Army.

After a thirty-day leave stateside and getting some wounds healed, I reported to MACV in June 1967. My first assignment at MACV was as advisor to a security company in the Bien Hoa area. My duties there were to instruct the South Vietnamese in the use of American weapons and how to set up fields of fire. For twelve months, I led squad-size nighttime ambushes. Yes, I did extend my tour for another six months. It was during this time that the 1968 Tet Offensive happened. This was where I learned house-to-house warfare, as we had to clear out all the houses in Bien Hoa looking for insurgents.

I spent the next six months in Bien Hoa advising the South Vietnamese until one night a friend of mine, who had been advising a battalion on the Cambodian border, convinced me over a few beers to extend my tour another six months and volunteer for his team.

So after another month's leave stateside, I went to Fifth Battalion of the South Vietnamese Army as an advisor. On this team there were only four Americans (a major, a first lieutenant, and two noncommissioned officers (NCOs). The major and senior NCO would advise the battalion commander while the lieutenant and the junior NCO (me) would advise different companies on different operations.

Our main objectives on these operations were to find base camps along the several infiltration routes coming in from Cambodia. We were to destroy their rice caches and capture any weapons and ammunition we could find. Occasionally, we would get into a firefight with a platoon-size Viet Cong unit, and once we got into a firefight with a Viet Cong company. Even though there were only four Americans, we were well protected by the troops as we were the ones who called in the artillery fire and airstrikes for them. In April 1969, I left the Republic of South Vietnam knowing that we were winning the war.

In closing out my chapter, I want to let my fellow Vietnam veterans, the warriors that they are, that I admire and respect each and every one of them, and I just want to say, welcome home. Let us not forget our fellow warriors who didn't come home. I also want to thank the vets at the Vet Center for making it possible for me to tell my story.

CHAPTER FOURTEEN

THOU SHALL NOT KILL AND THE GOLDEN RULE

Glen Jorgensen
CM2
US Navy
USN Mobile Construction Battalion 8
RVN 1967–1969

When I was first asked to write a chapter for this book I thought to myself, who would want to write about that? I found it difficult to tell others about my Vietnam experience. In fact, in the last forty years I have spoken about Vietnam to only a few fellow veteran brothers. My experiences there were not unlike that of countless other veterans sent to a place few of us even knew existed. We came from a multitude of backgrounds, but all from a culture that taught us core values such as Thou Shall Not Kill and Do unto Others as You Would Have Them Do unto You. Then we went to war. What follows is how I feel about Vietnam and a few of my experiences. Perhaps putting it on paper will help in my search for peace within.

The Vietnam War was a working-class war. Three million men and women served, most of who were drafted from the backbone of America, the working class. The sons and daughters of the upper classes and the wealthy and those who could keep up their grades in college were exempt from the draft. Many people from these exempt groups did choose to serve in Vietnam due to patriotism or perhaps the desire to be military professionals. Also, there were many who were already in the military as career soldiers and officers. However, overwhelmingly it was the draftee who paid the ultimate price in combat.

The rift in American society that emerged as the public grew to detest the war endures to this day. There was no welcome home for Americans who served and died selflessly to protect the freedoms of the people of the world. It didn't matter that we had fought to help South Vietnam establish a constitution of its own and to win freedom for its people.

After the Vietnam War, America would never be the same. The universal patriotism that drove America to victory in WWII was redefined by a public who harbored little support for America's military. I served twenty-two months and ten days in Vietnam. My experience in country was much like most others who served in the theater of combat. The daily duties, the intensity of contact, the number of days under fire, all vary greatly from unit to unit and soldier to soldier, but the one common denominator we all shared was the re-defining of our very souls. Only those who were there, those who actually served in combat, truly understand and have lived for more than forty years carrying a burden the rest of the country can never feel or understand. Our survival depended on our actions and the action of others. Others' lives were in our hands. We saw them die. We felt them die. We heard them die. We smelled them die. We sent them home to the tune of fifty-eight thousand dead. We sent home hundreds of thousands of wounded, sickened, poisoned, and demoralized soldiers. We sent them home to a nation that did not honor them as heroes. Then we came home to a nation who did not welcome us and even called us names: baby killer, war monger, and many others. There were no parades for us. No welcome home even from our families. Jobs were difficult for us to find. There was no help in our communities for soldiers whose bodies and souls had been torn asunder. We became the lost soldiers of a war that the media, the government, and the public wanted to sweep under the rug and forget.

I was drafted from a small town in Oregon in late 1966. I took the option of joining the navy. I like the water, boats, and fishing, so the navy seemed like a good choice. My family attended a small Protestant church, The First Methodist Church, where I would go to Sunday school, church services and youth group activities. I graduated from high school and the local community college with a technical degree. I had been married and already divorced from a girl I dated in high school. We had two boys, ages of three and one, when I became single again and therefore eligible for the draft. I was an assistant manager in an auto repair shop in our town. After passing my induction physical I went to the navy recruiter in our town and enlisted in the navy. The navy needed all the experienced technicians they could get for their mobile construction battalions. Since WWII and even today they are known as Seabees. My education and experience gave me an E-5 rating, a second class petty officer, equivalent to a tech sergeant in other branches of the service. The navy named those of us who enlisted with ratings IPOs (instant petty officers) and sent us off to training.

I went first to basic training in Mississippi. I soon found out that the goal there was to provide the navy with a construction company of personnel whose job it would be to build military infrastructure in Vietnam and defend it from the enemy while doing so. I was sent to Camp Pendleton, California, for automatic weapons training and learned to operate many of the tools of the trade: M60 machine guns, LAW rocket launchers, M79 grenade launchers. I was also taught how to throw hand grenades and became proficient with M1 and M16 rifles. I learned to use claymore antipersonnel mines and other types of mines and explosives. From Camp Pendleton I was sent to night combat training in the field at Vandenberg Air Force Base. There I spent three days and nights learning how to find the enemy and keep a squad of men together in pitch-black darkness. Upon returning to my homeport, Port Hueneme, California, I attended a week of classroom training in the skills used to kill or otherwise incapacitate the enemy. The total time I spent in weapons and combat training before deploying to Vietnam was less than one month!

In civilian life I was an automotive technician. My navy MOS (military occupational specialty) was construction mechanic. I was assigned petty officer in charge of the welding, radiator, and body shop of Alpha Company, Mobile Construction Battalion (MCB) Eight, Thirty-first Naval Construction Regiment (NCR), USN. I taught automotive repair classes to nonrated Seabees until the battalion was shipped to Vietnam. I was teaching basic mechanical fundamentals to kids who had never held a spark plug in their hand. This was their schooling before deployment to Vietnam. Other than rifle qualification on the rifle range and survival skills taught in basic training, they received no other defensive combat training. These were the kids who would become the men of my squad. Once I was in country, I became a reinforced automatic weapons squad leader. My fourteen-man squad was composed of four fire teams, one M79 man, and myself. One fire team was responsible for the machine gun and the rest were riflemen. My squad's job was to provide security at night for whatever the Seabees were building in the daytime. So that it would still be there tomorrow.

I first arrived in Vietnam on a C-130 that landed at night on a hot (under enemy fire) airstrip. This was near the city of Hue, during the Communist buildup for the 1968 Tet Offensive. All Seabees aboard rolled out of the plane onto the runway to face our first mortar and small arms attack. The plane did not even stop but simply turned around, opened its doors, let us out, and took off again. The first week my squad was in country, all the members of one of my teams were severely injured when a rocket landed on top of them. They were all airlifted out. I heard they survived, but I never saw or heard from them after that night. Every day our company would be hit with dozens of rockets and mortars, and almost every night our perimeter would be attacked by a few or sometimes twenty or thirty Vietnamese wearing black pajamas. The North Vietnamese Army (NVA) regulars, who were uninformed well-trained soldiers, bypassed our camp and went to Hue for their siege in the Citadel.

By the morning after a night raid, the enemy and any bodies would be gone. However, usually we found blood and sometimes clothing or canvas that they had draped over our security razor wire in an effort to climb over it. In the several months that this camp was our base, I only remember the VC getting through the wire twice. Once, several crawled through the hut where we slept and cut the throats of eleven Americans before they were discovered and killed.

The worst firefight came right after Tet started, when there was a push to overrun our camp. Several VC made it to the center of our compound but the light of our flares exposed them, and they were caught in a hail of crossfire.

For the first two months I was in country, we were under attack literally every day and night. A good deal of the time, we would sleep during the day in sandbagged bunkers. At night, we patrolled the perimeter or remained in defensive trenches that Seabees had dug with their road-building equipment. At Phu Bai, just south of Hue, we had a fortified tower, about fifteen feet tall, where we could mount the M60 and watch for enemy activity over a broad area.

When trucks were sent out to detachments with supplies, I would sometimes ride shotgun to return fire if the trucks came under attack. On the day before the Communists launched the Tet Offensive, I rode shotgun on the back of a deuce-and-a-half truck taking supplies to Camp Evans above Hue. It was an uneventful trip through Hue with the usual Vietnamese here and there walking along the roads or riding their little scooters. There were several Vietnamese selling whatever they had in the roadside shops. When we arrived at Camp Evans, it was on full alert and launching mortars as fast as they could from mortar pits, trying to slow the advance of the North Vietnamese Regulars headed for Hue. The mortar tubes were so hot they were smoking, but they never seemed to let up for the hour we were at their camp. On the way back through Hue to our base camp, the roads were so crowded with Vietnamese that we had to go slowly, literally pushing through the sea of people. I was sitting in the back of the truck with my M16 locked and loaded, and I never felt so helpless and alone. There were now thousands of people. Anyone of them could have thrown a grenade into the truck and ended life as we knew it, but for some reason they did not. We arrived back at camp just before sunset. Within hours, thousands of people would be dead in the city of Hue. The infamous Tet of 1968 was underway. After a few weeks of costly fighting, the Tet Offensive was put down and the area quieted down considerably. The attacks were only every few days and sporadically at night. I would go to the welding shop in the daytime if I had gotten sleep at night, and occasionally even did some welding on heavy equipment. The E-6 or first class petty officer of A Company was responsible for the day-to-day operations of the repair shop in my absence.

For the remainder of that tour of duty, our company accomplished its goals of building and maintaining roads, bridges, and landing zones in the area. We rotated back to Fort Hueneme, California, after eleven months. At that time, if you had less than a year left in the service, you wouldn't be redeployed to Vietnam. Our battalion was made up largely of people with two-year enlistments. We all left Vietnam with twelve months and a few days to go. We would return.

I began my second tour in the relative safety of the base camp at Red Beach, about seven miles north of Da Nang. We operated in detachments assigned to Seabees construction sites on Route One, the main north-south highway in Vietnam. My battalion, MCB 8, was assigned the task of repairing and maintaining Route One from Da Nang to the DMZ. I spent some time at a bridge site on the Perfume River, where my battalion was installing bridge pilings. The pile drivers were large steel cages that fit over the pilings. Each time the driver hit the piling, a diesel cylinder fired, pushing it up in the air a few feet again. These cages, or housings, would crack or break occasionally due to fatigue and would have to be welded back together. By this time I had been in Vietnam long enough to feel like, if it was my time to die, it was my time to die, and if not, not. I would set my helmet, flak jacket, and M16 down and climb up the pile driver with welding cables over my shoulder and go to work doing the repairs. Sometimes the sun would set before I came down, and the arc from the welding could be seen for miles. I would hear rounds banging around in the steel cage and try to stay on the opposite side of the poles from where the shots were coming from. I did a lot of that kind of welding. It just wasn't my time to die.

I have a vivid memory of working on the pile driver while three tanker aircraft flew overhead and sprayed me with a wet mist. I found out later they were spraying the infamous defoliant Agent Orange. At the time it just seemed like they were taking care of their job, same as I was taking care of mine. Another time, I was lying atop a bunker at Red Beach trying to get some sleep when I was sprayed with enough defoliant to soak through my clothing. I never gave a thought to there being any danger. What the hell—it wasn't bullets!

Of course, we now know that—especially in the part of Vietnam where the NVA could enter the country easily—the vegetation was constantly being cleared to give our soldiers easier access to the enemy. The crazy thing about it was the fact the enemy was largely underground, and it's questionable if we suffered more casualties from Agent Orange or if they did. We seldom had face-to-face contact with the enemy while operating out of Da Nang, but we would be pounded with rocket and mortar rounds quite regularly. We lost only a few people on that deployment, and those were usually out on a detachment somewhere.

Halfway through my first deployment I developed a persistent skin problem. Nothing I could get from the medics seemed to give me any relief. My skin would erupt with dozens of bright red bumps that would pop open and bleed. The usual treatment was to rub on the cream that was issued for heat rash, but it didn't help. In fact, sometimes it seemed to aggravate the problem. Even while back at Fort Hueneme, the treatment was always the same: Heat rash ointment and it will go away. By the time my second deployment was getting short, with only two weeks until the battalion rotated back home, most of my body had been affected. In Da Nang I happened by a mobile hospital and saw a doctor. I had to find some relief from the constant burning, itching, and nervousness caused by the rash. The doctor asked how long I'd had it, and when I told him a year and a half, he told me to return to my outfit for my belongings and report to Da Nang Air Base for a trip to the hospital in Japan. They looked at me in Japan and forwarded me to the Naval Hospital at Bremerton, Washington, where I was put in a large ward all by myself. I was examined by several people over a period of several days.

One day, the commander of the hospital brought a large book and opened it to a section that described my condition. That last sentence of the description read, "There is no known effective treatment for this condition." I was sent to Pier Ninety One, in Seattle, for processing out of the service. It was twenty-five months since I had reported for duty. For the next twenty-five years, I would seek help from civilian doctors who also could find no effective treatment. My rash persisted and it didn't matter if it was freezing or one hundred degrees. It would erupt, bleed and subside, leaving another round of scars before erupting again in yet another area. Blisters formed on the bottoms of my feet and would pop open, draining thick, clear plasma. There seemed to be no relief. Twenty-five years after Vietnam, someone suggested dry cornstarch as a treatment, and indeed it has helped ever since. I buy boxes of it, regularly, to this day.

I returned to civilian life and found a job doing what I did before I entered the service. I never talked about Vietnam. If it came up, and my co-workers found out I had been in Vietnam, they would invariably ask me, "How many gooks did you kill? How many babies did you kill? Do you like being a killer?" Always they asked me this. As if I was going to report some number that would satisfy their disturbing curiosity. I went deeper into isolation. I never told anyone I was in Vietnam. If anyone who knew I had served in the navy mentioned Vietnam, I would deny it. I didn't want to hear the same old questions again. Just like a million vets, I could not share the most important piece of my life with anyone. It was impossible to tell families, wives, children, grandparents, or others how you had a hand in the stench of a war. How can you describe to them the blood, the smell, the feel, the sound, the fear, or the brotherhood that makes other combat soldiers your closest family, your true brothers, until the day you die? We carry this common burden differently, yet the same. Within our soul we carry anger, depression, and laden with an uncommonly high number of illnesses and disabilities as reward for our service. Many of us found jobs that allowed us to work long hours alone, away from groups of other people.

Those of us who returned alive from Vietnam have as our constant companion the memory of those who did not. We are tormented by the same question: Why did they die and I come home? The lack of a welcome or acknowledgement for having paid the ultimate price for freedom and the public disdain of our fallen brothers and sisters, who are our heroes, is doubly cutting in our memory of those we left behind. Only in recent years have wonderful people started to welcome us home, treating our emotional and physical wounds in Veterans Centers, clinics, and hospitals, the same as the veterans of earlier wars. Throughout the nation, groups of Veteran Service officers are helping us with our VA claims. They have sponsored places where we veterans can be together again and feel like there are indeed heroes among us. In just the last four years, I have enrolled in the VA Health Care System and become a regular at the Modesto, California, Veterans Center. I have been diagnosed and successfully treated for chronic and severe PTSD, chronic depression, peripheral neuropathy, severe hearing loss, thyroid dysfunction, and reflex sympathetic dystrophy syndrome (RSDS). Medical professionals have determined that all of these ailments are connected to my time in service and exposure to Agent Orange. There are so many good people serving us now, thanks to the effort of a few who cared and worked relentlessly to ensure we and our issues were recognized. I and my fellow veterans are thankful.

Last Thoughts

Even veterans of prior wars tell us that our war was not a real war and that we "lost" our war. I can proudly tell you this: In Vietnam, we never lost a battle. We had our ass kicked hard sometimes but came back to achieve the objective. I am proud and grateful that our soldiers are treated better upon returning home now, but saddened that they and their families must continue to make the sacrifice and carry the wounds of war. The public of our great country should be reminded daily that it is the soldiers of the past, present, and future that have made and will make the sacrifices that allow the very freedoms they enjoy each day in this country. The majority must stand and be proud of our servicemen and women for being the heroes they are. They must never forget the fallen or the living soldier. May God bless them, the soldier and the United States, with freedom and the full strength of the Constitution that our forefathers fought and died for to establish and to live for.

This is largely how I feel about Vietnam and how it has affected my life. I cannot speak for others, but I can say I am proud of my Vietnam veteran brothers, one and all. We are truly the proud.

CHAPTER FIFTEEN

FLYING FOR FREEDOM

Carl W. Forgey
Spec. 5
US Army
First Aviation Brigade, 223rd Combat Aviation Battalion,
183rd Reconnaissance Airplane Company, Third Flight Platoon,
March 24, 1969–October 1970

My story began in late July or early August 1968, on one of those hot summer days in Modesto, California. I was home for the day after working swing shift the night before at Sharpe Army Depot. I sat reading the paper with the front door open when I heard the mailbox open and close. Getting up to see what the mailman had left, I found one lonely letter in the box. It looked very official with the United States of America printed on the envelope. When I reached in the mailbox and closed my fingers around the envelope to pull it out, I had this strange feeling come over me. I felt my death.

Opening the envelope, I found greetings from the President of The United States. He actually had time in his busy day to write me, personally, to ask me to join his military. To say the least, I was not overjoyed by his invitation. After sitting for some time thinking about my soon-to-come military service, I called my mom and dad. I told them that I had received my draft notice. Of course, their first thought was the Vietnam War.

Much to the dismay of my parents, I took full advantage of the time prior to my reporting date to drink as much as I could. It was party time! Being raised in a Christian home, they were not happy with my conduct. I don't think they understood what I was going through. I had just gone through a divorce, and now I had received my draft notice. It was a very hard time for me. As the time for me to report drew near, I did cut back on the partying, for which my parents were grateful.

On September 8, 1968, at 7:30 a.m., I was to go to the Federal Building in downtown Modesto, which also served as the main Post Office for our town. My mom, dad, and some friends were there to see me off. A large number of young men from Modesto and surrounding areas were reporting. Some I knew from high school, and some I knew from outside of school. Soon two buses pulled up in front of the post office, and someone from the draft board took roll call. We all said our farewells and loaded onto the buses. Our trip to the induction center in Fresno, California, took about two hours. We arrived in Fresno, and what lay ahead for us, I'm sure none of us knew.

We unloaded the bus and we were directed inside the center. Once inside, the day began with a physical exam. Waiting in line became the routine for the day: We waited in line to go into rooms for each part of the physical: one room at a time, one line at a time. To this day I can't tell you how long it took to get the complete physical. It seemed to go on forever. Once finished with that part of our induction, we waited in a large holding room. It was filled with the buzz of conversation. Same as on the bus, I'm sure the buzz was about what loomed before us.

Shortly, the room filled. The last young man entered, and a man in a military uniform followed. In a huge and loud voice we were asked to shut the hell up. He gave instructions as to what was going to happen next. He told us, with a laugh, that some of us would get the opportunity of our young lives. Some of the lucky few would get to be marines. After hearing what he said I became as small as I could, not even making eye contact with the front of the room.

Soon this badass-looking marine came into the room with a clipboard under one arm and this big shit-eating grin on his face. Again, he told us how lucky some of us were going to be. He pulled the clipboard from under his massive arm and began to call out names. With each name called, you could hear a big groan followed by a big sigh of relief. I did everything I could not to be seen, all but hiding under my chair. As the last name was called my heart rate dropped and my blood pressure went back to normal, as normal could be, on a day that would change my life forever.

Late in the afternoon, with everything done at the induction center except for the one big thing, that being the taking of the oath. We were called to attention and the oath was read. Our military lives had begun. Both the army and marine sergeants' attitudes towards us changed once we became new members of the US military. That attitude went from Mister Nice Guy to "I will kick your ass at any time I see fit." They changed from calm, soft-spoken men into loud barking dogs. I had never seen such a change in two men.

They divided us into groups. I think all of the guys from Modesto were put into one group. They selected one person to be the leader of our group. He was given a large manila envelope with our orders inside. Soon we loaded a bus for our trip to the Fresno Airport. We were to fly from Fresno to San Francisco. This was my first time flying, and I was excited and scared shitless at the same time. The flight from Fresno to San Francisco was short, forty-five minutes to an hour at the most.

When we arrived in San Francisco, if my memory serves me well, an army sergeant met us as we unloaded the plane. He took the orders from our leader and read them. He told us we were bound for Fort Lewis, Washington, for basic training. By this time the sun had set, and it was well into the evening. It was going to be a long night. Upon our arrival at Seattle, we were escorted to buses waiting for us. I'm not sure how long the bus ride was from the airport to Fort Lewis. It seemed as if time had stood still. When we finally arrived at Fort Lewis, it was well into the night. We were greeted by more barking dogs. I had never heard screaming and yelling like that. I knew the world as I knew it was about to change and, not knowing if it would be for good or bad, of course I feared the worst.

The next few hours would be a real learning experience for all of the young new recruits. In a large room filled with young men from around the country, we were yelled at and intimated. It was the beginning of the takeover of our minds and souls by the United States Army. It was the beginning of an experience that would last for the next two years for some of us, three years for others. And for many it was the beginning of the end.

Finally, in the early hours of the morning, we were given time to sleep, although it didn't seem we were allowed that much time. I guess some is better than none. We started our day off with our first army meal. All I can say is that it was not a five-star meal.

What followed was another long day: first the blood test to see what type of blood we had, then new uniforms, and so on. I'm not sure how many days I spent in the reception center. I was in a fog for my first few days of military life. I was given so much information to process; it was just too much to take in.

We were finally assigned to a basic training company. We were led around by what we called holdovers. Holdovers had just completed basic and were awaiting their orders for their next step in the army. We had many questions for them, being they were well-seasoned soldiers. I think their answers to our many questions were as honest as they could be with their eight weeks of basic behind them.

Before long, it would be time to meet our drill sergeant. On a late afternoon in September, I can't remember the date or time, too many years have passed, our platoon was out on the company street learning to march in formation. The trainer (a holdover) gave the order to halt and then called us to attention. We stood there at attention while this imposing figure came walking toward us. As he got closer I could see that he was a large, black man, and when I say large I mean at least ten feet tall. He was the biggest man I'd had ever seen with his Smokey Bear hat pulled down to the bridge of his nose and a big cigar in his mouth. His uniform was starched tight. Not a thing about him was out of order. I knew by his look that he was all business. We soon found out that he was. This man was so large that he cast a shadow over Mount Rainer, a large volcano in the state of Washington.

He told us his name: He was Drill Sergeant Riggins. He told us that he would be our mother and father for the next eight weeks. He informed us he would make men of us. We were going to be men for the first time in our young lives. As time went by, we heard rumors about Sergeant Riggins holding the record at Fort Lewis for driving recruits AWOL (absent without leave). We soon found out that he did have a knack for doing so, driving three from our platoon in the first month of basic. One returned for about two days, but after that we never saw him again. We never heard what became of the other two. That's how life was in the army: Now you see them, and now you don't.

I will not write about the rigors of the rest of my time in basic. All vets know how basic went. I'm sure we all have great stories about our time in basic, and I do have one last thought about Drill Sergeant Riggins. This man made marching fun. He could call cadence with the soul of a soul singer and the pain of a blues singer. Wow! What a joy to march when he would lead the company. Over the years I have thought about him. He was a tough man, but you knew that somewhere behind that tough exterior was a soft side, too.

When we got to basic training, we spent a day or so getting our uniforms, our shots and so on. Then came the day we took our aptitude tests. The tests were to identify our skills and help the army determine what schools we would enter during our next step in our military training. I scored high on two tests, one of which measured my mechanical ability. When the testing was finished, I was pulled aside by Drill Sergeant Riggins and the company commander. They told me that if would enlist for a third year that I could choose the school of my choice. I thought back to the day that I received my draft notice. The feeling I had of my death when I touched the envelope was a very real sensation. To this day even thinking about it or writing about it gives me that eerie feeling of seeing my own death. I made my decision very quickly. They gave me a list of schools to choose from, and on the list was a school for aircraft mechanics. I have always been in awe of airplanes. As a young boy I had a small collection of cards, much like baseball cards, with airplanes on them. I had always wanted to fly, and when I saw that training as an aircraft mechanic was available, it sounded close so it became my choice. I think God had a hand in the test scores I received that day. By his helping hand, I was spared my life and was able to come home and continue my life with my family and friends.

Being in the army all of three days, I was given an honorable discharge — but of course I had to reenlist for three years. My two minutes of being a civilian again was fun! Now I had to sign the reenlistment papers. My short-lived civilian life was interrupted by the growl of Sgt. Riggins telling me to get my ass back in formation. Looking back on my decision, it was the best one I had ever made. Graduation came, and what a good day it was for all of us. We were now old timers in the US Army, so we thought. I was to go from Fort Lewis, Washington, to Fort Rucker, Alabama, for my AIT (advance individual training) in aircraft mechanics.

Being from California, it was a shock to be in the Deep South. There were so many differences from what I was used to: the lifestyle, the food, the poor, the Confederate flag flying almost everywhere, and most of all the fact that the South had not fully integrated. I had no understanding of how blacks were treated in the south. It was so different from California. For the most part, I stayed on the fort. I had no desire to go into town. I just felt that it could be a problem I didn't need. Some of the guys would go to Panama City, Florida, and drink and chase women for the weekend. Again, that was something I didn't care to do. That would all come later in Vietnam.

In school, I was being trained to be a mechanic on the L-19 or as we came to know it, the O1-E-Bird Dog and a second plane, the U6-A, called the Beaver. The Bird Dog was designed to be a reconnaissance airplane. The Beaver was a personnel transport plane for officers and the like. I liked that the Bird Dog was my primary plane. It was a two-seat plane with a six-cylinder opposed engine, an updraft carburetor, and a tail dragger (meaning landing gear was at the tail of the plane). I still have a love for the O1-E Bird Dog, and most of the crew chiefs and pilots I have reunited with feel the same way. I'm not sure exactly how long AIT was, maybe nine weeks. I don't remember any graduation ceremony. All I knew was that my time at Fort Rucker was coming to an end. My guess was that Vietnam would be my next stop. I don't remember if I received my orders for Vietnam before I came home for leave or if they came to my parents' house while I was home. Time has blurred many memories of little things that I once thought I would never forget.

Home at last! What a great time it was to be home with my family, friends, and the girl I had met about two weeks before I went to basic. It all went too quickly. With a week remaining on my leave, my mom planned a farewell party with friends and family, to say goodbye. Again, I managed to mess up the party. I went out the night before and drank myself into oblivion. I was able to roll out of bed and I do mean roll out, but not much more. The guests arrived. I tried to greet them but their eyes began to roll around in their eye sockets as I greeted them. My breath smelled like an old Irish distillery. I realized I was in no shape to be around them so I found a corner and called timeout for myself. I could sense my dad's scorn. He took on the demeanor of Drill Sergeant Riggins. He was mad as hell and I knew that when the party was over, I would hear about my drunken stat. Boy did I. It made my hangover worse as he yelled at me and my brain began to bounce around inside my head. Oh, the pain of it all.

With two days of leave left, a friend from basic and AIT came out from Nebraska to spend time with me. His name was Roger Adams. We both had to report to Oakland Army Base to prepare for our trip to Vietnam. We took it easy. We hung around the house and enjoyed my mom's cooking. The time came for us to report to Oakland. The drive would be Roger's first time on California freeways. What a laugh he was. He was scared to death and held on tight. Of course, my dad did everything he could to make it a thrill for him. My dad had a way about him. He loved to mess with people. I lost contact with Roger after we were in Vietnam. He went his way, and I went my way. It was our assignment to different duty stations that separated us.

We arrived in Oakland to begin the final process to Vietnam, a place halfway around the world. What I knew about Vietnam was what I saw on the evening news. It was the first war we watched on televisions while we ate dinner. What we saw was the mayhem of war. It was a shock to a young man to know that soon he would be in the midst of a war that was hated by many in the country he loved. A political war, a war of greed, a war that—if only the military had been allowed to run it—I'm sure would never have lasted so long nor cost America the lives of fifty-eight thousand young men and women, soldiers who, with honor, stood for this great country and gave their lives for the rights of the many who fled to Canada like rats fleeing a barn fire. To this day, I still have great disdain for those who chose to run.

Roger and I said our farewells to my parents, and I said goodbye to Margaret, the girl I had met earlier. Making that long walk to the door of the reception center, Roger turned his head and remarked, "We need to look back and wave goodbye." I answered, "Not a chance, if we look back and wave, we both will end up crying." The last thing we needed, when we walked through the door, was to be crying.

We may have spent two days in Oakland before we got the orders to load the buses for the trip to Travis Air Force Base in Fairfield, California, where we would catch our plane for Vietnam. It always seemed like the army did everything at night. The buses we were on had metal grating over the windows like a prison bus. I really don't think any of us planned to jump out of the bus going down the freeway, or maybe the grating was there to protect us from the war protesters that we would see on the way. We arrived at Travis AB and were escorted from the bus by military police. I hoped that it was for our safety, but knowing the army, it may have been to keep us from running away. We waited in a long hallway with no seats, only the floor to sit on. I sat down and laid my head on my duffle bag and took a much-needed nap. It wasn't long before we were told to get ready to load the airplane.

I'm sure all of us recruits had the same thoughts as we formed a long line and walked toward the airplane: The thoughts of what lay ahead of us, going to a country and a war we knew very little about. The thoughts of family and friends we were leaving. What would the next year of our lives be like? It would be a year that would change the way we thought, the way we looked at life and death. It would change my life 180 degrees from how I was before I was taken to war.

The plane was loaded, and the door was pulled closed. It rolled down the runway to lift off. I was on my way to a new chapter of my life. Our first stop was in Anchorage, Alaska, landing only to refuel for our long flight across the Pacific Ocean. Our next stop was Yakota, Japan, where we were able to get off the plane to get something to eat, stretch, and get ready for our final flight to Vietnam. The whole flight was about eighteen hours, and it gave me time to relax some. I sat at the front of the plane with Roger. This gave us the opportunity to interact with the flight attendants, and we all played gin rummy for most of the flight. The attendants made us feel comfortable and gave us the idea that they cared about us. They had flown many planeloads of young soldiers on that long flight to Vietnam. I'm sure they did everything they could to make the soldiers comfortable, the ones before me and the ones after.

The pilot came over the intercom to tell us that we were now in Vietnamese airspace and would shortly be making our decent into Tan Son Nhut Airbase. Reality set in as we broke over land. I had finally arrived in Vietnam.

The plane touched down and rolled to a stop. The door was opened, and we lined up to deplane. Being that I was at the front, I was the first to walk down the steps. I walked out of the plane into a wall of hot humid air. The heat of Vietnam was a shock to the system. With the heat came the smell of Vietnam and the war. I guess you could describe the smell as being that of burning human waste. A smell that is still vivid today. A smell that none of us who were there will ever forget.

We gathered our duffle bags and threw them onto a waiting truck. We loaded buses for our trip to Long Binh Replacement Center. As luck would have it, my duffle bag was lost on its way to Long Binh. My first few days in Vietnam were without clean fatigues, soap, or toothpaste. I also had no towel to dry off with after a shower, so I used the drip-dry method. I would drip dry as much as I could then put back on my dirty stinky fatigues.

I went to Qui Nhon from Long Binh. Qui Nhon was home of the First Aviation Brigade, the unit for rotary and fixed-wing aircraft. Next, I was off to Nha Trang where the 223rd Combat Aviation Battalion was located. I think I spent two days at both places. I finally received orders to report to the 183rd Reconnaissance Airplane Company (the Seahorses). Landing at Cam Rahn Bay, I finished the last leg of my trip and arrived at the place I would call home for the next several months. I grabbed my duffle bag as I unloaded from the plane and wondered what to do next. In front of me was a building that looked like it could be the terminal for the air force base at Cam Rahn Bay. I walked inside and took a look around. It was a very busy place with air force and army personnel moving about. I saw an information counter. I approached the counter and asked the young airman behind the counter how one would get to the 183rd Reconnaissance Airplane Company. He pointed to a phone on the wall and told me to pick it up, dial one, and that I would get an operator. Little did I know that the operator would be a Vietnamese lady trying her best to speak English. It seems that when a person is unable to speak in your language we tend to talk loud to them. The more she was unable to understand what I was asking, the louder I got. Somehow, I finally made her understand that I was looking for the 183rd.

At last the phone rang and I heard a faint voice say, "183rd." A joy came over me knowing that soon my trip would be over. I gave the voice my name and said that I needed to get to his location. He then told me to wait outside and that somebody would pick me up. Thirty to forty-five minutes later a jeep pulled up. The driver and I made eye contact, and he asked if I was the one needing a ride to the 183rd. Nodding, I got into the jeep, and we both introduced ourselves. His name was Rudy Mendes. I told him my name was Spec. 4 Carl Forgey. We exchanged some small talk and I told him I was from California. I'm sure he told me where he was from, but after forty-three years, I don't remember.

After getting in the jeep, one of the first things I noticed—much to my dismay—was that he had no weapon. I asked him about it and he said, "Don't worry, we'll be fine." It was my first time in a war, and I was told not to worry about not having a weapon. *Worry* became my first name on our drive to the 183rd. my head was spinning on my shoulders trying to see everything at the same time. What made matters worse was the sand from Cam Rahn Bay to Dong Ba Thin was as white as snow. I soon was snow blind, which made it almost impossible for me to see. That did not sit well with this new, young warrior. Again, *Worry* was my first name.

We soon arrived at the company area of the 183rd, and he took me into the orderly room. I was introduced to the first sergeant and the rest of the personnel in the room. I was taken to what I learned was a *hootch*—the building where I was given a room, something I could call my own. The room had no door and only one bare light bulb hanging from the rafters, but hey, it was a room.

I heard a southern voice from behind me, and I turned to see who it was. It was this baby-faced boy wearing army-issue black horn-rimmed glasses. He introduced himself as Bill Keener. I introduced myself, and he said Froggy. I said, "No, it's Forgey." This banter went on for a few minutes until I gave in. Now, I was the Frog. It's a nickname that I carry with great pride. Bill and I became good friends. We had so much in common. We were both raised in Christian homes with the same values, and this helped to form a bond between us that would last. When it was time for Bill to go home, I had already left the company to go to a flight platoon. In 2001, I received a call from Bill. He had gotten my number from another vet, Al Cherin, who had made contact with me a year or two earlier. Bill's first question to me was if I knew who he was. Of course I knew. I said, "Bill Keener," while trying to fight back tears. He asked me how I knew it was him. I told him that I never forgot that southern accent, and that I thought about him almost every day, hoping that someday we could reunite. Later on that year, we did reunite at the 183rd first reunion. I reunited with not only Bill but also some of my other friends. A lot of crying and hugging went on at the four-day reunion.

April 8, 2008, my dear friend Bill Keener passed away at the age of 59. Hid body had grown tired from heart disease and a circulatory disease. When I knew that his time was short, I called him, and his wife Wanda let me talk to him on the phone. I was the only one she would allow to talk to him. I wanted to get back to Tennessee to see him, but I put off my trip by a day, and he passed away the day before I was to leave. I regret not being there to tell him goodbye. Even now, as I write about him, the tears are flowing. He was a true friend. Even through our time together in Vietnam was not that long, we formed a bond of brotherhood that lasted thirty-nine years and continues even after death. Even though he is not with me now, some day we shall reunite at the gates of heaven. Bill, I love you brother!

The next morning, after breakfast, Bill took me to the flight line and introduced me to Sergeant Wright, who was the flight line sergeant. Bill left us to talk. A short time later, Sgt. Wright took me to a revetment, which was a three-sided enclosure where aircraft were parked. Inside four soldiers stood around a Bird Dog, some working and some just watching. Sgt. Wright introduced me to the guys. He told them I was the FNG. For those who have no idea what FNG means, it means the fucking new guy. No doubt about it, I was the new guy. He told them I was now part of the maintenance team. Finally, I was able to do the work I was trained to do. I was working on Bird Dogs, and I could call myself a crew chief.

As time went on, we became a very tight team, and we worked well together. We always seemed to know what to do next without having to talk about it. We soon became the best team on the line. We had nothing to gain by it, but knowing we were recognized for being a good team was fine with us.

I don't remember a lot of details about the company, but we all seemed to get along. We seemed to always have fun. One thing I do remember is that on weekends we could take the company duce-n-half (two-and-half-ton truck) to Nha Trang. We would leave Saturday morning and return Sunday afternoon. I think I should tell my story about my first trip to Nha Trang in a way to protect myself from harm and let you read between the lines. We went to a bar to have a drink. The old-timers I was with told me that a tour guide would come to me and ask if I wanted her to take me on a tour of the city and also show me some of the customs of Vietnam. They told me not to go with the first tour guide that asked. In next to no time, a young lady came and sat down by me and asked me if she could be my guide. She talked about some of the sights she would show me, and my interest was piqued. She told me how much the tour would cost, and off we went.

She took me to parts of Nha Trang that this young soldier should never have gone. I had no weapon while going down small alleyways with the eyes of every man, women, and child on me. We soon came to a doorway, and she led me inside. She took me on a great tour, and although it didn't last that long, it was fun. After the tour, she wanted to take me to "Number One" movie. She told me that she would take me on another tour after "Number One" movie. I found myself, again, in a place that I should not have been. I realized that I was the only American GI in an all-Vietnamese movie theater. The next morning, she got a taxi for me and told the driver where to take me. I got back to where I think I started out the day before. The taxi driver pulled to the side of the road, and when I got out of the taxi I could hear two American voices yelling my name. They said, "Frog, you asshole, Where have you been?" They came over and grabbed me by my shirt and began to shake the shit out of me, yelling that they told me not to leave with the first tour guide and that I was to stay with them on my first trip to Nha Trang, I made only one more trip to Nha Trang, and that was the last time I went for a tour.

The company was always in transition. Guys were going home, and new guys were coming into the company. With the changes in staffing, I was made team leader. I was team leader for about two months before I was sent out to a flight platoon. I was sent to the Third Platoon at LZ Betty, located near Phan Thiet, a village on the coast off the South China Sea. LZ Betty was where the war became real to me. Sure back at the company we had some rocket and mortar attacks, but nothing real heavy while I was there. LZ Betty was different.

I was in Vietnam for eighteen months, twenty-eight days. I used to know the hours and minutes, but time has taken that from me. I guess I was at LZ Betty about fourteen months, twenty-eight days. Being a crew chief in a flight platoon, the work was almost nonstop. We seemed always to be down at the flight line, even on weekends, with not much time off.

We had six to seven crew chiefs and about the same number of pilots. The pilots would come and go. However, some stayed too damn long, and the ones we liked didn't stay long enough. I was crew chief for two pilots, Captain Anderson and Captain Tyler, both of whom were outstanding pilots. For years I have been bothered by one thing: The pilots always referred to us as *their* crew chiefs, and the planes as *their* planes. They had it all wrong; the plane was *ours*, and the pilots were *our* pilots. We allowed them to fly our planes.

The crew chiefs were like mothers or fathers to the planes. We nursed them back to health. We gave them their baths and we saw to their needs as a mother would. And we looked after them the way a father looks after a daughter: We gave the pilots permission to take the planes out for a date. We asked them to respect her, to do nothing to harm her, and to have her home early.

Capt. Anderson was my first pilot, and he was a good one. Flying the Bird Dog took rhythm. I suppose that is true of all aircraft, but I have only the Bird Dog for reference. He had a decent rhythm for a white man. One day, while flying, he thought we had flown into an artillery impact zone. He came over the intercom and asked me if I heard a round go by the plane. He was making a horrendous maneuver to avoid other incoming artillery rounds. I don't think I ever responded to him because my stomach was trying to crawl out of my throat. I couldn't talk. We did have some other close calls with ground fire. It didn't happen often but it happened enough to make you ask why you were up there flying over the jungles of Vietnam. One of my big thrills was to make rockets runs. I would be in the back seat, the pilot would drop the nose of the plane and go into a steep dive, and fire a rocket. We would stay in the dive for a second or two watching the rocket when suddenly he would pull back on the stick to climb out of the dive while banking to the left or right. Oh! What a rush that was.

In recent years, I have been able to reunite with Capt. Tyler. We had a mini reunion in Jasper, Tennessee, the home of my dear friend Bill Keener, where about ten of us from the 183rd gathered for three days. Thirty-nine years had been good to Capt. Tyler or Don, as I now could call him. I was walking by one of the rooms at the hotel where we were staying and noticed the curtains were open. I glanced through the window and saw him sitting on the side of the bed. Without thinking, I turned back to the door and walked inside without knocking. I said, "Capt. Tyler?" I immediately added, "Hi, I'm Carl Forgey." He jumped up from the bed. We came together in a hug, patted each other on the back, and then the tears started to flow. We were both so excited to see each other. We were talking and asking questions as fast as we could get them out of our mouths.

At LZ Betty, the other crew chiefs and I decided to give Capt. Tyler a nickname. We decided on Capt. Magnet, but of course we never said it to his face. He seemed to have a way of drawing fire from the enemy. One day, just after sunset, we were flying south on our way back to LZ Betty. We were west of the LZ's perimeter, flying over a large Vietnamese cemetery that ran almost the length of LZ Betty. The Vietnamese buried their dead above ground, which created large mounds of earth throughout the cemetery. These mounds gave the VC places to hide behind and fire from. Suddenly, while making our final approach over the cemetery, we saw green tracer rounds coming up from the ground. The bullets flew past on both sides of the aircraft. It looked like the whole North Vietnamese Army had opened fire on us. We could not tell where the VC was located, other than on the ground beneath us. The intense fire petrified both of us but we landed safely. Both Capt. Tyler and I made an inspection of the plane. We were lucky. We were not hit by any of the rounds. We both decided that what had just happened to us was too close for comfort. How close we came to being shot down was frightening, and to this day, I have recurring dreams of that evening.

Life at the LZ could be downright boring or exciting or fearful. It ran the whole gamut of emotions on an hour-to-hour, day-by-day basis. You never knew what to expect. I'm sure that must have been the same for all of us who served in Vietnam. The never-knowing factor was my biggest fear. The fear that a VC round would hit the plane or hit me or even the pilot was always there with you while flying. Your worst fear as a crew chief was if the pilot was wounded and how bad the wounds were because you might have to fly the plane to safety. I had no training to fly, although once, Capt. Tyler did give me a chance to fly from the back seat. He taught me how to control the plane once in flight. Trying to land it from the back seat is a whole different story. I feared that I would have to do that someday. I could see myself putting the plane nose first into the ground while trying to land and killing both Capt. Tyler and myself.

I extended my time in Vietnam six months. I came home on leave in April of 1970. I'm not sure for how long or how I got home, but I did get home. It was good to take a break from the war and spend time with my family and friends. The odd thing I do remember is that no one asked me questions about Vietnam. I'm not sure why they didn't ask. Maybe it was my fault because I didn't bring it up in conversations, so maybe they felt they shouldn't bring it up.

My time was growing short at home, and I got ready to go back to Vietnam and be with my buddies. I had six more months of the war, six more months of the smells of Vietnam. I knew I could do six more months, but at what physical or mental cost I couldn't say. My return to country was uneventful. On May 3, 1970, I landed at LZ Betty in midafternoon. I climbed out of the plane and was greeted by my buddies. We talked for a few minutes, and then I went to the hootch to put away my things. After getting settled back in my room, I walked back to the flight line and took a look around the LZ and out to the South China Sea. I began to wonder if my decision to extend for another six months was the right one. But it was too late now to question that decision.

Later that night, after a few drinks down at the flight line, I went back to the hootch to get some sleep. I lay down on my bunk with my fatigues on, which I had never done before. I always lay down with my boxer shorts on. I soon fell asleep.

Sometimes after I fell asleep I was awakened by a *thud* sound. It was the sound of a mortar launching from its tube. For those of us who have been in a mortar attack, you learn to tell the difference between incoming rounds and outgoing rounds. I heard a second thud, and as soon as I did, the first round hit with a big explosion. Then the second hit, and all hell broke loose. I jumped from my bunk, grabbed my M16, and ran to the bunker located just outside the door of my hootch. I met all the other crew chiefs there. We sat in the bunker assessing the situation and deciding what to do next as we listened to the sounds of outgoing and incoming rounds and small arms fire. The night sky lit up with red and green tracers and flares. You could hear the cries of "incoming" all around. GIs were running to bunkers yelling and screaming, trying to decide what to do next. We probably sat in our bunker all of two minutes. We decided we needed to get to the flight line as fast as we could to help the crew chief at the hanger get the plane out and ready to fly. We always had both a pilot and crew chief on duty at night. We jumped into our three-quarter-ton truck with me at the wheel. Jean Kent sat in the front with me, and the other guys jumped into the back. We drove alongside the runway with explosions going off all around us and tracers streaking over-head. That night is just as real to me today as it was forty-three years ago.

I drove as fast as I could, and within minutes we arrived at the flight line. Gordon Green, the crew chief, already had the plane ready to go. Gordon and the pilot were standing by the plane along with our Vietnamese observer. We all jumped from the truck and ran to the plane. There was a problem with the Vietnamese observer, who was a second lieutenant in the South Vietnamese Army, as he was refusing to get in the plane. The observer's job was to go up with the pilot and direct artillery fire on the VC and NVA who were launching the attack on the LZ. I told the pilot that I would go up with him and be the observer but I would not be able to direct the artillery. The pilot told me no and said that the second lieutenant had to go. This left me only one thing to do: I had to get the Vietnamese observer into the back seat of the plane. I used a little force and with some struggle I somehow was able to get him in the back seat. During the attempt, I found his second lieutenant insignia in my hand. It had come off during the struggle. I must be the only US Army Spec. 5 to bust a Vietnamese officer. I still have it today and wear it on my Seahorse hat with great pride.

That night I knew that if our pilot was willing to risk taking off with all the shit going on, then that coward needed to go too. I thought the next day I would hear about it, but not a word was said. The business of the day went on as normal. I'm proud of how I handled the situation that night.

The night of May 3, 1970, was the worst I had been through. That night the VC and NVA launched many attacks at LZs and military installations throughout Vietnam. The attacks were to coincide with the war protests back home. The attack on LZ Betty was the most intense of all that night, but it got little to no attention back home. What did make the news headlines was the National Guard shooting of the students at Kent State on May 4. The night of May 3, seven young GIs lost their lives, thirty-five were wounded, and several helicopters were destroyed along with some vehicles. The memory of that night brings on the dark side of the war dreams. I dream of explosions, the sight of tracers going through the LZ, and the cries for help. What I'm left with, some forty-three years after the war, are not only nightmares and sleepless nights but also this thing we call PTSD.

On an afternoon in June 1970, a Huey set down on our tarmac in front of the hanger. The side door opened, and a person in flight Nomex stepped out. He began walking towards the hanger, and as he got near I could tell that he was a pilot. He came inside and spoke with one of our pilots and with Sergeant Wright. Sergeant Wright told us that the pilot had made an emergency landing with his plane on a road about a half-hour flight from the LZ. I'm not sure of the unit he was with, but I think it was the 219th, which was a Bird Dog unit. Sergeant Wright asked for two of us to fly out and see if we could determine what the problem was. I said that I would go and Jean Kent said that he would also go. We gathered some tools and put them in a tool bag, grabbed our M16s and an ammo box, and walked to the waiting Huey. We climbed in and the crew chief slid the door closed. The Huey lifted off and headed for the site of the abandoned chopper. On our way out, the crew chief told Jean and me that he would give us a green smoke grenade, and when we were ready to be picked up we should pop the grenade. The Huey made a circle over the site of the Bird Dog before beginning its decent to the ground.

The chopper didn't quite touch the ground and the door slid open. Jean and I jumped out with our tool bag, M16s, and ammo box in hand. We ran to the plane, and the Huey lifted off leaving us alone on the ground. Jean climbed into the cockpit of the plane and he made several attempts to start the engine. Finally it turned over and with the engine running I lifted the cowling with a grease pencil. I drew a line on each of the manifold tubes. This would let me know if we had a cold cylinder. We found no real problem so Jean ran the plane for a while to let the engine heat up. With the RPMs up the engine seemed to be running fine. While Jean sat in the cockpit, I crouched on the ground with M16 in hand, ready to fire at any movement. On each side of the road, tall elephant grass meant you couldn't see if the VC were near. We were on our own. Jean shut down the plane and got out. We both stayed as low as we could. The Huey seemed to be miles high and away from our location. I pulled the pin on the smoke grenade and threw it on the ground. It was a long wait for the Huey to return and pick us up. It may have only been minutes but to the both of us it seemed that time stood still. After our return to the LZ, we both had a cold beer and reflected on what we had done—two young GIs taken to a remote location in Vietnam to work on a downed Bird Dog. To make matters even worse, we had no combat training. Sure, we had learned how to shoot the M16 in basic, but to what skill level was the question. After the pilot returned to the plane, he flew it back to the LZ, and we did some more checks. We found everything to be in good running order except for maybe one thing (the pilot).

With my time growing short and American forces turning over the war to the Vietnamese, the Third Platoon was moved to Phan Rang Air Force Base, located north of Phan Thiet. We spent about two days getting ready for the move. We loaded our gear into conex metal storage containers, and they were taken down to the docks at the LZ to be loaded onto a barge for the trip to Phan Rang. The pilots flew the planes, and our vehicles were driven by two crew chiefs. The vehicles joined a convoy on its way to Phan Rang, and the rest of us were taken out to the barge by a LARC (a vehicle that could travel on land and in water). Our trip, by barge, on the South China Sea was an overnight trip. It was a time to relax knowing that the next day we would have to work hard getting everything to its right place, our personal things to our new hootch, and our tools and parts to the flight line. The Second Platoon had been at Phan Rang for some time, so we shared space with them.

Moving to Phan Rang Air Force Base was like being stateside. It had paved roads, sidewalks, a movie theater, a large snack bar, and the EM-NCO club. The club was great. You could get a steak and lobster dinner for about $5.00. What a treat! We even had hot water for showers and flushing toilets. Taking cold showers and crapping over a fifty-five-gallon drum that had been cut in half were things of the past. The air force really knew how to go to war.

Sometime close to October 21, 1970, I was told it was time for me to leave. I packed my gear and other belongings that night. I was to leave Phan Rang in the morning and fly to the company headquarters at Dong Ba Thin. The morning I was to leave not much was said, but it was rather surreal having to leave friends I had grown to know and respect over the last year and a half. I was going home to be with my family and friends. The time for my departure came, and we said our goodbyes. I loaded my things into the plane and waved a final wave goodbye.

Two emotions came over me as we taxied to the runway, guilt and joy. They were the guilt of leaving my friends behind, thinking I would never see them again and wondering what might happen to them after I left and the joy of knowing that soon I would be home enjoying my family and friends. I would be back stateside, safe after eighteen months and twenty-eight days of fighting a war. I would be home safe from a war that was halfway around the world. Home from a country called Vietnam, a country of jungle, rice paddies, mountains, and the smell of a third world country that still lingers in my memory forty-three years after the war.

I arrived at the company headquarters just before noon and checked in at the orderly room. I talked with the first sergeant, and he told me that after I had finished lunch I would be driven to Cam Rahn Bay to make my way back home. Lunch was one of my last meals in Vietnam and what a treat—another meal of dehydrated shit.

After lunch, I took my M16 to the arms room, and then I went to the supply room to turn in my helmet, gas mask, and flak jacket. I said my goodbyes to the rest of my friends in the company. I returned to the orderly room to wait for my ride. The time came for my ride to Cam Rahn Bay. I was excited to be on my way. The drive back to Cam Rahn Bay seemed to take longer than when I first arrived in country. I was dropped off at the replacement center, and I reported in to begin the routine of going through customs and preparing for my departure from Vietnam. After that, the waiting game began. Because of the cutback in troops and so many soldiers going home, there were no bunks left in the barracks. So for the next two days I waited, sleeping outside on the ground. I used my duffle bag as a pillow. I am not sure how much sleep I was able to get on those two nights. I thought that this was a hell of a way to treat someone who had spent over a year in a war zone. I should have known that I was just a number, and that the army couldn't have cared less about my comfort. To them I was like an old used tire, taken to the dump and replaced by a new one. The morning of day three, I looked to see if my name was on the manifest for any of the flights leaving that day. I saw my name on the first flight of the day. My heart rate jumped. I would soon be on my way home. Roll call was taken, and with that we loaded the Freedom Bird to home. I didn't know anyone on the plane, and I really didn't care if I did. I wasn't on the plane to make new friends. All my thoughts were of getting home.

When the plane lifted off the runway, a big cheer could be heard throughout the cabin. For the two hundred or so on board, this meant a year or more of war was over. For many, their time in the army was over. Others, like myself, still had time remaining on our enlistment. The flight back to the States could not go fast enough.

We flew into Sea-Tac International Airport in the state of Washington. I can't remember any of the stops on the way to Washington but there must have been a few. Again, too many years have passed. Once on the ground, we were bused to Fort Lewis, where my army life began. I was hoping not to run into Drill Sergeant Riggins. I'm sure that if I had, he would have made me drop and give him ten or get down in the duck walk position and go around in circles saying, "I'm a shit bird, tweet-tweet. I'm a shit bird, tweet-tweet." Oh, he was such a fun-loving man.

Once again, I had to stand in line to go through the process of reentering the States. It must be a control thing because it seems that lines, at least in my way of thinking, were developed by the military to make it easier for them to harass those standing in the lines. After finishing up with the return process, I got that much-talked-about steak dinner. It was good to have real food again, a good steak with a real baked potato. But it would have been better if it had been prepared by my mom. My journey home soon continued with a flight to San Francisco. Once in San Francisco, I caught a thirty-minute flight to my hometown of Modesto, California. As the plane touched down at the Modesto Airport, my feeling of excitement grew. I know both my heart rate and blood pressure went up after getting off the plane. I grabbed my duffle bag and suitcase and made my way inside. I made the phone call that I had looked forward to making for a year. I hung up the phone, gathered my suitcase and duffle bag, and went outside to wait for my mom and dad. I no sooner got outside than they pulled up. My dad must have driven like a bat out of hell. I walked to the car with both of them standing at the curb. My mom looked the same, but my dad had changed. His hair was longer. He had always worn it short, and he had grown a mustache. All I could say was, "Damn, look at you." Needless to say I was as happy to see them as they were to see me. Hugs and kisses from both of us. Home at last, I thought, thank God I'm home at last. We talked on the ride home. Mom asked me if I was hungry, and I told her I wasn't. This seemed to disappoint her; being a mom she probably thought her son needed something to eat. All I wanted was some sleep after my long eighteen months and twenty-eight days away from home. After getting home we talked for a while and then I made my way to my old room, which I found to be the same as it was when I left on September 8, 1968. I undressed, got in bed, and soon fell asleep.

When I awoke in the peaceful surroundings of my old bedroom, it was a shock not to hear the sounds of helicopters and airplanes warming up or flying over the LZ. The sweet aroma of the bedroom was a welcome replacement for the smell of burning shit. I knew it was going to be a good day when I got up and ate a home-cooked breakfast. After breakfast I called Margaret to let her know I was home. She was working so I waited and picked her up for lunch. We made plans for the evening. She was as excited to see me as I was to see her. I was happy to hold her in my arms, but my feelings were different. I wasn't sure what my feelings were, all I could say was that they were different. We really enjoyed our time together the month I was home. When time began to get short, I received orders to report to Fort Leavenworth, Kansas. I arrived in Kansas in December, which meant I would miss another Christmas at home. The good thing was that my enlistment was almost finished, which meant no more holidays away from home.

I quickly found that my last months of military service at Fort Leavenworth would be made easier because of my rank being Spec. 5 (equal to a sergeant in pay). I didn't have to make morning formations, and all I had to do was go to Sherman Air Field and perform maintenance on Cessna 172s. This plane was a four-seat aircraft, which was not too different from the Bird Dog. Fort Leavenworth was the perfect place for somebody who had just returned from Vietnam. It seemed to be rather laid back for the army, perfect for me.

While at Fort Leavenworth I injured my knee and required surgery. After the surgery and some rehab, I was able to return home on a short medical leave. I flew into San Francisco, and while waiting for my connecting flight to Modesto, I got to meet some war protesters up close and personal. They decided to take me to task for my military service. They came to where I was sitting, swore and spat at me, and called me names like baby killer.

They even tried to get physical with me. I was on wooden crutches at the time, and they were excellent weapons as these protesters soon found out. A few well-placed strikes to their heads and balls let them know I was no one to fuck with. Security came to break up the skirmish and helped me to my connecting flight. The incident was my first and last encounter with war protesters.

During my remaining months in the army, I took time to reflect on my experience in Vietnam. I could sense a change in my mental state. I was having nightmares and dreams of Vietnam. I was hyper-alert, always on guard, and I also noticed that I was quick to anger. I started to think about my relationship with Margaret. My feelings for her had changed. I wasn't ready for another commitment. She was not the right one for me at this time in my life. I felt she was not strong enough to deal with the changes in my personality. With the demise of our relationship my only regrets were of the pain and hurt I caused her. The pain of living with a person with PTSD, and the roller-coaster of emotions caused by PTSD, would have caused her much greater pain. It would take an extremely strong person to deal with these symptoms of war. The decision to end the relationship was not easy, but I realized that bringing her into a life of pain and misery wasn't what I wanted to do.

In September 1970, I was discharged from the army after three years of service to my country. I was about to begin a new chapter in my life. I went through the discharge routine of medical and mental examinations. I talked to the doctors about the dreams, nightmares, and the hyper-alertness I was going through. The doctors didn't seem to care about what I was feeling or what I was experiencing. They had a look on their faces as if they could give a shit. I signed my DD214 (my record of military service) and I was now, officially, a civilian.

The next morning, I loaded all my belongings into my 1967 VW bug for the drive home. I was all alone on the drive from Kansas to California, and it was great. The first day I drove to Denver, Colorado, and spent the night. The next morning I was up at 4:00 a.m. and on the road. I made it to Provo, Utah, before stopping for the night. I was back up at 4:00 a.m. again and back on the road. The drive from Provo to Modesto was going to be a long one, but I was on my way home, and I knew I would make it. I pulled in front of the house at 4:00 p.m. and walked to the door and rang the bell. My mom came to the door and when she opened it, I said, "Surprise." Boy, was she surprised! I had called home before I left Kansas and told my mom and dad that I wanted to do some sightseeing so it would take me five days to make it home. However, while on the drive home, I decided to get there as fast as I could, thus the three days. I had been away for three years, and all my thoughts were of getting home. That last day of driving was getting harder as the time wore on, but while driving through Nevada, I was able to pick up a San Francisco Giants baseball game on the radio. Being a lifelong Giants fan, the play-by-play helped me make the last few miles plus gave me another reason for getting home. My mom and I waited for my dad to get home from work. I wanted my arrival home to be a surprise for him also. We had a great time talking for a while and then we went out to dinner. It sure was nice to be home!

After a week or so of getting used to civilian life, I went back to work at Sharps Army Depot, where I had worked prior to my stint in the army. I'm not sure how long the job lasted before I was laid off because of cutbacks in the war. That led to a history of jobs that never lasted more than five years.

In June 1973, I met a beautiful young lady, and I was taken by her. I knew I had to get to know this incredible-looking girl. A month or more of persistence paid off when she finally had time for me. Our first date went great, and after about a month of dating I knew I had her. Once a week I would go to Mom and Dad's for dinner. She would come by my place on those nights. When she showed up one night mad that I hadn't been there exactly when she expected me, I knew she was mine! Six months later we were married. We've been married for thirty-seven years, and our marriage is as strong as ever. I know God brought her into my life. She was the strength I needed in my life. I give my wife, Janelle, all the credit for saving my life. She has stuck by me for these thirty-seven years. She held me tightly in her arms at night to comfort me when the nightmares took over. She was there for me in my times of depression. She would talk me down when the slightest thing would get me angry. She even stood by me when I went from job to job. I think of the hardships I put her and my daughters through every day. I think of the financial hardships, my demanding ways, and my PTSD symptoms they had to endure. She is my rock and foundation. I thank God for her every day.

In 2001, the 183rd planned its first reunion, and it was to be held at Fort Rucker, Alabama. At first I didn't want to attend, but with the urging from Janelle and my daughters, I decided to go. Janelle seemed excited about us going, and she made all the arrangements. We flew into Birmingham, Alabama, where three of my friends, John Bradley, Al Cherin, and Bill Keener, met us at the airport. It had been about thirty years since I had last seen them. As Janelle and I started down the escalator, my emotions began to take over. Because of an overhang, I couldn't see the bottom of the escalator. Once we got past the overhang, I saw the three of them waiting. My eyes filled with tears, and when I glanced at Janelle, I saw tears in her eyes also. A man from Birmingham had sat next to us on the flight and asked about our trip. I had told him I was about to reunite with some of the men I had served with in Vietnam. I mentioned to him that three of them were to meet us at the airport. He was ahead of us going down the escalator and I noticed him talking to my friends. He had stopped and told them how excited I was about seeing them. By the time we reached them, all five of us were in tears while hugging each other. We stopped and looked at each other and realized that finally, after so many years, we were reunited. You could feel our joy of being together again. I glanced to the side and saw the man from our flight standing there with tears flowing from his eyes. Our eyes met and he gave me a big smile and a thumbs-up. I wish now that I had gotten his name and phone number so I could have let him know how things went.

While at the reunion the guys could see that I was troubled. They began to talk about their troubles and of how they began to seek help through the VA. They told me that I needed to go to the VA and seek help. After Janelle heard this from them, she said that she wanted me to look into what was available for me. When we got home from the reunion, Janelle told our daughters about what the men had said about the VA being able to help me with my problems. The four of them began to tell me to go to the VA and at least look into what was available. It took them four years to finally convince me to go to the VA, and in 2005 I was entered into the system. I started with one-on-one counseling and then added group therapy. I have been in continuous counseling and group sessions for the past six years. These six years have been the best for me. I have met some wonderful veterans and have made new friends. They are friends that understand the problems I have. We all have the same things in common, and we know what each other is going through. One of the most important things to come out of the help I've been getting at the Vet Center is that I've come out of my bunker. I have been able to resume somewhat of a normal life. I'm now able to go out and be around others and spend time with family and friends. For all the years prior to the VA Center intervention, I was only able to interact with others in periods of time lasting about an hour or two. Those short intervals were all I could take before I had to return home to my bunker. Not only is the VA taking care of my mental needs, it is also taking care of my medical needs caused by my exposure to Agent Orange. I must say that the VA has taken good care of me.

For all of us who served in Vietnam and suffer from mental and health issues, there is help available for us. There are veterans who have put off seeking help because they think they don't need help or they have heard stories about how dealing with VA is difficult. Don't let the stories stop you from seeking the help you need and deserve. Some vets may have had problems with the VA, but I am sure their numbers are small compared to those who have received great care.

Flying for Freedom was the motto of the 183rd Reconnaissance Airplane Company (the Seahorses). I'm sure that man for man we believed we were doing just that. Our missions took us over rice paddies, waterways, mountains, and the jungles of South Vietnam. We were flying to protect the people there from the Communists of North Vietnam. During the eighteen months, twenty-eight days I was in country, I would like to think that the pilots and crew chiefs of the 183rd had that in mind. The 183rd served in Vietnam from 1966 to 1974 and disbanded in 1974. Most of the soldiers from the 183rd came home. We did leave behind some MIAs (missing in action) along with a number of KIAs (killed in action). However, in 1974 the remains of our last MIA came home from the war. He died Flying for Freedom.

As the war was drawing to the end, reading and watching the news accounts caused me to think about the numbers of young soldiers who lost their lives in a country halfway around the world. The fact that they knew little or nothing about this country didn't make their loss rest any easier. They went to fight this war because they thought is was their duty to their country. They answered the call from President Kennedy when he said, "Ask not what your country can do for you, but ask what you can do for your country."

This question stayed with me, and when my country came asking me to serve in its military, I knew that was what I could do for my country. I was willing to give three years to the greatest country in the world. I was willing to lay down my life, if need be, and pay the ultimate sacrifice for my country. Unlike the cowards who ran north to another country, more than fifty-eight thousand gave their lives in duty to this country. These young men and women would never be able to live out their lives, have a wife or a husband, or experience the joy of having children. Yes, I do carry the guilt of surviving the war, but I am learning to understand that I can use my survival to help other veterans find the care they need. I hope that by writing this account concerning this chapter of my life, those veterans who need help will have the courage to find the door into the VA system.

I know there are still many Vietnam veterans who for whatever reasons haven't sought out assistance yet. They need to realize that they no longer have to hide their thoughts and feelings. Telling your experiences will not only help you come to grips with your emotions, but it will help countless others you may come in contact with. The system of Veterans Centers located throughout the United States is a great place to start. They work independently from the VA and can help you start your journey through the VA system. I attend counseling and recreational opportunities at the local Veterans Center in Modesto. After a tough night of nightmares, I can walk through the front door and a sense of peace comes over me. Talking with my counselor and sharing stories with my fellow veterans, who have the same experiences, is extremely helpful. The Veterans Center is my safe haven!

A look from a Vietnamese graveyard out over a valley in the war torn countryside

Carl Forgey standing in front of his beloved Bird Dog

A Bird Dog lifts off on one of the many missions it was assigned to complete

CHAPTER SIXTEEN

A MASS OF OLIVE DRAB: A MEMOIR TOUR 1969–1970

Marc Mitchell
Spec. 4
US Army
First Aviation Brigade, 223rd Combat Aviation Battalion
183rd Reconnaissance Airplane Company (Combat)
Republic of South Vietnam
1969–1970

I was a passenger traveling in a car with a total stranger. But the stranger was also a brother, and all was well. Randy, at the wheel, and I were heading south along a dark South Carolina highway. The destination I was not quite sure of. Someplace called The Seawee. I asked, "Seawee, what is that?" Ranger Randy Mills answered back, "It is an out of the way place where locals go for real good low-country cooking." He quickly added, "I promise that you'll like it." I didn't know Randy from Boo, but here I was with him, and I knew all was well. Like I said, he's my brother!

This is one of those short trips we all have taken. You know the kind; it seems to take forever to get there, but the return trip is just a hop, skip, and a jump. Amazing how that works, isn't it? Randy asked me where I was from, but knowing he was local to the Charleston area I simply said Northwest Louisiana. Randy answered, "I got a great brother in that area, but I don't know the name of the town." Randy rambled off a few names of some small towns and finally gave up after saying, "It starts with an H and that is all I can think of." I immediately said the name of the town is Haughton. Randy excitedly said, "That's it! That's it! It sure is. Regis lives in Haughton." He wanted to know how far I lived from Haughton. I told him that I was from Benton in Bossier Parish, about ten miles from Haughton.

We kept traveling down the dark highway and decided to check on the convoy of Nam vets who were traveling behind us, all heading to the same place, The Seawee. All the ducks were in a row with each automobile in sight of our point man, Randy Mills, army ranger vet from Charlie Company, Seventy-fifth Ranger Battalion, and all seems well. I'm riding in good company. Randy hit his directory on his cell and immediately I could hear a disembodied voice emanating through the darkness. "Regis, its Randy, and I've got one of your neighbors with me from your corner of the woods." Randy handed me the cell, and I was introduced to another brother, Regis Murphy Jr. We had a quick but very pleasant conversation. I noticed the left turn signal blinking, and Randy slowed down for his turn. We were within sight of The Seawee. Regis and I concluded our conversation, and the convoy exited the highway for a late low-country meal. The Seawee is a very nondescript place, pretty plain looking, really. If one were to pass it in daylight, I doubt you would even notice it. However, Randy promised it had great hospitality and food that would rival any low-country cooking. This was where the locals ate! The rest of the group of Nam vets and their wives pulled in next to us. We all gathered to count heads and then proceeded to join our point man and enter The Seawee.

The Super DC-8 Stretch airliner rocked in the darkness, buffeted by an invisible pocket of air turbulence. The mike crackled to life as the pilot keyed it and addressed his passengers. A number of the passengers had made this same trip before, but for the most of us it was our first and last time. Our destination was a place most of us had only heard of from Walter Kronkite on the evening news. The smoking lamp was extinguished, and the buckle-up sign flashed as the huge jet with 268 souls, all dressed in olive drab BDUs, prepared for the descent into Cam Rahn Bay airfield.

Welcome to South Vietnam. The plane lurched, and we felt the massive tires touch down. We all got that same sick feeling in our gut. We're screwed. We're helpless, and there is nothing we can do about it. We are officially in South Vietnam for 365 days, more or less. Sadly, for many it will be for less, and for a nation, our nation, it will be much too long. Tour 365 had begun.

Throughout that first night, hundreds of America's sons—the sons of America's greatest generation—disgorged from planes in olive drab mass. With a tightly stuffed duffle bag for a pillow or seat, those who wished to recline or sleep chose from a concrete slab, PSP (perforated steel panel), or crab-infested sand. But sleep visited very few of us that night. We lay there contemplating our fates. Far in the distance, we saw flashes of light. Nothing resembling lightning, just an quick glow that rose and spread then faded into darkness and then moments later, a dull rumbling sound, not unlike thunder. Meteors appeared to pierce the darkness at Mach 2 speed, only to arch in the sky and disappear. Meteors? No. These had color, colors of red crossing green on a black pallet of sparkling stars. Somewhere in that dark void, fear, pain, suffering, and death awaited us. The visitors dressed in olive drab.

Father, I have sinned and I am frightened
I fear the future, I fear the unknown
I am alone, though I am with many
Father, stay with me for I need you

Then the threatening dark pallet, ever so slowly, began to morph into the faint but familiar pastels of a new day. Our surroundings began to acquire familiar shapes. A generation of American youth began to stir and mingle, quietly absorbing the sights and sounds of America's largest combat and logistical base in Southeast Asia. An uncommon smell assaulted the senses, coming from every direction on the compass. Everywhere we looked small dark chimneys of black smoke rose to the sky, ugly and growing, multiplying tenfold. When the sergeant began barking his orders we felt thankful for the familiar and now welcome sound of military authority, bringing order to the disarray. It was time to suck it up.

Hours passed as each troop waited to hear his name called. One by one, the olive drab mass shrank in size as men were assigned to the troop transport aircraft that would disperse us throughout South Vietnam. We couldn't stay here. In short order, more and more planes would arrive, bringing in more troops and taking home the lucky, the living and the dead. With orders in hand, I had my first destination: headquarters of the Seventeenth Aviation Group, First Aviation Brigade, located at Nha Trang Army Airfield, Republic of Vietnam. It was May 5, 1969. One step at a time, one day at a time. Headquarters was a relatively short hop away, forty miles tops. I was placed in a hold status, awaiting further orders. I would be here a few weeks then I would relocate. Don't get too comfortable! I wasn't. I was nervous, but I was OK.

My first duty was guard duty, which lasted a full week. It was really weird. The perimeter was scant yards from the personnel barracks. The guard tower was literally on top of the concertina wire and no more than ten feet, on the other side, was the city of Nha Trang!

I'm here with a loaded M14, looking right into people's homes, like it's a peep show. The inhabitants carry on as if I didn't exist, and to them I probably don't. That tower has been manned around the clock for years. A few days, then a week, and before I know it May 19 arrives. There is nothing significant about that day. It's just another day and closer to home. Slowly but surely, day turns into night and all is quiet and restful. I've been given a break from guard duty so I get to visit with some other troops, trade smokes and small talk, and later hit the rack.

Around 2200 hours (10:00 p.m.), I could hear the thump, thump of impacting rounds being walked right into us. The alert siren sounded, men were running in all directions and hollering, and I had no idea what to do. This was Charlie's first visit for me! I grabbed my gear and tried to run somewhere—anywhere. *Where the hell is the bunker?* Rounds were still coming in, but now rounds were going out, and more and more sirens screamed their song. I was running, BDGs barely hanging on my body, one boot on and one in my hand, a rifle in the other hand, and a steel pot bouncing around on my head. I had to be a hell of a sight! I found a bunker and jumped in and sucked up into a knot. Rounds slammed into the ground, and all oxygen seemed to disappear. I was gasping for air and at the same time felt myself levitating above the floor of the bunker. I felt like I was hanging in the air. Then I was dropped to the floor. I caught a breath and—*thump*—it started all over again. Until, as sudden as it began, it stopped, the sirens continuing to wail.

Adrenaline was pumping, and my brain was spinning, trying to absorb what had just happened. Slowly, other men began to stir. Cuss words were flying in the dark, fucking-bombs being hurled at Ho Chi Minh like confetti on Broadway during New Year's Eve. Suddenly, I learned the significance of May 19. It was Uncle Ho's birthday, and Charlie had an unwelcome way of celebrating. I was still sporting a naked foot, so I fumbled around until I found my other boot and tried to put it on. My foot was wet, slick, and sticky, and it was starting to ache. I'd been in country fourteen days, and I was already eligible for a Purple Heart! The medic cleaned the wounds, bathed the foot in monkey blood, stitched it up, and I hobbled around for a week. Oh, yeah, I got to return to guard duty.

Once again, troops assigned to guard duty fell into formation. The sergeant of the guard barked the order to come to attention. We snapped to, squared our shoulders, dressed to the right to obtain the proper arm's length distance, and prepared for inspection. The sergeant of the guard did an about face, saluted the officer of the guard, and informed him that all guards were present and accounted for and ready for inspection. The inspection was quick, precise, and thorough. The OIC (officer in charge) returned the command to the sergeant of the guard, and we were posted to outposts.

This guard duty was starting to wear on me, but I knew the work was deadly serious. There was still an hour before dark settled in, and I was wondering what could take so long to cut orders? I was ready to move on to my so-called permanent duty station. A few hours slipped by, and the nightlife returned, as did the peep show. Mama san stepped out of her tin and cardboard shanty and slung waste and trash into the concertina wire. The concertina wire was truly multifunctional. One, it served as a warning to infiltrators. Two, it helped to separate the good guys from the bad guys. Three, during the daylight hours it served as a clothesline for the civilians. Four, it was their waste and garbage dump. The rats loved it. I'm talking big rats—seriously big rats—and lots of them. Manning the tower each night, I watched cats literally flee for their lives from those monster rats. Between the peep show, the rats, and cats, I had no problem remaining vigilant. Something was always moving inside or around the wire.

Finally, I received my orders. My destination was to some place called Phu Hiep Army Airfield, where a company needed a clerk-and-tag. I was it. With my worldly possessions slung over my shoulder, I loaded into a CH-47 Chinook chopper. This flying machine was a big one with twin rotors, one in the front and one in the rear. There were quite a few men being ferried to new homes or returning to familiar ones. The RPMs began to build in the huge motors, and the blades turned in ever increasing speed. The Chinook lifted off the ground and we were on our way. The ride was uneventful, but when the pilot had us flying at treetop level, I began to get a little nervous. I wondered out loud, "What's this?" But a Specialist 4 sitting next to me said, "All is cool, man." He continued, "In Nam, we do a lot of flying at treetop level. It keeps Charlie from getting a good shot at us. We get on him so fast and we're so close to him, he doesn't have the time to shit or go blind. Cool, huh?" I nodded my head, took it all in, and sat back in the sling seat for the duration.

We gained some altitude as the pilot vectored across the South China Sea. Before long, the image of Phu Hiep appeared in the distance. The first thing I noticed was the rusted, reddish-brown hulk of a partially sunken cargo ship. It was a Japanese ship that had been sunk in action during WWII. We reached the airfield at Phu Hiep, and the pilot brought the chopper around, and it slowly settled to earth. I and a few others exited the chopper with our duffle bags in tow. I heard a voice call out, "Spec. 4 Mitchell?" I instantly sounded off and was waved over to a waiting army jeep. I piled into the jeep, and the driver, a PFC (private first class) with a menthol cigarette dangling from his lips, greeted me with real encouraging statement. He said, "You're not going to like this place, man. It's the shits." I didn't say a word but kept looking around my new home. Rusted fencing hung everywhere you looked. The airfield was located near a beach on the South China Sea with a fishing hamlet on one side and some farming hamlets on the other. The base was crowded with conex boxes, avionics trailers, hootches, and revetments. You name it and it was here. This place was ugly and packed tight. I thought, if Charlie gets a fine zero on this place, he could do some real damage. Big time!

The driver began talking about one crazy soldier stationed on the base. No one knows who he was but he had been given a name. You know, kind of like when the cops give a name to a serial killer. "What's he called?" I asked. Above the drone of a nearby Mohawk engine, he says, "The Mad Bomber of Phu Hiep." He quickly added, "Every once in a while the dude wanders around in the dark and throws frags. You never know when it is going to happen. Hell, they can't catch the guy!" I took it all in and knew I wasn't going to like this place, period.

I was dropped off at the company orderly room, where I walked in and presented my orders to the clerk. He was a sandy-haired guy with nothing to say. He looked at them and called out, "Top, the new clerk is here." Top (first sergeant) walked over and shook my hand in welcome. He seemed to be a real pleasant guy. He explained a few things about the company then introduced me to the CO (commanding officer). He told me where to find my quarters, the mess hall, latrine, bunkers, and other things. I found that I would be bunking with the clerk that took my orders. The clerk guided me to the hootch and pointed out my bunk. He then told me where the supply room and the arms room were and left me to myself. This guy either was not having a good day or had an attitude problem. Time would tell. I made a trip to the supply room for bedding and web gear then to the arms room for an M16 and four magazines of ammo. With the rifle slung over my shoulder, I headed back to the hootch to get settled in. Top had told me to chill out for the rest of the day and report to work the next day. That sure sounded good to me.

Everything on the post was within easy walking distance. I learned of an EM (enlisted men's) club, and I headed over to it and spent the rest of the day there. There were other soldiers there and more came in as the workday came to an end. I began to meet other troops from the company and saw that they all wore a breast patch with the company logo on their BDU jacket. They called themselves Hawkeyes. There was a tiny Vietnamese girl, named Kim, working in the club as a waitress. She was constantly going from table to table, popping off lids from the beer containers with her church key. She had a great personality and got good tips. It was too bad she hadn't long to live.

The next day was a new day and a new job. The clerk still had little to say, and that wasn't going to get any better. He tossed work on my desk and told me that the forms were in the file cabinet. That was the extent of our conversations. To be honest, I didn't like the guy. It was a first-impression thing with me. Maybe it was the same with him. We never had a good day or evening in the hootch together. He was a jerk, and along with that, a smart ass. Each subsequent workday was like the last, uncomfortable and hostile. It was starting to wear on me, and I wanted to kick his ass. But this wasn't high school. I was a Spec. 4, and I didn't want to get nailed for busting someone's chops.

Duty rosters were posted on an information board outside the orderly room, and troops were required to check them daily. One of my jobs was to make the daily updates to the duty rosters, including the guard duty roster. Since there were two company clerks, one was available for guard duty and one was not. I caught guard duty, as did most of the men, about every one and a half weeks.

Guard duty was unlike the duty at Nha Trang; it was pretty laid back. The guard crew consisted of four men who were responsible the tower/bunker. We would meet at the arms room and check out binoculars and an M60 machine gun with oversized ammo can filled with five thousand rounds. Everything was loaded into a three-quarter-ton truck, and we were driven out to the perimeter. The driver, sergeant of the guard, dropped us off at the post and helped us get all squared away before he left. Unlike Nha Trang, our post sat atop a raised mound that sloped a hundred yards to the razor wire. To our left, about two hundred beyond the wire, was a very small hamlet. Maybe fifteen or twenty thatched-roof hootches total. Looking out toward the west was a beautiful verdant green valley of rice fields. Perhaps a few miles beyond the valley, the central highlands rose well above sea level.

The final step in setting up our position was to put a belt of ammo in the M60 and fire a short burst. Everything worked fine, and the machine gun was ready. The mess hall had left us with two urns of drinks. One was Kool-Aid and the other was coffee. On top of the drinks, they had given us a plentiful supply of sandwiches.

We were all sitting together when the vets started to tell the new guy, me, what guard duty was like at Phu Hiep. Several hundred yards away to the right were towers manned by ARVN troops. Every night and at any moment of time, the ARVN had what was called a *mad minute*. Up and down their area of responsibility, they would cut loose with automatic weapons fire, which naturally included machine guns. The purpose was to intimidate Charlie and let him know that he might wish to infiltrate somewhere else along the line.

The three other troops had turned their attention to the hootches in the hamlet. They were asking, "Is she out there yet?" They bantered back and forth, with each as eager as the other to spot her. I asked, "What's the deal?" One answered, "Mitchell, you won't believe it until you see it. Every night, just before dark, this girl comes out from between those two closest hootches." Another soldier jumped in and says, "She takes her top off and stands there, facing us, and motions for us to come and visit her. The whole time she is squeezing and rubbing her tits. Damnedest show you've ever seen." He quickly continued, "She keeps waving for us to come into the hamlet, but we know better. She is trying to sucker us in. Just watch. Charlie is down there." We kept watching, and once in a while some movement could be seen between the hootches. Anyone she lured into that hootch was dead meat. This was not Nha Trang, but the peep show was real, and the consequences of succumbing to it were deadly.

Two of the guards badly wanted to go down to the hamlet, but not to the hootches. They wanted sex, and they had a way of getting it. They explained to me that there was a fenced off lane which was open to the locals during the day. It was closed each afternoon at a certain time. The lane allowed the locals to travel between the fishing village and the farming hamlet to visit and exchange food items. The lane was sunken from the surrounding terrain due to the back and forth traffic of generations of locals. Where it met the perimeter, concertina was strung across. Each day, this was opened and closed when the time came. "We get the girl to come down to the concertina gate where she crawls under, and we can have our fun!" One of the men remarked, "Mitchell, this is wild, man." He explained that two of the men would go down there, and the other two would remain with the M60 and keep an eye out for Charlie. They paid the girl with mosquito repellent and sandwiches. Hell of a deal! We also use a switch: While one guy is getting his jollies, the other stands watch with his M16. Then we change places."

As we watched her, she waving to us and backing towards the hootches. However, if we sat there long enough and kept waving, she would finally give in and move closer. Eventually, she would strip naked and if we continued to wave and watch, she would come up to the wire. That was exactly how it worked, but I didn't want any part of it. These guys were stupid. When the first two came back, the one who stayed with me wanted to go down, but I told him that there was no way I was going down there. We had a sharp exchange of words between the two of us. One of the first two men said that he would go and watch the soldier's back. This was a nightly thing and had been going on for quite some time. It was still going on when I was medevaced out, and I'm sure it was going on, as a regular event, up to the day the company struck its colors and was shipped out of Nam in 1970.

It is now July, and I've been in country for two months—too soon to start my short-timer calendar. Most men start the calendar when they hit six months. However, some can't wait until then and start damned near as soon as they get here. I guess it's normal because most want out of here and out of the army quickly. I am no exception. Four of my high school class-mates have already died in this war. My best friend, LCPL Harold O'Neal was killed September 15, 1968. He was setting up a night defense perimeter around a disabled marine tank. His squad had been brought in to secure the tank just before dark. The task of setting trip wires was a job for two men teams. However, it was getting dark and time was of the essence so the two-man teams split up to expedite the job. Harold had his frag tied off and the pin crimped closed, but somehow in the dark, he hit his own trip wire. His marine buddy from Rutland, Vermont, Gregory Barsanti was the first to get to Harold. It was over. He had absorbed the full blast of his own grenade. Harold had a short-timer calendar; he just had no idea how short his time would be. He had been wounded during the Tet Offensive in 1968, in the battle to recapture Hue. To die in this country because of a mistake! I still miss him. His services were closed casket and held in Henderson, Tennessee. When Harold Sr. wanted to see his son before he was taken to the cemetery the funeral home honored his request. Poor Mr. O'Neal, he couldn't even recognize his own son. A short-timer's calendar can really prove to be an oxymoron. There were over 58,200 calendars in that war.

Life can be full of unfinished business. For me, some of that unfinished business was locating the grave of my friend and brother, LCPL Harold O'Neal Jr. On July 4, 2011, that business was completed. In the company of my wife Kathy, we placed flowers at his VA headstone. Time has tarnished that stone but not the loss. Forty-two years, ten months. I love you brother. Harold is resting next to his mother, Marguerite, and Harold Sr., in Memory Garden Cemetery, Chester County, Tennessee, a few miles from the town of Henderson.

The pain was intense as the medic and doctor worked on my left shoul-der. So intense, they placed a rolled cloth in my mouth to bite down on. With each jerk I clamped down on that cloth. I was strapped to a gurney, immobilized at the Phu Hiep Dispensary, and I began to think back to what had put me here.

It was late at night and I was returning, from showering, to my quarters. I stumbled on the paved walkway and tumbled down the concrete steps, slamming my left shoulder into a fifty-five-gallon drum filled with sand. These drums lined the walkway next to the outer walls of the hootch. They were placed there to deflect and absorb shrapnel from exploding rocket and mortar rounds. They were also good for separating shoulders if a troop fell against one. The doc just can't figure out why he can't reset what he thinks is a "dislocated" shoulder. *Hell man, it isn't dislocated, it's separated! There is a profound difference between the two.*

The army doctor was determined to reset that dislocated shoulder and he got serious about it. He told the medic to help brace him as he placed his foot squarely into my armpit. Have you ever looked at the logo on a pair of Levi jeans? There are two mules tethered to a leg of Levi jeans. They are attempting to pull those jeans apart in order to demonstrate the strength of the jeans. Well, this doctor did the same thing to me, and it hurt. It really hurt. His efforts seemed to make the injury even worse, far worse than it originally had been. I was exhausted and the doctor decided there was nothing more he could do so he called for a dust off. It wasn't long before I could hear the blades of a Huey setting down on the medevac pad. My left arm had been tightly secured across my chest to immobilize it. I was now a walking wounded. I was so tired and hurting from that armpit maneuver, but I also was so glad to be getting out of Dr. Jekyll's care.

The pilot and copilot remained at the controls while the medic and crew chief helped me into the chopper and sat me on the floor. I'll never know whether there are straps available to secure patients in a Huey. The crew chief gave the pilot the thumbs-up, and in a shot we were airborne. The pilot mad a hard left. It was after midnight and I was tired. I could feel gravity working against me as the pilot made his turn. Suddenly I felt myself sliding, sliding out the damned door of the rescue chopper and I couldn't even see ground. I was screaming so loud that the noise from the rotor wash couldn't drown me out. My legs were outside the craft. I was clawing at the stripped-naked floor of the chopper, attempting to find something to grab on to. My buttocks were getting closer to the edge when a pair of hands grabbed my shirt and pulled me back in. He said, "Get back in here Specialist, you're not going anywhere!" That man saved my life. No ifs ands or buts about it. I should have been dead! I was so upset that I can't recall the rest of the trip to the Sixty-seventh Field Evacuation Hospital in Qui Nhon. Lord my God, I pray that man made it home and has been blessed with all of life's fruits.

I was taken into the ER where I was triaged, and X-rays were finally taken. I don't even recall being able to speak at that point. I may have been in shock from the pain and the fear that gripped me during my near free-fall. I do recall the ER doctor commenting, not kindly, about the care I had received at the Phu Hiep dispensary. There was nothing that could be done for the shoulder. It would become my life long souvenir of my service in Vietnam. The doctor prescribed intense physical therapy. I was treated for pain and assigned to Ward W. It was a short trip, just through the swinging doors and twenty feet across the hall from the ER. A nurse and orderly helped me into some pajamas and helped me into bed. I was spent. I slept.

I awoke to my good shoulder being jostled and the sound of an American girl's voice speaking to me. Through blurry eyes I saw patients scattered throughout the ward. There were more empty beds than not. She talked to me for a bit, but I didn't understand a word she has said. She left and I closed my eyes again. It seemed like a short time later when I was awakened again by voices all around me. There was stuff being moved about, and someone was repeatedly calling out, "Tom-Tom, Tom-Tom, come over here." I opened my eyes again and looked around. Most of the patients were awake, doing their thing, and calling this little Vietnamese boy. I found out he was a patient also. He had been caught in the crossfire between our troops and the VC. One leg had been shot off at the knee, and most of the muscle on the remaining calf had also been blasted away. He had several other wounds that were healing, but he wasn't letting it slow him down. He was hopping from patient to patient helping where he could. He was smiling and seemed happy, but he looked so pitiful too. I thought maybe he was going to come over to my bedside, so I rolled over and put the pillow over my head. I wasn't prepared to see a child so mangled. I asked God to guide the child away from me. Tom-Tom passed on by, and I was glad. I spent the rest of the day and night without being bothered. I really needed that time. Of course, the nurse would roll her pill cart around and administer the prescriptions, and I was glad to get them. I had no appetite and eventually they removed my food trays.

Day two rolled around, and my physical therapy was to begin. My doctor told me it would entail weight lifting and heated whirlpool baths. An orderly helped me to my feet, and we walked to the therapy room. Once there, a specialist took over and discussed the program in detail. I was to start with a half-pound weight on a cable pull. I was to draw the weight for so many sets of so many repetitions. I never imagined how hard it was to lift eight ounces. It was hard and excruciatingly painful, but it had to be done. With each rep it felt as if bone was ripping flesh. After finishing this, it was time for the whirlpool. I had never been in one of those before, but it felt good. The heat of the swirling water was a relief to the shoulder. I was scheduled to have two of these sessions a day. Upon returning to the ward, I found out that the walking wounded would help the staff with the seriously wounded soldiers in another ward that was connected to W.

These men were battlefield casualties. You name the wound, and someone in there had it, and they needed care. I was honored to help them. They didn't complain. They deeply appreciated anything and everything that one could do for them or their buddies. Also, they insisted that their buddy, on either side, be helped first. It is called brotherhood; the brotherhood that is born from love, respect, honor, and him-first qualities. We would feed those who couldn't feed themselves; light and hold their smokes as they took a drag; reset and fluff their pillows; scratched their nose and anything else that itched that they couldn't get to; read a letter to them, or write one for them. There were several troops in there that made me think of Harold. These men had so much shrapnel in their bodies that the wounds couldn't be dressed. The wounds were left open so they could drain. Linens were not even permitted to touch their skin. Hoops were arched over their beds holding the sheets that would give them a minute amount of cover. They had tubes protruding from every orifice of their bodies.

Little by little I was gaining some strength back in my shoulder. I had graduated to two pounds on the weight pull. I was still receiving the whirlpool baths, but now I had company. There were some civilians brought in who had been caught in a Napalm strike. These individuals had special baskets for them to be lowered and raised from the whirlpools. It reminded me of boiling crawfish back home except the crawfish didn't scream in aguish when the water hit them. The surging water helped remove the fried, baked skin and flesh. When their time in the whirlpool expired a button was pushed and they would be winched out of the pool. It was like I said, 'like boiling crawfish and just as red'.

I had been told that I was doing better, and in a few days I would be placed in a medical convoy to an airstrip outside of Qui Nhon. From there I would be taken to the Sixth Convalescent Hospital in Cam Rahn Bay for recuperation and return to duty. Before I left, Ward W had some new patients. They were three South Koreans and a suspected Viet Cong. The South Koreans loathed Communists and enjoyed nothing more than killing them. Lights out in the ambulatory ward was 2200 hours (10:00 p.m.), and the nurses demanded quiet. My arm was still immobilized. To find a comfortable spot that would enable sleep was an annoying chore, but I didn't complain. At least I wasn't feeding crabs and sharks in the South China Sea. Restlessness ruled the night for most of us, so if something unusual happened during the night, it would be noticed.

Very late that night, well after midnight, something did happen, and the sounds were strange. It sounded like a muffled and subdued struggle. I rose from my pillow, as a few others had done, and through the dim light of the nurses' station I saw the three South Koreans. Two of them were holding the suspected VC hard against the mattress and the third was deftly smothering the thrashing soul with his pillow. They seemed determined to kill him, and nobody had an urge to stop them. Just about then and for no apparent reason, a nurse entered the ward and saw what was happening. She immediately called for staff to help. It was a show, at least. The VC survived, and he was wheeled out of the ward. They posted an MP in the ward for the rest of the night.

The next morning, the ward was buzzing about the incident with the Koreans and their victim. News traveled fast through the soldiers at the hospital. The Koreans were moved somewhere away from us. We never saw them again.

It was close to the end of July and it was hot. I was ready for a change of scenery. By now, I was up to five pounds on the weight pull. I was told that I would probably be on a convoy leaving the next morning. I had two more sessions of therapy broken up by some work with the combat wounded. They were the greatest guys in the world; there wasn't a selfish bone amongst them! From time to time, I walked outside and sat on a bench. I took in some sun and lit a borrowed smoke. The days were long, time dragged, and I would have enjoyed a cold beer. A few of us had set up a watch post, for lack of a better term, and watched the medical staff quarters. The off-duty doctors and nurses would lounge around and socialize. We saw plenty of horseplay, giggling, and we could hear plenty of laughter. With American round-eyed girls, plenty of beer, and Jack Daniels with Coke, we wanted to be over there. But it was not to be.

Once again, night settled in, and we got to watch a little AFTV (Armed Forces Television). Then it was lights out. I thought to myself that in the morning I would be out of here. Around 0100 hours (1:00 a.m.), I was awake, restless, and not finding that comfortable spot that enabled me to sleep.

I heard several Hueys coming in, and the ER staff was hustling. A lot of casualties were being brought in from the field. Gurneys, lots of them, were wheeled out to the dust-off pad. Blood-soaked canvas litters, loaded with more of my generation, were placed on gurneys and rushed through the same doors I had been pushed through a week before. However, this was different. Urgency cut through the night as more and more troops were brought in, scores of them. These were men from the 173rd Airborne Brigade, and they had been chewed up. The men were gently but firmly removed from the litters to the operating tables. The place was swarming with activity, each staffer had a task, and they went directly to it. Men were suffering, some crying out in pain, and many others with a blank look upon their faces as if they were resigned to their fate. I stood there watching all this life and death drama before me. It was galvanizing.

For some reason I felt myself drawn into the triage room. No one noticed; everyone was too busy. I just stood and watched it all. Now, years later, the scene returns to me in inescapable dreams. Most people don't think that blood smells. Well, it does, and there before me was lots of it. It was all over the place. Bleeders were spurting blood onto anything in their path. The staff was stained with it, the floor was awash with it. It was on the walls. It was on everything and everybody. The bodies in the room had sustained trauma wounds, and bowels and bladders released their contents. It was overwhelming. I got out of there and noticed an orderly, with a water hose in his hand, standing to the side of the swinging door. He had washed the canvas litters that had been used to carry my brothers from the field. They now stood on end, drying. The Americans' blood had been hosed off and into a drainage ditch. I felt sick to my stomach.

Morning finally arrived, and I found the army ambulances with their big red crosses were assembled in a convoy outside the ward. Patients on litters were loaded first, at least four to an ambulance, maybe six. It's been a long time. Finally, the walking wounded were loaded. There were six ambulances in the convoy, which was led by an armored MP vehicle, and another brought up the rear. If you were prone to claustrophobia, the ambulances were not your ticket. We were led out the gate of Qui Nhon and began our trip to Cam Rahn Bay. The first leg of the trip was rather short. It seemed that we were in convoy for less than an hour. Boxed up like Kentucky Fried Chicken and unable to see a thing, time and distance were difficult to discern. We left the ambulances and boarded an Air Force Medevac C130 for the second and final leg of our journey. We lifted off, and the big Hercules did its job. We touched down in Cam Rahn Bay and taxied to a stop. The ramp dropped and exposed a few army buses waiting for us. With military organization, we were promptly loaded onto the buses for the drive to the convalescent center. Unknown to me, another life experience was waiting for me. This experience was one that my folks and the audience of the nightly news would learn of—and that hundreds of us in blue pajamas would never forget.

The army's Sixth Convalescent Center was located along the beach of the inner bay of the Cam Rahn facility. It was our nation's largest military base in the Pacific Region and was considered the safest combat and logistical center in all South Vietnam. The hospital was composed of all wooden structures, and the wards, on one end, faced a black-topped road. The opposite end of each ward opened onto a wooden walkway. The buildings were long structures that held dozens of patients each. At one end of the road, a mess hall stood next to a chapel, and across the road were some medical offices. The other end of the road turned right, toward the beach. Fronting that short section of road, were the mobile home quarters of the officers, doctors, and nurses. Just a few hundred yards further was the beach with its blinding white sand and a guard bunker. The bunker was supposed to be manned by permanent party (those stationed at the base), but it wasn't. Instead, it was manned by patients. These were men who were sick, injured, or wounded and recovering so they could return to duty. The patients were allowed to mill around throughout the day. They could lounge on the sun-bathed sand or visit inside the wards. The only restriction was that patients had to be in their racks at pill time. That was when Captain Linda Gail Boddie made her rounds with our prescriptions. No one wanted to miss Captain Boddie. She was gorgeous and an absolute knockout in combat boots and tropical fatigues! She made us all damned glad to be there! She was known to us as simply Captain Body, a vision of beauty, grace, and dedication. I doubt that any one of us has forgotten her.

I arrived at the convalescent center around July 30. America was at war in her streets at home, and her sons and daughters were at war in South Vietnam and throughout Southeast Asia. However, there is no war here. This place was for healing.

Unknown to any of us, the Viet Cong had plans to the contrary. A squad of trained sappers attacked the haven of healing on the night of August 6, 1969. It was a horrible experience, and hundreds of America's sons and daughters were unarmed, defenseless, and undefended.

Charlie slipped his sampans into the bay after dark. He stealthily worked his way to the Sixth CC beach, undetected by the patient guards, who were asleep. The sappers left their footprints in the sand around the guards and worked their way to the mobile house quarters. The attack commenced with an assault on the nurse's quarters. The sappers knocked out windows and tossed dynamite in through the broken windows. Then in rapid succession, the other quarters were hit. The sappers split into two teams and attacked the wards. One team ran down the road, and the other used the walkway. They threw explosive charges into each ward as they passed. Simultaneous explosions filled the night as almost every ward, including the mess hall, was hit. Charlie escaped untouched, but in his wake, he left two patients dead and ninety-nine wounded.

As fortune would have it, the safest patients of the Sixth CC were the sleeping guards. The medical staff rushed to our aid. Brothers were helping brothers, and doctors and nurses spread throughout the wards. But there were more casualties than there was staff. The wounded were rushed to the air force hospital, and the rest of us were left, in shock, to soak up the enormity of the attack and wonder at the brutal desire of our enemy to kill us no matter where we were. On August 9, the assault upon the Sixth CC made headline news in the *Stars and Stripes* along with the murders of Sharon Tate and the La Biancas by Charlie Manson's tribe of misfits. I still hadn't begun my short-timers calendar.

I received orders, and it was back to Qui Nhon. This time it was the home of the 223rd Combat Aviation Battalion. Finally, some sense of normalcy began to return. I was assigned to a job that I was trained for. Also, I had a bunk with a roommate and a mess hall. This might not be too bad, after all. I was nervous, but I slowly began adjusting to new faces and personalities. I found the enlisted men's club, which meant beer—cheap beer, like seventeen cents for 3.2 beer. What mattered was that is was cold and plentiful. There was a nightly game to see who could build a Schlitz or Budweiser pyramid faster. Once in a while, we snuck in a Pabst Blue Ribbon pyramid. The club always had a Vietnamese band that played nightly and did their best to sound like Cher or Nancy Sinatra. We did enjoy the bands and looked forward to them every night.

The best I can remember, the Qui Nhon Army Air Field was laid out like a huge football field. Like Nha Trang, the perimeter abutted the civilian hootches on three sides. The east side opened to the South China Sea. On the west side, past the village and the coastal plains, were the mountains of the central highlands which rose gently from the valley floor. During the Tet Offensive, Charlie had made a big push to capture this city, and the battle damage was quite visible. Within the perimeter to the south side of the airfield sat the USO building. The Donut Dollies made all the troops feel welcome there. If you were in transit, the USO was a good place to catch a shower, shaves, and get some rack time. They also had one television, but it received only one channel, The Armed Forces Television. Programming was quite limited, with programs such as *Gun smoke* and a series called *Combat* with Vic Morrow. *Combat* was about a squad of American grunts fighting the Germans in France. For some reason, that show didn't feel as real to me as it had back home in Louisiana. Go figure! I can't forget the commercials. There were three that I recall. The first was about the prevalence of VD, and believe me, there was a bunch of it. So much so that the city of Qui Nhon was strictly off limits the entire time I was there. The second commercial was an order to be alert for animals with rabies—as if the Viet Cong and the North Vietnamese Army wasn't bad enough. Now the zinger, the mother of political correctness: An attractive Asian actress would stress the importance for American soldiers to remember that they were guests in this country and were required to honor and abide by all local customs. Hello, hello? If we were guests here, why were you trying to kill all of us?

While I am on the subject, lightly, of killing: The Sixty-seventh Field Evacuation Hospital was located a few hundred yards east of the USO barrack. The entire time I was at battalion, never did I imagine the role that hospital would play in my life outside the military. Strange how being young and dumb kept a soldier from recognizing how traumatic events could revisit him later. Like any other enemy, the memories of those days bided their time, hiding in the crevices of my brain. They waited, waited, waited. Then crept into my days and stole into my nights. The war ended, but the specter of Vietnam never did.

"Top, can't you do something about this E-8 who keeps coming in here and making a nuisance every day?" I asked the first sergeant one day. I continued, "He pulls up a chair and parks it right at my desk and seems like all he wants to do was ask a bunch of questions. It's damned near like being interrogated."

This guy was being a pest, but I didn't have the rank to move him out. What's the deal? I thought to myself. Just give him some tokens and send him to the NCO Club.

The first sergeant replied, "Mitch, he's in transit and awaiting orders. He'll be gone soon. He's just bored."

"Yeah," I said, "I'm sure he could just as easily be bored somewhere else." The first sergeant immediately said, "Mitch, I'm too short to worry about it." He added, "I'll be heading home in a few weeks and I want to make sure everything is squared away for my replacement."

I quickly said, "Top, please tell me that he's not going to be your replacement."

"No, no, no," he said. "He's headed for the 183rd. He'll be gone in a few days."

I decided to drop the subject. Like top said, I would just have to deal with it. Top was on his short-timers calendar. In fact, most days." Top wasn't even in his office. An added reason for joy when his rotation date rolls around was the fact that he also was retiring from the army. It was mostly Captain Tracy and I. Captain Tracy was a cool dude, and I really liked him. He was a good commanding officer. However, on his desk he had a human skull he said he got from a Montanyard Tribesman (a group who fought alongside the US). Supposedly, it was the head of an NVA officer. The Yards hated the VC and the NVA. Heck, they hated all Vietnamese. They were more than happy to join forces with us. I pondered the thought of asking Captain Tracy to do something about my pest, but I decided it was best to just drop it. Like Top said, he would be someone else's problem soon enough.

September was half history now. Harold had been dead a year. I got a letter from dad, and the folks were doing fine, plus the summer heat in Louisiana was breaking. Dad said another boy I went to Woodlawn High School with had been killed in Nam. That made four from Woodlawn. I remembered him. He was a quiet guy and very likeable. I wondered if he had a calendar.

The day had come for the pest to leave, and I was happy until I heard about a small hitch. The SOB had gone directly to the battalion sergeant major and made a personnel request to take me with him. I was sitting at my desk, not suspecting a thing, when the E-8 Top Pest strode into my orderly room as if he were on a mission. He broke the news to me and handed me orders transferring me. He gave me five minutes to have my duffle bag stuffed and out front to meet the jeep that would take us to the airfield. I looked at him, and he said, "Orders are orders, Mitch. I personally asked battalion for you, and it was granted." He continued, "The 183rd has a slot for you and it is a damned good unit. Better hustle, don't want to keep the jeep waiting." I knew that Top and I would be parting soon but I hadn't imagined I would be the first to go. He was a Louisiana boy also, and he was from Oakdale, which was located between Fort Polk and Lake Charles.

I headed to my quarters to pack. Duffels don't take long to stuff, especially if the clock is ticking against you. It wasn't like we had a lot of possessions! I slung the bag over my shoulder, grabbed my lid, and headed back out to load into the jeep. There *he* stood like he was Patton or Abrams. (Take your pick—each was an arrogant ass!) Unfortunately for the men of the 183rd, *he* was in Nam. But fortunately *he* had an extremely short short-timer's calendar. The driver popped the clutch, and we were on our way to the airfield. We found an Otter from the Eighteenth Aviation Company waiting for us. We loaded into the plane, stowed are gear, and buckled our lap belts for the flight. We taxied to the runway, and the Qui Nhon tower gave the warrant officer the green light for liftoff. The Otter gained speed, and we rose from the runway. I looked down and thought to myself that I hadn't even had time to say goodbye to my friends. They were all at their duty stations when I was packing. We flew over the Sixty-seventh Evac, and my thoughts were on my brothers below. I know they would care for each other. That was one of the few constants a troop could depend upon, his brothers.

Our destination was Don Ba Thin Army Airfield. It straddled National Highway One, better known as The Street without Joy. Dong Ba Thin also sat directly across the inner bay of Cam Rahn Bay, and the Sixth Convalescent Center was directly across the water from the 183rd. Our pilot received his landing instructions from the DBT tower, and he swung around to make our approach. The Otter sat down, and we taxied to the 183rd revetments. Troops in the aircraft maintenance facility were too busy to notice the arrivals. They were quite accustomed to troops and planes coming and going. Myself and *It*—yeah I renamed him—walked into the orderly room and we are warmly greeted. The outgoing top was quite delighted to welcome his replacement. Pleasantries were exchanged among us all. I met the company clerk with whom I would be working. His name was Terry. Terry seemed like a swell guy. He was from Nashville, Tennessee, and he told me that most of the guys in the company were Southerners, and that I would feel right at home. This was a big difference from the welcome I had received at Phu Hiep! The unit had a fine mess hall; in fact, it was the best in battalion. Terry took me to the hootch where each troop had his own private quarters. Terry and I would be neighbors, and he liked Jack Daniels as much as I did. I was given the rest of the day off to get squared away. As always, it was a trip to supply for linens, towels, and a pillow, followed by a trip to the arms room for my weapon. I was issued an M14 with four magazines of ammo and a fragmentation vest along with web gear and a helmet. I took all the stuff back to my quarters. Noon chow rolled around, and I fell in line with the others. I was warmly received, but it was just more names and faces. That was one thing about the army; there were lots of names and faces. Time and years rob the memory of most of the names and faces, but there would always be one thing a soldier will never forget – RA15634732 – his serial number. Just ask one!

Locating the latrine was a simple process. I could either follow my nose or observe where the mamasons hung our washed BDUs to dry. The concertina wire was a great place to hang clothes in DBT, just as it had been in Nha Trang or any other place in Nam. Trust me that scent in your freshly washed BDUs wasn't Tide Ultra Spring! A short recon of the company grounds quickly revealed the community latrine and the clothesline. Some things were just a constant! I opened the door of the latrine and selected a seat. This one had six holes and I could sit anywhere I wanted. I chose the middle. There was plenty of elbowroom and I could see left, right, and straight ahead I was sitting there tending to my business when I suddenly heard some indistinguishable chatter. The voices drew closer, and from between the hootches appeared five mamasons. Each had on her conical rice straw hat, pastel silk or cotton shirt with black or white silk pajama bottoms and flip-flop sandals. They were all jabbering at the same time. I didn't know how one could discern the words of the other. They were obviously in good spirits. I noticed that as they talked, they seemed to be walking in my direction and getting closer with each step. I was sitting there thinking, No, they aren't coming in here, are they? I repeated that thought a couple of more times when the screen door swung open and in they all entered. Three of them to my left and two were to my right. The jabbering never ceased but they did manage a smile and a "Hi, GI." They all climbed up on the bench, dropped their PJs and lowered their ass's right down into the remaining five holes. They squirted, they spewed, and they farted, all the while never missing a word. They quickly stood up, pulled up their pants, and out the door they went. Just that quick! I don't know what they had eaten but the flies were swarming around those honey buckets. I decided it was time for me to didi mau, and I did it in quick time. That screen door didn't catch me on the way out, I can promise you that!

September was gone, and I had grown accustomed to the new routine. Being a company clerk in one company wasn't much different from doing it somewhere else. The job was enjoyable, and there were always plenty of troops in and out needing our services. We had a mail clerk who would bop in twice a day. He was a communication specialist and spent his days in the commo shack. The commo shack was easy to find. All you had to do was locate an olive drab conex trailer with antennas galore festooning it. It was also the only duty post that required air conditioning that was maintained at fifty degrees. There was so much electronic gear in there: radios, teletype machines, and other commo equipment. I can't name it all, but it had to stay cool. Maybe that was why the communication/mail clerk talked so fast. He was trying to thaw out. His name was 'Short Round' aka Allen Cherin from Des Plains, Illinois. He was the only twenty-six-year-old draftee I had ever met. One of the unforgettable, 'Short Round' never had a bad day. He would fuss about stuff but never to the bad-day level. He was smart as a whip, had a great wit, a quick laugh, a very keen memory, and he loved everybody. He has kept these great attributes until this day. Al was a classic — our classic.

When his birthday arrived on October 8, two sergeants decided it was time for Al to experience the intimacy of a woman. A three-quarter-ton truck was drawn from our motor pool, and three 183rd Seahorses went on a mission; One jabbering ninety to nothing, and the other two laughing their asses off. The truck pulled into a nearby village and parked in the rear of a bar out of sight of MPs and anyone else that may have been prone to ruining a good time. Into the bar they went, and there was mamason and her barmaids — uh, professional purveyors of flesh. The treat was on the two sergeants, and mamason was only too happy to provide her finest employee for the occasion. A five-dollar MPC (military payment certificate) was handed to Allen, and he and his lady in waiting passed through the beaded curtain and disappeared.

The party was on, and the two gifters were celebrating with glee. Mamason couldn't keep those cans punched fast enough. Oh, they were having a great time, with laughter filling the place. All of a sudden, the beaded curtain rustled and out stepped Allen. He returned with three dollars in change, which he handed over and then he quickly turned and disappeared behind the beaded curtain, again. The NCOs were absolutely falling off their stools with laughter, and thanks to Al, they had three dollars more to spend on beer. Isn't that right, Short Round!

Top Sergeant It didn't waste any time before he showed his colors — his ignorance and disrespect for the enlisted men. Terry had left the orderly room for some reason and it was just me, Top, and the CO. Top stood in the commanding officer's doorway for most of the time, brownnosing. It was a pathetic sight. I have never had tolerance for ass-kissers, but this was above my pay grade and out of my control. Oh yeah, the CO ate it up. On this particular time Top felt he had the major where he wanted him, and this was what was said. "Major, I've been taking notes and have done a lot of observation of the company. I think we need to make some changes with respect to our weapon safety around here." The major had been listening and asked Top what he proposed be done. Top answered, "Sir, we don't have men here. What we have is a bunch of boys with guns and ammo. They keep the guns and ammo in their quarters, twenty-four hours a day, and I think that needs to be changed before someone gets hurt." Top's voice became firm. "I have given this a lot of thought, and it is my opinion that all weapons be surrendered to our arms room where they can be secured, and all the magazines of ammo should be placed in padlocked footlockers kept in the orderly room. This company has never been assaulted and never will be. In the case of an emergency, we have NCOs and officers we can depend on as a first line of defense. The guards on duty can hold the line while the enlisted to draw weapons from the arms room and run over here to get the ammo. The sergeant of the guard will have the keys and be able to issue ammo." The major sat for a few minutes, thinking over what Top had just said to him, and finally said to the Top, "Carry out your plan." That afternoon we were called to a company formation and everyone was told to turn in their weapons and ammo.

The stage was now set, and Charlie would find out about it the next day. He planned his attack, set the date and time. He knew he had plenty of time; Charlie valued the virtue of patience, which was an Asian tradition. The order didn't sit well with any of the enlisted men. Nobody was happy, but there was nothing to be done.

However, several of us had knives, and one man, a cook named Dale Jurney, had a WWII M3 grease gun, a .45 caliber with about three hundred lose rounds of ammo, and one stick magazine. We were subject to surprise searches of our quarters where they looked for so-called contraband. But we were able to find ways to hide our stuff, and it was a rare day when any contraband was confiscated. My contraband was a bottle of Jack Daniels and a fixed-blade knife. Since my room had no door on it when I arrived at the 183rd, I constructed a sliding door so that I would have some privacy. When the door was closed, my knife and bottle sat on a two-by-four nailed between the wall studs. It was in plain sight but only from the inside. When the NCOs came through for a search, they would find the sliding door closed, and after they fumbled around some, they realized the door would slide. However, when the door slid open, it conveniently hid my stash. At night when I was in the room, I kept the door closed for three reasons: One reason was the aforementioned privacy. Another was to keep my contraband hidden from prying eyes. And, lastly, remembering what had happened at the Sixth CC, it would keep Charlie from tossing a bundle of explosives in on me. How Dale was able to successfully hide that grease gun I will never know. Dale died of cancer several years ago. I often wondered which troop acquired that weapon later.

October passed quietly and everything was routine. Pilots were constantly in and out, and once every month there was a commander's call. This required all available pilots to fly in from outlining platoons. The unit had flight platoons in Nha Trang, Phan Rang, Phan Thiet and, I believe, Da Lat and Ban Me Thout. With all the brass present for commander's call, we all stayed pretty busy. I was never privy to the info coming from commander's call, but I understand that for the most part, it was standard stuff. Questions like, Are you getting your supplies? How is your aircraft maintenance section performing? What was your percentage of downtime with repairs? What types of missions did they fly? Were any areas showing signs of enemy activity? There was more, but I think that covered the basics.

On numerous occasions the guard detail would notice that our claymore mines had been turned toward our company area instead of pointing toward the perimeter. The claymore was an anti-personnel mine that had two scissor legs on each end. The plastic case, which held the C-4 explosive and ball bearing shot, was curved. The front of the mine was the outer curve. Finally, we decided to fill ammo cases with cement and stab the scissor legs into the wet cement and stand them on their end. That ended the turning of the mines.

Another daily routine, before climbing into the guard tower, was to walk along the concertina wire searching for areas where the wire had been cut. Generally, that was where the wire met the ground. Charlie would slip in and cut the wire prior to an attack. They would camouflage the cut with soil, mud, grass, or weeds. We would look for areas where the grass or weeds looked like they had been laid onto the wire. We were always looking for the minute signs that foretold trouble.

November arrived and throughout Southeast Asia the North Vietnamese Army showed no sign of slackening their efforts. Body counts were on the rise on all sides. Morale was slipping among American troops, and protestors still marched the streets of America. Contrails of white striped the sky from horizon to horizon. They had no pattern and reminded me of my days as a child, in Texas, when I played pick-up sticks.

This was a long way from Tyler, Texas, and I wasn't a child anymore. Each morning black towers of smoke would rise to foul the air. Not even the breeze from the bay could suppress it. Burnie, a Vietnamese worker, used a metal rod with a hook on one end to drag the honey pots from the latrines. He would douse them with diesel fuel before he set them ablaze. Another chimney was born, and the blackened, foul column arose to join the others. This country literally stunk. We kept an eye on Burnie. We kept him around because we knew what we had. If we got rid of him we wouldn't know what we would get. Burnie was old but probably not as old as he appeared. However, he had been around for a long time. He had fought against the Japanese in WWII and with the Viet Minh when the Indo China War was raging against the French. He always acted like he didn't understand us, but we knew he could. Even Jessie, our mongrel dog, didn't like him. That should tell you something! But Burnie unknowingly had a way of forecasting trouble. Every once in a while, he would come into the orderly room and ask for some time off. He said he had a cousin who lived in the coastal town of Phan Rang. He was always given the green light to di-di (take off). We all would become more vigilant when this happened. We knew Charlie would be up to something. I wondered if he had gone to Phan Rang the night Charlie visited us at the Sixth CC, while we were in our blue pajamas. After all, it was right across the water.

Our Seahorse brother Bill Keener, from Tennessee, was sergeant of the guard two weeks after the first attack on our haven of healing, the Sixth CC. The guards on duty that night noticed small boats in the bay slowly moving towards the convalescent center. Bill climbed into the tower and watched the boats with binoculars. He was convinced it was the enemy, attempting to slip in again for another shot at our brothers in blue pajamas. Bill ran to the orderly room and informed the officer of the guard and then contacted base security at Cam Rahn Bay. They told him that they were friendlies. However, Bill had a feeling and repeatedly did his best to alert Cam Rahn Bay, but each time he was told they were friendlies. Soon, mortar rounds were launched onto the hospital grounds from the boats. When base security still insisted they were friendlies, our brother from Tennessee screamed into the phone, "Does that look like friendlies, now?" He did the best any soldier could do. I had left the Sixth CC before the second attack, and I never knew about it until Bill told me.

A few of us had noticed that our dog Jessie had been acting strange. She kept barking and pacing up and down the perimeter road. Back and forth she would go, just yammering away. Someone said that we ought to give her a beer before she lost her voice. GIs have a way of finding humor in most situations. It may have been sick humor, but it garnered a laugh or two. We all needed that. It was November 30, and another month could be crossed off someone's calendar, but not mine. I still had four days and a wake-up before I could create my short-timers calendar. My tour, 365 days, was almost half over.

A tall NCO from California, who was on TDY (temporary duty), was the sergeant of the guard that night. Most of us didn't know him because he had been there only a few days. He posted the guard detail, and Jessie calmed down a little bit, but she still didn't like something. The rest of us hung out at the enlisted men's club. Only Seahorse enlisted men were allowed in the club, but there was one exception. He was a South Korean officer who was a Bird Dog pilot. The ROKs had a reputation of being mean as hell, and none of us let him buy a beer! On days he was scheduled to fly, he would arrive in a shiny jeep. The jeep had the regular issue canvas canopy, plus something extra. It sported golden tassels all the way around! His driver was required to stay with the jeep until the officer returned from his completed mission. The driver spent the day mothering that jeep. When the pilot got back from his flight, he would inspect the jeep, and then off they would go, golden tassels and all.

That night we broke off one by one and headed to our quarters. It was getting late, and Jessie could probably still use a beer. I slid the door shut, cut the light, and soon fell asleep.

The first explosion shook me out of my sleep, and when the second one went off, I rolled off the rack onto the floor with my mattress on top of me. My first thought was mortars, but my inner voice ordered me to get up and get out. I suddenly realized what was happening. A shot rang out, and I threw my fatigues on as fast as I could. I hollered for my brothers to get out. It was sappers, and they wanted our Bird Dogs. A burst of AK-47 fire raked the top of the guard tower. More explosions followed, but we were all jammed against the window of the arms room, retrieving our M14s as fast as the clerk could hand them out. Then we found ourselves sprinting the hundred yards to the orderly room for ammo. As we were running, a big explosion erupted as an RPG round ripped into the officer/NCO latrine and shower house. Another explosion and the house trailer where the CO and XO lived was cut in half. I was worried about the gook with the AK-47. We made it to the orderly room only to find the footlockers still locked. Someone located an axe and chopped the footlockers open. By this time, I noticed some more small arms fire had erupted from behind the officer's latrine, which was now a pile of splinters. I grabbed my ammo and ran as fast as I could to that area.

I leaped into the drainage ditch that ran alongside the road, for cover. I had to figure out where I was needed the most. All of the men of Seahorse were on the move. The sirens came to life; mortar flares from across the road popped overhead. They burst above us and the flares drifted overhead, hanging from their chutes. Their luminescence spilled an eerie green light that danced to and fro on its descent to earth. Another popped, and another, and another. They were popping all over the place, and more could be heard as they exited the tubes. Heat from the dying flares ignited the grass, and fires spread through the camp. Everything was a sickish green color, but I was thankful for the light. For the first time, I was able to fight. Suddenly, I caught a glimpse of an object—not just one but five objects, only feet away from my face. My mind raced as I tried to understand my situation. Common sense told me they were hunks of baked shit from the blasted latrine behind me. I looked again, and in the light of a flare I saw exactly what they were. It was a bundle of C4 and chi-com grenades. I dropped back into the bottom of the ditch and crawled inside my steel pot as deep as I could get and then went in deeper. I waited for the explosions that I knew would suck the air out of my body and heave me upward. The gook was trying to roll that shit into the ditch with me. I told myself that I was not going to lay there and die like that, not in a ditch. I leaped up and charged across the road, determined to fight my ass off and kill those bastards.

I wheeled left and right, but no one was there but me. Where was he? Where was he? I shouted, but there was nothing. I was alone. I collected my thoughts and I heard more rifle fire from in front of the orderly room. I sprinted in that direction ran past the orderly room, and dropped into another drainage ditch. This time I had company. I found my friend Terry in the ditch. More flares were popping open in the sky over us lighting up the area. I saw a figure running and both Terry and I fired at it. The sky darkened, and it grew quiet with the only light coming from the burning grass fires scattered inside and outside the wire. Pilots began moving among us, checking on us and then moving on. We held our fire, caught our breath, and took stock of the situation.

I thought that the CO and the XO were goners because I saw their quarters ripped apart by a ball of flame. We had some NCOs missing, and the troops in the guard bunker had taken a beating. I was sure they were casualties. The sirens continued to wail from all points on the compass. I heard someone say that it was past midnight. A captain from Washington state began to regroup us, and he was calling for volunteers. He needed seven men to form a team and sweep the company area. It was a job that had to be done, and I was fired up and ready. I yelled at him and joined the forming group. The only other volunteer I can remember was my buddy Jim Benoit.

The captain gave his orders: We were to work our way through, around, and under every building regardless of what it was. Each individual sleeping quarter was to be kicked in and searched. Nothing was to be left unsearched. After the search of the company area was finished, we were to proceed to the revetments, check to make sure the planes were intact, and make sure Charlie wasn't hiding in them. Then the motor pool and vehicles had to be checked before we moved on to the perimeter. At first light, we were to repeat the search. All of us were wired, but we were determined. It was nerve-racking work because most of the time we were probing and feeling our way in the dark. We didn't have any night vision goggles so everything was black. We were ready to shoot, beat, or club any gook we found to death. Someone found some flashlights and brought them to us. They gave little comfort because they made us easier targets, but I was willing and I took the chance.

I never liked playing boogieman back home in Texas a child's imagination could run wild with him and so can an adult's. This was real, and the boogieman was near. But all the buildings were clear; so were the motor pool and vehicles. Now, we were moving towards the revetments. Here the flashlights gave us our greatest comfort. If Charlie was in our revetments, he was trapped. There was only one way out, and that was through us. Slowly, we swept the paved revetment pads with our lights. If he was in one, he would be found very quickly unless he crawled into a plane. Soldiers shouted *clear* as each revetment was checked. We got to the last one, and as we moved closer, we heard the sound of shuffling feet. We wheeled around the corner, and there was our cook, Dale, with his M3 and a sack of ammo. We all breathed a huge sigh of relief. For a short moment and no more we relaxed our muscles and breathed. Seahorse was secured, and our brothers were on the first line of defense. Those "irresponsible boys" had saved Seahorse's ass!

Jim and I and our five Brothers moved out, abreast, through the perimeter. Blood trails were plentiful, but it was hard to count how many Charlie's had been hit. The trails intermingled and all led to the wire. Charlie had infiltrated through several cuts in the wire and exited the same way. We began finding stuff Charlie had left behind and policed it up. I stepped on what felt like a stick, and I flashed the light down at my feet. I was standing on a bamboo Bangalore torpedo. Further investigation revealed it contained seventy bars of C4, lashed together with vines. Each bar looked like a small bar of soap. AK-47 magazines and satchel charges were also found as well as grenades and more C4. Charlie had snuck in very slowly but left with his tail between his legs. Jessie was still charged up, running between the company road and the perimeter. She sniffed the blood trails but refused to go through the wire.

When dawn broke on December 1, 1969, visitors had arrived from battalion, and in the faint gray light I recognized two of them. They were the battalion sergeant major and the battalion commanding officer, accompanied by the battalion S2. They sure hadn't wasted much time getting here. I kept my distance, but there was much I wanted to tell them. I was sure that the truth would surface once the after-action report was read and questions began to be raised.

Now that we had daylight, another sweep of the company was launched. Evidently our sweep team did a very good job in the dark. Nothing else was found. We all, at one time or another, walked through the perimeter. The blood trails were more detailed, and we found flesh beside the bunker immediately below the tower. The generator that had produced the light within the perimeter was a wreck.

The guard in the tower had been posted for no more than twenty minutes when he discovered the penetration. The previous guard had retired to the bunker below and had joined the third member of the team for some rest. At about 2330 hours (11:30 p.m.), the tower guard heard the sound of an AK-47 bolt as it slammed a round into the chamber. The guard swung his spotlight to a point, in the darkness where he believed the sound came from and lit it up. The floodlight caught the sapper in full beam. He then rolled over and released a hail of automatic fire into the tower. The tin roof was literally stitched form end to end. The guards in the tower came to life and grabbed the clackers that, when squeezed, would set off the claymores. By this time, more sappers had surrounded the bunker. However, before the guards could crank the clackers and fire the mines, the sappers grabbed the detonation wires and pulled the clackers from their hands. The sappers began hurling C4 charges up to the tower, but they struck the chicken wire around the base of the tower repelled and dropped back onto the sappers and exploded. While the guards below scrambled for their lives, sappers tossed more C4 charges inside the bunker. The force of the detonations hurled the guards out the door. One caught a satchel charge between his shoulders as he was exiting the bunker and slammed into a Charlie and knocked them both senseless. Our tower guard, Spec. 4 Butch Graef, was tossed repeatedly into the air as more charges exploded around him. But the chicken wire had done its job, and Butch was safe.

Butch spotted a Charlie squatting behind the officer and NCO latrine and fired a blast from his rifle that took the gook's right knee off. The gook dropped his explosive charge and crumpled in agony. Butch reached for the M60 machine gun and got off one round before the gun became inoperable. The latrine erupted into a flash of fire and explosives. At this moment, my buddy Jim Benoit was headed for the shower and latrine when the entire thing disintegrated in his face. The concussion slammed Jim into the sand. He was naked except for his towel and sandals, but he was unscathed! Sappers ran past him as he lay in the sand, one even used his prone body as a stepping stone as he and others rushed towards the CO's trailer to set charges. Jim was terrified but determined to get into the fight. He leaped forward and rushed to his quarters to grab what he needed to fight back, including his pants and boots. Another soldier rushed to the arms room and secured another M60 machine gun. He returned to the tower where he and Butch got it set up and released a storm of fire throughout the perimeter. Seahorse was alive and swarming like a mound of fire ants to repel our invaders. We were alive and well and determined to send Charlie to hell or home whichever came first. The collective response of a bunch of boys had secured the night, and now we owned it.

Walking through the area, I went to the ditch where hours before I was climbing inside my helmet. I saw several plastic wrapped packages of C-4 tied with vines and the blasting caps in place, strewn before me on the road across from the ditch. They were the size of large Idaho potatoes and scattered among them were the chi-com grenades. Also, there were pieces of bone and a lot of blood spattered about the scene. This was where the gook was squatting when Butch shot him. Further survey of the area revealed the damage to the NCO hootch. The roof had collapsed from the blast and, while digging through the rubble, we found our three missing NCOs. They were dead, dead drunk. The battalion commander and sergeant major were furious. Quickly, these NCOs, the first line of defense, were hustled off and none of us ever saw the three of them again.

With the new day fully born, we stood in front of the orderly room when an army deuce and a half pulled off the highway. The truck came to a stop, the tailgate dropped open, and a platoon of CIDG (Civilian Defense Group) troops sprung out of the vehicle. They formed a skirmish line and slowly but methodically worked their way back and forth through the brush. They used the enormous spatters of blood as a guide. They were out there several hours when we noticed a flurry of excitement and heard loud voices shouting in Vietnamese. They had discovered a Charlie cowering in the dense bushes. He was ordered to come out, but the militia didn't wait for him to act. Automatic weapons fire slammed into the hiding place. Two of the troops rushed forward and tied a rope on the prostrate body. Quickly, the two militiamen clutching the rope began running towards the platoon's location and ripped the body from its last repose. More troops from the platoon rushed forward to search the area more thoroughly. It was clear of any more enemy soldiers. The militiamen dragged the body to the highway, where it was left to send a message. Several of us asked for and received permission to take a three-quarter ton truck, and we drove to the highway to look at the dead sapper. In the left side of his chest were three precisely spaced bullet wounds. He was nude from head to toe and his skin was darkened with charcoal.

Further examination revealed a surprise. We recognized this sapper! He was the South Vietnamese pilot that had been training in the back seat of our Bird Dogs. Our enemy walks with us, or in this case, had walked with us. I felt anger in my chest, and I had no compassion for the corpse before me. I wanted to punish him, desecrate him. I wanted satisfaction. But the best I could do was to locate a stick and shove it up his ass, as if it was a flag. It made me feel better then and it still does. Up your ass, Charlie!

The following day, suspicions arose that the sweep, conducted by the CIDG platoon, hadn't been as thorough as it could have been. US Army grunts were trucked in to conduct a follow-up search. The suspicions were quickly proven to be well founded. Nine more bodies from the sapper squad were pulled from the weeds and brush of the battlefield. Just a few miles away, three months ago, my sleeping army brothers had been murdered and many wounded in their hospital beds by a group of sappers. The location of this group indicated they were the same group. The loss and agony suffered by my brothers at the Sixth CC had now been avenged. The lord works in mysterious ways, and he saw fit for me to have the satisfaction of being personally involved in their demise. Never again would this sapper squad be a fighting force in the Cam Rahn/Dong Ba Thin area.

The month of December saw our perimeter guarded around the clock. Approximately one half of our men were on the line at any given time. Everyone was tense, but we had a lot to be proud of. Christmas Eve brought us a Christmas gift from Battalion. The commanding officer, responsible for the November fiasco, was relieved of command. We had a new commanding officer, and he was a keeper. There was no formal change of command ceremony, no passing of the colors. One silently exits stage left, and the other enters stage right. Shortly afterwards, First Sergeant It was gone as well. Later that day, the company was called into a formation. The acting first sergeant called us to attention, did an about face, and saluted the executive officer. The executive officer turned and presented the men of the First Platoon to the new commanding officer, Major Manley. After an exchange of sharp salutes, Major Manley commanded the formation to be at ease. He stood before us and addressed what had transpired in the last few months. He didn't go into detail, but we knew what he was saying. He was proud of us and assured us he was there for us. He announced that at no time would his men be without weapons. His orders were loud and clear. He said, "When this formation is dismissed, each of you will report to the arms room and withdraw your weapons and as much ammo and magazines as you can carry." He quickly added, "You will never be defenseless on my watch. Company dismissed!" I happily obeyed the orders and went to my quarters. I could mark nineteen days off my short timers' calendar!

The closer I got to my DEROS (Date of Estimated Return from Overseas) the slower the days seemed to pass. We had a new president, and he was determined to extract all American troops. Johnson was gone and Richard Nixon was fulfilling his pledge to bring the troops home. Short Round and I were excited because the day was getting closer. December was gone, then January, February, and March passed, and my calendar now sported a lot of X's. It was April 1, 1970 and I received a fantastic surprise. My DEROS had been pushed forward from May 4 to April 8 and Al and I were set to leave together. We were excited. We were going home, and our brothers were happy for us! As the official date drew nearer, we did what all brothers had done before us. The belongings that we couldn't carry with us were passed to our buds, and it only took minutes to stuff the duffel. We said all our goodbyes, shook hands, exchanged man hugs, and headed for our transportation out of the unit. As we left the company area, we didn't want to look back for fear that our tears would be seen.

The returnee station was abuzz with activity and giddy soldiers. We had returned to Cam Rahn, but this time it was our portal to home. All we had to do was sleep one more night and then we would be bused to that great Freedom Bird, that beautiful Flying Tiger Airline that will carry us home. Short Round was beside himself, and his happiness had no bounds. Prior to now, I only had thought he could talk fast.

Once again, we were part of the olive drab mass, and it felt so good, so right, and so long in coming. The sun slipped behind the central highlands, and the coastal plain became cloaked in darkness, but the sun was still shining inside the many barracks, holding the men in olive drab who continued to revel in excitement. Slowly, most of us found a rack to stretch out on. There were no sheets, no blankets, no pillows, just a military mattress and bunk ends. It was 0200 hours (2:00 a.m.) when the earth began trembling, the sirens began to wail, and explosions reverberated from across the bay. We all rushed outside to see what was happening, thinking and praying, "Dear lord, not now, not now. We've come so close!" Allen and I were standing shoulder to shoulder; each had a lump in our throat and a tightness in our gut. The noise was coming from across the bay: Our brothers of the 183rd Reconnaissance Airplane Company were being slammed by Charlie. Short Round went silent.

"Mr. Mitchell, we are trying to help. Tell me, what is it that keeps your anger so bottled up? You are so quick to cry, and you lash out. Tell me about it." Just like all the other sessions. I can't express myself. This tightness in my chest makes me feel like I will burst wide open at any moment. I don't know this person in front of me and I don't trust him. My nightly visitors come into my brain each night, and I toss and kick, trying to break away. Kathy wakes me, and I am sitting up in bed, arms across my chest, rocking back and forth, back and forth. Blood drips from the ceiling. It rises through the floor. It coats the walls. All is red, and my nostrils inhale the smell of pain, suffering, and death, but there is no one there.

TIGERLAND

Mark Mitchell
Sp. 4
US Army
Convalescent leave specialist
Fort Carson, Colorado
April 1970-June 1971

I completed my tour in Vietnam in April 1970. Following my DEROS leave, I reported for CONUS (Continental United States) duty at the Forty-seventh MASH (mobile army surgical hospital) at Fort Carson, Colorado. I was assigned to duty at Fitzsimmons Army Hospital in Denver. My job as a convalescent leave specialist required me to interview patients in order to assess their status in qualifying for such leave. Also, I had to arrange travel pay and the time period of the leave. The vast percentages of these patients were combat-wounded veterans. The fourteen months that I spent in the unit were very rewarding. These were my brothers in arms, and I would go to any length to assist them. A lot of them were anxious about returning home. They weren't the same young men anymore. A great number were amputees, with many of those double and triple amputees. You imagine a combat wound, and I worked with all of them.

In late spring of 1971, a patient came to my desk with his request for convalescence leave. I was absolutely shocked at his appearance, but I made an extreme effort not to show it. Thankfully, for his sake, I was able to assist him with his leave request, and I was able to insure his personal comfort as well.

Having personally been medevaced in Vietnam to the Sixty-seventh Evacuation Field Hospital and later transferred to the Sixth Convalescent Center Hospital in Cam Rahn Bay, I was accustomed to seeing our combat wounded. I had seen raw wounds straight from the battlefield, and I thought I had seen it all. However, before me sat a young soldier that had survived an absolute nightmare, and I was sure it was going to be never ending. His destiny was to be reminded of it every day for the rest of his life. As he sat there, he noted my First Aviation Brigade shoulder patch and my ribbon bars. It seemed to comfort him knowing he was sitting with another Vietnam veteran, and he knew I would take care of his needs. As we worked together, he shared with me his horrendous experience.

He and his squad had set up for a night ambush. Though it was late at night, the air was still hot and humid and filled with the ever-present nuisance of mosquitoes. As he lay in silence, anticipating the enemy, he was silently being stalked and never aware of it. Suddenly, he felt something hot and unusual on the back of his neck. As we all tend to do, he reached back and swatted at his discomfort. Immediately, he was in a fight for his very life! He had just slapped the snout of a Bengal tiger straddling his prone body.

The silence of the night was broken by his screams and the snarls and roars from the cat as it sank its fangs into his skull and ripped at his scalp and face. As he fought to pry the cat's jaws from his head, he forced his right hand into the big cat's mouth. He desperately fought to open the powerful jaws, but it was to no avail. The tiger ripped his thumb and index finger from his hand. He knew he wasn't winning the fight. The huge animal was just too powerful. Everything was happening at lightning speed, yet it seemed to last for hours. When he thought that all was lost, the air filled with sounds of rifle fire. His brothers had immediately rushed to his aid and miraculously they were able to kill the tiger without wounding the animal's meal.

The squad stood and looked at the exhausted soldier, mauled beyond recognition. But he was alive. His head injuries were extremely bloody, as was his hand. His scalp had been ripped from above his left earlobe, across his head, to the right side. Gone was his outer right earlobe and the flesh from his right cheek. Fangs had penetrated the skull but fortunately not the brain. First aid was immediately applied as the tiger was pulled from across his body. His scalp was draped over his skull and tight bandages held it in place. More bandages covered his face and mauled hand.

A dust-off picked him up and transported him to the nearest field evacuation hospital. His surgeries were extensive. His scalp was reattached to his skull but he was minus his right outer earlobe. Plastic surgery had repaired the missing flesh and skin to his face. The small finger, on his right hand, had been surgically amputated and transplanted to where his thumb had been. This would at least allow him to use what was left of the hand.

I have often thought of him over the last forty years. How could one not? Do his grandchildren caress his scars and ask those questions? Has he shared with them his night of horror and the nights he hasn't been able to sleep? Has he shared with them the night he escaped the jaws of death?

During the war, stateside antiwar protesters created a very popular anti-US Army poster. The poster displayed the skeleton of a soldier that had been assembled with metal rods, pins, artificial limbs, hands, feet, leg braces and such. Above the picture were the words, *The Army Builds Men.*

Thank God, it does!

CHAPTER SEVENTEEN

GO DEVIL

William "Bill" C. Shepherd, Sr.
Sergeant
US Army
2/60 4/39, Ninth Infantry Division
1967–1968 and 1968–1970

In 1965, I decided to quit high school. I had been talking to an army recruiter for months when I finally made my choice to enter the United States Army. I enlisted and was sent to Fort Ord, California, for my basic training. Upon graduation from basic, I was sent to Fort Gordon, Georgia, for my advanced individual training (AIT) as a mortar crewman.

After I completed all my training, I was sent to the conflict in Vietnam from 1967–1968. When my first tour ended I was sent back to the United States. I spent three months in CONUS and was sent back to Vietnam in August 1968 for my second tour.

While in Vietnam, I spent the majority of my days traveling through the jungle looking for the enemy. We were fighting two kinds of people. They were the North Vietnamese Army and the Viet Cong guerrillas. Most of the time, they were extremely elusive. They were good at appearing from out of nowhere and disappearing just as quickly. At times, they lived in underground tunnels. They would pop up, engage us, and disappear back into the ground. They also lived in the local villages either by choice or by force. Here they could meld easily into the general population. We didn't know who was who and usually found out the hard way. Their ghostly activity could make things difficult for a soldier tasked to protect and defend, or search and destroy.

During my two tours of duty in Vietnam, I saw people blown up, shot, and dismembered. These sights have remained with me as I tried to return to my life as a citizen in America. Problems and nightmares have plagued me since my return from the war. I have suffered through loss of family and broken relationships and even ended up in the gutter as a drunk.

After Vietnam I was trying to find my way in a country that didn't accept me when I was found by an old girlfriend. We are now married and because of her, my life is on the upswing. She and her cousin managed to get me connected with the Veterans Administration. I now attend several group sessions, and I have been able to make a lot of friends among the other Vietnam veterans at the Center. Between my new friends and the Vet Center, I receive the needed assistance with my problems.

The last thing I want to say is that Uncle Sam gave amnesty to the cowards who dodged the draft. They are now living among us, which causes me to ask two questions: Are these people you want behind you if something happened in our country? How can they live with themselves?

I and other veterans, even as senior citizens in our community, are still ready to defend this great nation of ours at a moment's notice. Freedom is forever, but sometimes you have to fight for it. This short story is how I feel and will always feel.

Bill Shepherd (L) relaxing with a friend at base camp

CHAPTER EIGHTEEN
A STRESSOR LETTER

NOTE: A stressor letter is required from some veterans who have applied to the Veterans Administration for recognition of the service-connected disability called PTSD (Post Traumatic Stress Disorder). The letter describes those incidents that the veteran thinks caused him/her to have PTSD. The following are some of the incidents pulled from his stressor letter filed by the veteran named below.

Jim Corso
Sergeant
US Army
Ordinance Specialist
Attached to Third Battalion
173rd Infantry Division
August 1968–May 1969

I was born and raised in Tracy, California. I was a Cub Scout, a Boy Scout, a Sea Scout, and a Junior Assistant Scout Master. I graduated from high school in 1966 and was drafted in 1968. I had gone to see a recruiter for a candy bar and a Coke. He proceeded to talk me into another year by saying the school would be next to the WAC (Women's Army Corps). Right next to the fence, he emphasized. However, he failed to tell me that it was 150 miles away!

While coming home from Alabama for a short leave before heading for Vietnam, I was on the plane with who I thought were a very nice couple. When we landed in Oakland, California, I was standing outside the terminal when a taxi stopped in front of me. The same couple that was on the plane were inside the taxi. The women stuck her head out the window and yelled, "We hope you die in Vietnam." It was a huge surprise to say the least. What a thing to say to a young soldier whose was going to war!

During my tours in Vietnam, I had four kills, three in combat, and one I will keep to myself. The reason I stayed so long was that I had two brothers in the marine reserves, and as long as I was in Vietnam, they wouldn't be able to send them there. Also, the army gave me five months to fill out my three-year commitment, and I was discharged upon returning home.

This is my statement of what happened during my two years, two months, and six days in Vietnam.

I began my tour in Cam Rahn Bay, in August of 1968, where I spent three weeks on the swing shift as a crewmember on a projectile loading crew.

Cam Rahn Bay Event

Got done with all loading and blocking of trucks about 2:00 a.m., and was kicking back in an old Quonset hut. Someone lit a pipe of marijuana and passed it to me. I had never smoked marijuana before. The guy said, "If you're going to be on this crew, you got to smoke!" Wanting to fit in, I went ahead and started smoking. Later that night, a helicopter gunship was working an area in the mountains, a distance away. I could still see the lines of tracers coming down. After leaving Cam Rahn Bay, I would smoke my whole time in Vietnam. I would only do it at night and then only if I didn't have guard duty or if we wasn't "on alert." It helped me sleep when I had a chance to sleep. I did do it one time when I was in A239 SF camp. A sergeant there offered some to me one night when an airplane, shooting three mini guns, was making its way around the camp. It was Puff the Magic Dragon. I was so scared there that the smoking didn't help.

Ban Loc Event

August 1968. I was sent on TDY (temporary duty) to Ban Loc in Lam Dong Province and assigned to the Third Battalion, 3/503, 173rd Airborne BF for Task Force South Operation in that area and other units under MAV, Team 38. I was one of five men to run the ammunition point for the LSA (logistical support area).

Duties were to run ammo dump, M60 machine gunner for our compound and for convoys. Guard duty every other night at a two-man post if E Troop, Seventeenth Cav., Second Platoon was there, otherwise every night by yourself if they weren't there. Guard duty was three hours on and four shifts. I performed EOD (Explosive Ordinance Disposal) in our area. Also, had to help GR (Graves Registration) at times, built bunks, sprayed defoliate around the perimeter and anything else assigned to do.

I was on a plateau with a small steel airstrip for two-engine planes only. There also were two FAC air controller airplanes there. The compound was to the left of the strip, one hundred yards by 125 yards. There were about thirty LSA personnel, two quad-50 machine guns, and one searchlight jeep from Arty Group, E Troop, Seventeenth Cav., 173rd Airborne, Second Platoon. They had jeeps with M60s; two had .50 calibers, one had a 106, and there were three men to a jeep. I think they had about ten jeeps, off and on, in the compound. All the men in E Troop were grunts on their third six-month extension of their tour of duty. We, in the LSA, all learned to fire all these weapons the Cav had. Every third man in the LSA group, my group, was issued an M60. I was one of their gunners. The guy who taught me to shoot my 60 was a guy named Rusty or Cowboy. I learned his real name twenty-five years later Charles David Braiser. I have pictures of that day. We were friends and would sometimes smoke together, in a bunker at the end of the compound, with the other heads that were there. Rusty was a driver at the time. His T/C was S.Sgt. Mendez. Mendez was a hell of a good trooper in the field, the guys would say, but when he stayed in the compound, he would stay drunk. He had been in Vietnam since May 1967. One night we got a movie projector and were watching a movie. I had to go to the p-tube and when I got back, Mendez was in my chair. I asked him nicely, a few times, if I could have my chair back. He got up and left. A little later and I had to go to the tube again. I was walking between the hootches when suddenly Mendez grabbed me and put his knife to my throat. He said, "I don't need any of your FNG (fucking new guy) shit. I already knew he was a stone killer and nuts. After I pissed my pants, I talked him out of killing me.

Mendez would sometimes get a hand grenade, say he was going to do himself, and go over the berm that was around our perimeter. Guys would go talk to him, but after a while they said the hell with it, and if he wanted to, let him waste himself. On July 14, 1969, drunken Mendez grabs a white-phosphorous grenade and goes over the berm. He comes back later and goes in the hootch, sits on Rusty's cot because Rusty is his driver, and starts talking to him. Mendez drops the grenade. Nobody knew that he had pulled the pin. I don't know if he knew. When I heard it go off, I ran to the sound. At first, I heard a lot of screaming, but as I got closer, I could hear the name *Cherie, Cherie!* Over and over and I knew it was Rusty because that was his girlfriend's name. When I got to the hootch, Rusty and Mendez were laid outside. Guys were getting water and towels to stop the phosphorous burning on them. Some of the guys had it on them, also. Rusty and Mendez were really messed up. Their bodies were burned, smoking, and bleeding all over. Rusty kept screaming *Cherie*. After seeing Rusty, I turned around and walked away. I knew he was a dead man. Rusty and Mendez died later that night. I cried to myself all night. Rusty was a good friend, any time I hear the name Cherie, I think of this event and get tears in my eyes. I still have nightmares about this. Rusty and Mendez were the two who took me to the evacuation hospital when I got shrapnel while blowing up an enemy cache of mortar rockets. That was my fault because I didn't test my fuse (test the burn speed) before I set them up. Luckily, I just got one piece of shrapnel in my right elbow and a small one in my back. Also, for two days, all I could hear was ringing in my ears.

On the morning of April 7, 1969, a guy I knew as Red, one of three Graves Registration (GR) guys for the LSA, asked me and my partner, Red Downs, for help because the other two had escorted bodies back to Cam Rahn Bay. A short platoon of the Third Battalion of the 173rd had been overrun and had eleven KIA, and Red from GR needed our help. We got in a duce-and-a-half truck and headed for the chopper pad. When the body bags got there, we loaded them into the truck and took them to our compound. Now, the small refrigerator unit never worked and should only hold six bodies. Graves Registration usually would get a plane out loaded with the bodies so they wouldn't have to use the refrigerator. We unloaded the bodies from the truck onto the ground and learned there would be no plane that day. The first six bodies weren't too bad. But one of us would have to pull the other five back into the unit and stack them. The three of us drew straws to decide who would do it. I lost! I got the short one. To get the last three bodies in, I had to lie on top of the other bodies. Lying across them, I felt the slickness of the bags, the shapes of the bodies. I could smell all the shit, piss and death. When the eleventh body wouldn't fit, we put it on top of the unit. To get out I had to crawl over number ten, and I couldn't get out fast enough. Beer time, and I didn't care what time it was.

Red and I had just finished our warm beers when GR Red came into our hootch. Not wanting to look at us he said, "I got to take the bags out and Take their personal things." He thought the 173rd had already done this. I first went to the back of the bunker and did two pipes of dew and then joined the others to pull the bags out onto the ground. When GR Red unzipped the bag, the guy's left eye was gone and the back of his head had been blown apart. Parts of his brain were lying mixed with blood. GR Red went through his pockets. The second bag revealed a guy's face that was just red and white pulp. I said, "I can't hang with this," and so did Red D. We told GR Red that when he got done, we would help put them back in. When the time came around for the bodies to be put back in the unit, I told them both, since I had already done it, that I would go back in and pull the bodies. By then it was almost noon and hotter than hell. The first time I had gone in the unit, I ended up soaked in sweat. My shirt and pants were completely wet. This time in the unit was no better. I was soaked wet again. I was breathing hard and my heart was pounding. We asked GR Red how they had died. He told us that all of them had superficial wounds, but then they all were executed. Five had been shot in the left eye, five were shot behind the left ear, and one had looked like he was beaten in the face with a gun butt (no face, bag number 2).

After two days, I finally went to sleep. All I could feel were those bodies on my body all the time, day and night. I only slept a little while because of a nightmare I was having about what had just transpired. The nightmare starts with me on a pile of body bags, and it was hot, hot, hot. I am screaming, *Open up! Open up!* There is the stink of death in the heat. I finally get to the door and start pounding, and then my chest blows up. That's when I wake up with cold sweats all over my body. My heart is pounding and for a moment I am disoriented. I've had this nightmare for the last thirty-two years. I had it quite often in Vietnam and after I got home. Through the years, I can only say that I have had it between five times a week and once every few months. It comes and goes. I guess I don't yell out because nobody says I do. A few soldiers and or wives do say I jump up in a cold sweat and look around. I found those eleven soldier's names twenty-five years later.

Cam Rahn Bay Event

During July 1969–August 1969, I was on a thirty-day extension of leave. I was sent as a machine gunner on the JP-4 gas convoy to Gia Nghia. I was then dropped off for TDY in Ban Me Thout. I worked in LSA ammo dump. Again, I performed EOD work for the sergeant of the guard for LSA perimeter one to three times a week.

I was back in Cam Rahn Bay on a thirty-day extension leave. I reported to my new unit when I found it. I was transferred again in thirty days. The first sergeant asked me if I could handle an M60. Being on TDY and going back to it was part of the agreement for my six-month extension. I said, "Yes," and he answered, "Good," with a smile on his face. That evening, a runner came and got me, saying, "The first sergeant wants to see you at the CP." When I arrived at the CP, I was informed that they were sending me TDY to Ban Me Thout, but first they wanted me to machine gun for a convoy that was going to hook up with a convoy in Ban Me Thout. I could drop off my personal stuff and then continue on to a place called Gia Nghia to drop off the cargo. I would then return to Ban Me Thout, leave the M60 in the truck, and start my TDY duty. I said, "Fine."

I woke up early the next morning and went down to check out an M60, which I didn't get to test fire (that pissed me off) and one case of ammo. The runner then took me to a deuce-and-a-half truck, and I was introduced to its FNG driver. The driver was told to take it to the fuel dump. I was thinking to fuel up the truck, but when we arrived there were sixteen or eighteen trucks, and all of them had M60s with them. This seemed strange to me. As we were sitting there, I started to grab some sandbags that were around the office and began throwing them on the floor of the cab. The FNG driver asked what I was doing and I told him that they might save my ass if we hit a mine. Then we all went into the dump and loaded five-hundred-gallon bladders of JP-4 (jet and helio fuel) on the back of the trucks. I looked down at the sandbags and thought these sandbags won't save shit if we hit a mine. Never before had I seen a convoy hauling JP-4. By now, I was upset. We made Ban Me Thout before dark, and we parked outside the LSA. I dropped my stuff off at the ammo point and spent the night.

The next morning we hooked up with the other convoy. It was an RVN Army convoy. Things just kept getting better all the time. They were carrying ammo and re-supply items like most convoys except they were on five-ton trucks. We followed them out of town and hauled down a paved road for a good hour before we turned off onto a side road, or I should say, a little dirt trail. We climbed up a mountain and then started down the other side into the valleys. We went through some bamboo tunnels, some as long as a quarter mile. Coming out of one of these tunnels there was a big curve. Jungle was all around us. There was an explosion, and I saw a black cloud rising up from around the curve. I jumped out of the truck and headed up a hill. The FNG was just looking. I wanted to get as far away from those trucks as I could. While running up the hill, I realized that there was no small arms fire, only that one blast. This wasn't an attack, or was it? I squatted and waited. An American medevac chopper arrived along with some gunships and lifted out the wounded. I walked back to the truck and then on down the road to see what was up. About five trucks up from the RVN end of the convoy was a truck bent double. It was the one that was hit by the mine. The enemy were down in the bush picking out which truck to blow up. Just great! We managed to get the truck off to the side of the road so we could pass. It took about an hour. The truck was burned as soon as we passed. Not long after we started going and they did it again. Another RVN truck in the middle of the convoy was picked out. It didn't make any sense to me. They usually blew up the first and last truck, and then they tore up the middle. At least that's what I'd been told. After this second attack, the gunships stayed around until we got to Gia Nghia. We arrived about two hours before dark.

Upon arrival, a second lieutenant told us to follow his jeep. We went up this steel airstrip, just like the one in Bao Loc. We went down the right side of this great big sandbagged bladder. The trucks would back up, un-strap the bladders, push the blocks away, and roll them off to the side of this big one. We had to stop, once, when a Caribou airplane landed and taxied up to us and let their tailgate down. Inside was this big bladder. They hooked up a hose and connected it to a pump. There was a colored soldier there, who was running the pump, and I asked him, "Hey brother, how often do they run a convoy up here with JP-4?" He said that they never do and that we were the first. I can't tell you how I felt. I was violated, abandoned, used, and pissed off, all at one time. I then found the first lieutenant (an FNG also) and started asking him questions. Why all this? What was the reason for risking all our lives? This is what he said: "The general said to get this convoy together. Each unit in Cam Rahn had to put up one truck and an M60 gunner. The JP-4 was the only thing Cam Rahn was supplying." He then added, "We're real lucky. They were expecting more action. In fact, there was a pool going on at the Cam Rahn Officer's Club on how many trucks would make it back." When he was finished, I asked when we were leaving and the reply was, "In the morning." It seems the team there didn't want to feed us all. However, the RVNs would be there for the next few days while they completed their resupply. I found some cardboard, laid it out in the back of the truck, and rolled up in my poncho liner. I finally fell to sleep, but the body bag nightmare came again and woke me up soon after. I just lay there until daybreak.

The lieutenants were trying to figure out how to clear the road of mines so we could go. I told them how we did it at Lan Dong. I said, "Let the dink busses go through, getting a head start, and we would follow in their tracks. Never hit any mines that way." But then again, at Lan Dong, we didn't have Charlie sitting in the bush pushing the button, either. Plus the RVN convoy wouldn't be leaving with us. We went down to the main road and waited for the buses. We let two go by, and the team sent two men to stop any more busses from passing until we left. Also, we let the two busses that had passed travel some distance before we started so we could drive fairly fast. We were near the front of the convoy; I believe the fourth or fifth truck. I was standing in the back of the truck when I noticed I was the only one doing this. The rest of the group had their guns pointing out through the front windows of the cabs. As we were traveling down the road, I suddenly heard a couple of gunshots. I looked out in the valley and saw a black figure in a grove of trees pointing a rifle at us. I said, "Hah!" I turned my M60 on the area and started to shoot. Then the FNG driver hit the brakes. I was flying all over the back when he stuck his head out the window and asked me what I was shooting at.I yelled, "Go,go,go!" I jumped back up, but I couldn't see the guy anymore. When we got to Ban Me Thout, I threw the M60 into the cab in disgust. As the driver started to say something, I flipped him the bird and walked away.

Ban Me Thout Event

November 1969. I was sent from Ban Me Thout, by convoy, to Special Forces A Camp 239 in Duc Lap for three weeks. Duties: Set up re-arming point for helicopters working in the area. I became a rigger for incoming and outgoing loads by helicopter. Aided with re-arming helicopters, helped fire 81-mm mortar in daytime, manned 50-caliber machine gun at night.

It was the end of October or the beginning of November, and we were humping the ammo day and night for some action that was going on up by the Cambodian border. A fire support base, Fire Base Kate, and a Special Forces camp, Camp Bu Prang, were fighting for their lives. The LSA colonel (Leaf) drove up to the dump. He said that the SFB (Special Forces base) next to the LSA and airstrip wanted to send an ammo person to one of their A Camps near the action. The person would build a re-arming point for the helicopters in the area. They wanted an officer. There was a lieutenant from Cam Rahn Bay who had come down to make sure the dump was running good because the new battalion commander was coming in November to inspect the place. The colonel asked him about going to the A Camp, but the lieutenant answered, "No!" His orders were for the ammo dump only. Then S.Sgt. Allen and the NCOIC were asked, but they also said they had to run the dump. Then they made me a hard stripe (Sgt.) instead of a specialist. With that, I was the chosen one. The colonel told me that I would only be there for three days, and that he would send a replacement. The best news of all was that I would be going by artillery convoy.

I got up in the morning, packed my basic load for my M16, some C-rations, my poncho liner, towel, and water. I got a ride to the artillery unit located at the end of the airstrip. I found the trucks lined up with 155 projectiles and pounder tubes, pallets of C-rations, and other stuff. I reported to the second lieutenant, and says, "Good, put your gear in the rear jeep. You can man the machine gun." I answered, "Yes sir," and turned away shaking my head.

The convoy traveled down the same paved road I took to get to Gia Nghia, only this time I was sitting in the back of the last jeep, with a mounted M60. We passed Gia Nghia and turned off the main road and kept going. We finally turned onto a dirt road and started climbing the hills. They had given me a pair of clear goggles to wear, plus I wrapped a towel around my nose and mouth. The dust was just terrible. Trying to get out of the dust, the lieutenant driver and his lieutenant passenger decided to drive as far to the right as they could get. Well, he gets the jeep stuck in a rut, and the vehicle bottoms out. I was sent flying over the M60, over the front of the jeep, where I landed in the road. I was skinned up a little. Someone came running up and I began cussing him out when I suddenly realized it was the lieutenant. I was only a sergeant, and he told me that I couldn't talk to him that way. I quickly said, "We best get going before we lose the convoy." As the jeep began catching up to the convoy, I was telling myself that this would be the last convoy I would travel on. I vowed *never* go on another convoy even if it meant I would go to LBJ (Long Bin Jail).

We went over a ridge and entered into a valley. Before us, about the middle of the valley, were two big mountains that looked like a set of breasts, with the road running between them. There was a small steel airstrip at the base of these mountains where a helicopter pad area was located. The convoy passed through the front gate and the trucks turned to the left. The jeep stopped and let me off and I went to the right to the A Camp. As I was coming up the road, I noticed a searchlight jeep on the artillery side. The cover on the light said Sunshine Superman. I knew I was at Boa Loc. The soldier who ran the jeep was called Sunshine by everyone. That evening, I walked over to the jeep and saw that it was all shot up, holes everywhere. I walked over to the artillery unit's CP and asked, "What happened to the guy that was with the jeep." I was informed that he had been killed, along with the lieutenant and first sergeant, the day before. To make sure it was Sunshine, I described what he looked like, that he was from Michigan, and had a young daughter. The S.Sgt. assured me it was Sunshine. He added, "He was killed in a mortar attack by a small piece of shrapnel, the size of your little finger, went between his flak vest and helmet, into his head. Poor Sunshine, he had a pretty wife and kid to go home to. I never knew his real name. I just knew he was the weapons specialist for the team.

The captain told me that higher command wanted a re-arming point set up in order to keep the helicopters in the area longer. I was told there were two loads of 2.75 rockets, which had been dropped by chopper outside the perimeter, and he wanted them brought in before dark. He gave me two trucks and ten yard soldiers. The trucks were located at the bottom of the hill. I jumped in one truck and a colored dude who had been dropped off like I had drove the other one. We drove out onto the same road we came in on and were directed by a yard to turn right. It wasn't too far before we came to the loads. The loads were still in their slings, but some of the boxes had broken open. Two yards were on guard, and the rest of us loaded the rockets onto the trucks. We headed back to the camp and drove up to the team house. Now, I thought that they wanted the rockets in the main ammo bunker; however, there were lots of rockets but not much room in the bunker. I went into the team house and said to the captain, "I got the rockets outside." He looked at me and says, "What?" I repeated what I had said and he immediately starts to yell, "Get them trucks to the bottom of the hill! If the enemy sees them, he will drop mortars on them and blow the hell out of everything, team house and all." I ran back out to the trucks feeling like the biggest jerk in Vietnam. This was real embarrassing to me. I told the colored dude that we had to get the trucks back down to the bottom of the hill. Luckily, there was enough room to get the trucks turned around. We drove off, only this time he was in the first truck and I was in the second one.

After turning around, my truck ended up going down the hill first. The hill was pretty steep, and I was holding the brake pedal down. I kept hearing the beeping of a horn. I looked in the mirror and saw the other truck hauling ass. I had just enough time to move as far right as I could when the truck flew past me, breaking my left mirror and his right mirror. The driver was working the brake pedal for all it was worth. As he was passing, our eyes caught each other's, and you could see the look of terror all over his face. I think anyone would have had the same look if they were hauling ass down a hill with a load of rockets and no brakes. By now, it was getting dark, and they had put the wire up at the front gate. That was what stopped the truck.

We finally got the trucks safely parked. Beer time! I went into the Team House Bar, grabbed a couple, and headed for the artillery hill to see Sunshine. It had been one hell of a day. As I walked, I found I as moving slowly because I was sore all over.

Duc Loc Event

I first met First Lieutenant Schnably (Dutch—what he wanted everyone to call him) during an attack. I had started back to the team house when the attack began so I jumped into a trench that was next to the road. Suddenly, a jeep drives up with a 106 recoilless weapon mounted on it. Dutch was driving, and the big colored guy who I had met earlier was with him. I noticed Dutch didn't even have a helmet on, and the S.Sgt. had a helmet and a flak vest on. I only had a helmet on.

Dutch was going to fire the weapon and the S.Sgt. was going to load. Dutch yells, "FLYSHIT," around the muzzle load." The S.Sgt. turns the time fuse to zero and loads the shell into the gun. I don't know whose fault it was, but the S.Sgt. was standing right behind the 106 when Dutch fired it.

Now, before I went to Vietnam, I had seen a training film on the 106, and when fired the back blast blew a wooden box to pieces. Anyway, this big S.Sgt. is sent flying, head over heels, for about twenty-five to thirty feet. I jumped up and ran to him as he was trying to shake the cobwebs out of his head. I grabbed his vest and got him in the trench. Dutch then yells, "You!" He pointed at me. "Get up and load the gun!" I jump up like I'd been told, grab a round, pull the cardboard protector off it, and put the round in the already open breech. I slammed the breech closed and jumped out of the way. As soon as the breech was closed, Dutch fired the tracer round and then fired the weapon. I opened the breech, grabbed another round, loaded it, closed the breech, and Dutch fired the weapon again. This action was repeated about three more times before the helicopters started showing up.

The enemy had been so close you could hear the mortar rounds coming out of the tubes and see the smoke coming out of the trees that landscaped the valley. Beside the three to four mortars, they had also fired a recoilless gun. As soon as the action ceased, Dutch jumped down off the jeep and looked into the trench, but the S.Sgt. was gone. I later learned that the S.Sgt. lost both eardrums, and that his vest had saved him from further injury. The enemy did manage to blow the shower up, I mean blew it away. It would be a little over two weeks or so before I would get another shower.

Duc Lap A239 Event

One night, Dutch came into the bunker and mortar position where three men (two were well diggers from B Company) and I were located. They stayed at the team house, and I was sleeping in an underground cement bunker for a while. Dutch told me to throw an illumination round toward the front gate. He grabbed the .50 cal. and pulled the bolt two times. I turned the tube toward the gate, grabbed a round, and dropped it down the tube. I immediately ran back into the bunker and got behind Dutch, just as the round popped off. Then Dutch opened up with the .50 cal. I watched the round tear up the dirt in front of this bush just outside the perimeter. We saw a tracer and a couple of rounds enter the bush, and then an arm flying up into the air. It was like a majorette's baton twirling in the air. Dutch smiles, says "Thanks," and leaves. I won't go to any high school or college football games or parades because I see that arm when any majorette throws a baton in the air.

Dutch would go out on patrol with a squad of yards and sometimes one other man from the team. They would leave early in the morning, and by no later than noon they would engage the enemy. One day, I asked him why he was still going out. I had found out he was a short-timer with a month or less. When he answered, his eyes got big and he told me, "I've got seventy-seven confirmed kills and I would like to get a hundred before I go." He added that the army was going to send him to helicopter school and make him a gunship pilot. "And then I can really grease the shit out of them." I only knew one person who got this big eyed when they talked about killing, and that was S.Sgt. Mendez.

Phet Thiet Event

While I was drinking beer with the crew at the hootch, the LSA major came running in and said a guard on duty thought he saw and heard gooks in the ammo dump. Since the L2 had been overrun about two months before I had arrived, he wanted the dump checked out as soon as possible. Everybody volunteered at once, but there were only three guys that weren't married. They were Rodgers, Tatum, and I. Tatum was passed out so that left Rodgers and me. I grabbed someone's M16, a bandoleer of ammo, and a flashlight. We ran outside and loaded into the front of a jeep and headed for the dump. We jumped off the jeep and opened the gate. I yelled at the major to get back and wait while we checked the place out. I told Rodgers that we'd check the HE pads first and then work our way around to the other pads. Besides Charlie, we also had to watch out for cobras and the like around the area. We didn't see anything except a few snakes, but they took off as soon as the light hit them. We came out in half an hour and said, "All clear." The major put us both in for the Bronze Star with a V. Since we didn't get a kill or the dump didn't blow up, they just gave us the star only.

I have to talk about the nightmares that I have been having during the time I've been writing this statement. Sometimes I'll jump up sweating all over, and my heart is pounding and I can't remember what I dreamed about. Now, sometimes I experience night terrors, where I think I'm awake and see people in silhouette, but in the time it takes me to reach my gun, they are gone. I go to work, come home, start drinking my beer and smoking my dew, to try and chase away the stresses of the day and the memories of the past. I have found this has become more frequent over time. I've been doing this since I've been home from Vietnam. It is really hard to be around groups. I just really can't trust people in large groups or the government that tries to run everything in your life. When I hear or see how the police beat down people, it reminds me how we treated the gooks in Vietnam.

I can no longer sleep with my wife. I sleep on the floor on a thin mattress. I went to the VA in 1985 and started going for counseling. They said I should go to Menlo Park for a program they have there. I said I would like to go, but it's in a zone for Mike, November, Alpha, Mother Nature's Ambush, an earthquake. Going to Menlo Park for three months would be hard to do because of this. I went back to the VA in 1991 because things started to get out of hand, and they told me about Menlo Park again. I asked for someplace else, but they said no, so I told them the same thing. I now go to the Vet Center, and a guy named Mike Miracle, in Sacramento, once a month.

This Statement of Facts I have given is true to the best of my recollection.

GLOSSARY OF TERMS

AFVN-TV - Armed Forces Vietnam Television
AIT - Advanced Individual Training
AO - Area of Operation
APC - Armored Personnel Carrier
ARP - Areo Rifle Platoon
ARVN - Army of the Republic of Vietnam
AWOL - Absent Without Leave
Beau Coup - Vietnamese for 'many'
BLT - Battalion Landing Team
Boom Boom - Want sex
C-4 - Plastic Explosive
CAP - Combined Action Force
Cav - Short for Calvary
Charlie - Name given to the South Vietnamese Insurgents
Chicom - Chinese Communist
Co - Company
CO - Commanding Officer
CP - Command Post
CQ - Charge of Quarters
CWO - Army rank of Chief Warrant Officer
CPR - Cardio-pulmonary resuscitation
DBR - Don Ba Thin Army Airfield
DD214 - Official Record of Military Service
Diddy bopping - Walking along
Dinky Dau - Vietnamese for 'your crazy'
Diddy Mau - Vietnamese for 'get out'
DMZ - Demilitarized Zone
Doc - name given to a Medic
EENT - Eye, ear, nose, and throat
ED - Exempt from Duty
EM - Enlisted Man
ER - Emergency Room
FNG - Fucking New Guy
FSB - Fire Support Base
Gook - Name given to the Viet Cong Soldiers
Hootch - Name given to the living quarters of the soldiers
Huey - Short for helicopters
KIA - Killed in Action

LA - Los Angeles
LARC - Vehicle for land and water use
LCPL - Marine rank of Lance Corporal
LP - Listening Post
Lt - Army rank of Lieutenant
LZ - Landing Zone
LRRP - Long Range Reconnaissance Patrol
MACV - Military Assistance Command Vietnam
Mayday - Request for help
MCB - Mobile Construction Battalion
MCRD - Marine Corps Recruit Depot
MD - Medical Doctor
Medevac - Medical Evacuation Helicopter
MIA - Missing in Action
MOS - Military Occupational Specialty
MQF - Mobile Quarantine Facility
MP - Military Police
MPC - Military Payment Currency
MPH - Miles Per Hour
NCO - Non Commissioned Officer
Nam - Short version for Vietnam
NCR - Naval Construction Regiment
NDP - Night Defensive Position
NVA - North Vietnamese Army
OCS - Officer Candidate School
OR - Operating Room
PAVN - Peoples Army of Vietnam
PFC - Army rank of Private First Class
POW - Prisoner of War
PRS - Primary Recovery Ship
PTSD - Post Traumatic Stress Disorder
Punji Traps (Pits) - Camouflaged holes dug in the ground with poisoned sharpened sticks pointing skyward which would penetrate into any human body parts that happened to fall or step on them
PX - Post Exchange
ROK - Republic of Korea Army
ROTC - Reserve Officer Training Corps.
R&R - Rest and Recuperation
RTO - Radio Transmission Operator
RVN - Republic of Vietnam
Second Louie - Nickname given to the Army rank of Second Lieutenant
Sgt - Army rank of Sergeant
S.Sgt. - Army rank of Staff Sergeant
STD - Sexually Transmitted Disease
S&W - Smith and Wesson
TET - Vietnamese Lunar New Year

TNT - Explosive
UCD - University of California at Davis
UC Davis - University of California at Davis
USDA - United States Department of Agriculture
USMC - United States Marine Corps
USN - United States Navy

Made in the USA
Columbia, SC
23 September 2024

42258964R00120